Racism

From Slavery to
Advanced Capitalism

SAGE SERIES ON
RACE AND ETHNIC RELATIONS

Series Editor:
JOHN H. STANFIELD II
University of California at Davis

This series is designed for scholars working in creative theoretical areas related to race and ethnic relations. The series will publish books and collections of original articles that critically assess and expand upon race and ethnic relations issues from American and comparative points of view.

SERIES EDITORIAL BOARD

Racism

From Slavery to Advanced Capitalism

Carter A. Wilson

Sage Series on Race and Ethnic Relations

v o l u m e   1 7

SAGE Publications
International Educational and Professional Publisher
Thousand Oaks   London   New Delhi

For information address:

SAGE Publications, Inc.
2455 Teller Road
Thousand Oaks, California 91320
E-mail: order@sagepub.com

SAGE Publications Ltd.
6 Bonhill Street
London EC2A 4PU
United Kingdom

SAGE Publications India Pvt. Ltd.
M-32 Market
Greater Kailash I
New Delhi 110 048 India

Printed in the United States of America

Library of Congress Cataloging-in-Publication Data

Wilson, Carter A.
    Racism: From slavery to advanced capitalism / Author, Carter A. Wilson.
       p.   cm.—(Sage series on race and ethnic relations; v. 17)
    Includes bibliographical references and index.
    ISBN 0-8039-7336-5 (cloth).—ISBN 0-8039-7337-3 (pbk.)
    1. Racism—United States—History. 2. United States—Race
relations. 3. Capitalism—United States—History. I. Title. II. Series.
E184.A1W514 1966
305.8'00973—dc20   96-10053

      98 99 10 9 8 7 6 5 4 3 2

This book is printed on acid-free paper.

Sage Production Editor: Diana E. Axelsen
Sage Typesetter: Marion S. Warren

Contents

Series Editor's Introduction

Carter Wilson's book, *Racism: From Slavery to Advanced Capitalism,* is an important example of how much new ground must be broken in regard to the historical social scientific study of racism in the United States. This study certainly demonstrates how overly simplistic past historical groundings of social, political, and economic analyses of racism have been. This work is an excellent model for shaping future research in the underdeveloped area of the historical social scientific study of American racism.

JOHN H. STANFIELD II
Series Editor

Acknowledgments

I am grateful for the support that I received from both Denison University and the University of Toledo. The administration of these two institutions provided the resources in time and money that allowed me to complete this work. Faculty and students at both institutions gave me the encouragement that motivated me to complete this manuscript and the constructive criticism that led to improved versions of it. I am especially thankful to Dave Wilson, who read and critiqued my first drafts of Chapters 1 through 5 and urged me to complete the remaining chapters, and to John Stanfield, editor and scholar, who believed in my work.

Introduction

The literature on racism is voluminous. Books have been written on the psychological and cultural aspects of racism (Reich 1970; Kovel 1984; Katz and Taylor 1988); the individual and group dynamics of prejudice (Allport 1979; Katz and Taylor 1988); individual and institutional racism (Carmichael and Hamilton 1967; Knowles and Prewitt 1970; Feagin and Feagin 1986); the historical and socioeconomic features of racial oppression (Cox 1970; Blauner 1972; Steinberg 1989); and the political and ideological foundation of racism (Staples 1987; Omi and Winant 1990). Recent studies have analyzed changes in racism in different historical periods (Wilson 1980; Kovel 1984).

This extensive literature has been contentious. Debates have raged over issues of whether racism is changing form (Pettigrew 1979; Willie 1979; Kovel 1984; Omi and Winant 1990) or declining (Wilson 1980). Economists have debated whether racism is endogenous to capitalism (Boggs and Boggs 1970; Reich 1981; Williams 1987; Cherry 1989) or whether competitive markets drive out racially discriminatory firms (Becker 1957; Sowell 1981). Sociologists have disputed whether racism is a class phenomenon (Cox 1970; Wilson 1980) or a caste phenomenon (Dollard 1949; Myrdal [1948] 1975). Political scientists have disagreed over whether racism is a type of political ideology (Omi and Winant 1990) or simply a function of working-class authoritarianism (Lipset 1963). Marxists have argued over whether racism benefits the ruling class at the expense of all workers (Baron and Sweezy 1968; Reich 1981) or whether white workers are the prime beneficiaries of racism (Bonacich 1976; Shulman 1989).

Despite the numerous studies on single aspects of racism and despite the contentiousness of the literature, little has been done to integrate the literature or to resolve some of the more controversial issues. Few studies have attempted to connect the psychology of racism with the economics of racial oppression. Few have linked racial politics with the culture of racism. Multidimensional, historical studies of racism and racial oppression are rare.

However, there are a few of these studies; most notably, William Julius Wilson's (1980) book, *The Declining Significance of Race,* and Joel Kovel's (1984) book, *White Racism.* Wilson examined the ideological, economic, and political dimensions of racial oppression in three historical periods: slavery, Jim Crow, and industrial capitalism. However, he said little about the cultural and psychological dimensions of racism. Kovel provided one of the most brilliant analyses of the cultural and psychological dimensions of white racism for the same three historical periods but said little about the economic and political processes that sustain racism.

We attempt to integrate the literature—combining economic, political, and psychocultural dimensions—into a single model that explains racism in four historical periods. We try to illustrate the process by which racism is sustained throughout history. More specifically, we attempt to accomplish four tasks.

First, we try to make a contribution toward resolving some of the debates over racism. We demonstrate that racism is changing form rather than disappearing; that it is not entirely reducible to class conflict; that its reproduction involves politics and ideology; that it does have an economic base; and that it benefits both the upper class and the white working class, depending on the historical context.

Second, we attempt to demystify racism. That is, we try to define it, clarify it, explain it, and unveil its origin and modus operandi. We argue that racism is more than just a practice of exclusion, a form of discourse, or a system of ideas that denigrate the excluded. It certainly entails exclusion, discourse, and ideas; but it also involves economic structure, politics, and culture. It is sustained by oppressive economic structures; it is legitimized and supported by the state; and it is perpetuated by culture. Moreover, it is a historical phenomenon. That is, it originated in a definite stage of history, the postfeudal or modern era, and it is historically specific. It changes form from one period to the next.

Third, our primary task is to understand how racial oppression is sustained in various periods of history. We argue that racial oppression is perpetuated within the context of an oppressive and exploitative economic structure. This structure shapes the development of personality types and cultural forms that support racially oppressive relations. The state, constrained by this structure, generally protects these relations. However, this state role is open to political challenge, and it fluctuates with the balance of political power. We construct a theoretical model that accounts for these dimensions of racism: economic, political, and psychocultural.

Finally, we apply our model to four historical stages: slavery, Jim Crow, industrial capitalism, and advanced capitalism. We argue that racism takes a different form in each stage and that these differences can be explained by changes within the economic, political, and psychocultural dimensions of racism.

METHODOLOGY

In this study, we use an eclectic approach, set primarily within a historical materialist context. We use a variety of approaches because one method or framework may be appropriate for explaining one dimension of racism but inadequate for explaining others. We use a combination of methods to develop the strongest explanatory model.

In building our model, we draw from a number of different conceptual frameworks, including the Marxist, Weberian, and neo-Freudian frameworks. Where need be, we use the approach of cultural anthropologists and political scientists. We rely on those social theories that link the three dimensions of our model and that explain changes in different periods of history.

Marxist Framework

We use a Marxist framework, although this approach has been criticized for reducing racism to a simple matter of class conflict, for dismissing the culture of racism as a product of the economic base of society, for ignoring racial politics altogether, and for requiring activists to subordinate nationalism to the international struggle of the proletariat. In the past, with a few exceptions—most notably, Fromm, Marcus, Fanon, Sartre—Marxist scholars have offered little insight into the cultural, ideological, political, and psychological dimensions of racism. Recently, post-structuralist Marxists have moved beyond economic determinism. Some, having discovered Gramsci, have focused on the cultural and political dimensions of racism—Hall, Marable, Miles, Smith, Solomas,

Wolpe, Omi and Winant. These dimensions play important roles in the reproduction of racially oppressive economic arrangements.

In spite of the controversy surrounding a Marxist approach, three features of this framework are useful in an analysis of racism. First, Marx's social theory has a dualistic or dialectical aspect that best captures the dialectical or dualistic nature of racism. On the one hand, Marx maintained that culture, law, and politics are shaped by the economic structure of society. From this framework emerges the view that racist culture, laws, and politics are shaped by racially oppressive economic structures. On the other hand, Marx argued that human actions and decisions change circumstances and socioeconomic arrangements. For example, criticizing materialists for their belief that men are nothing more than the products of the material conditions of society, Marx ([1888] 1974, p. 121) said, "The materialist doctrine that men are products of circumstances and upbringing and that, therefore, changed men are products of other circumstances and changed upbringing, forgets that it is men that change circumstances." Marx ([1852] 1959a, p. 320) contended that "Men make their own history," but not "under circumstances chosen by themselves but under circumstances directly encountered, given, and transmitted from the past." This perspective provides the framework for understanding the role of social movements in assaulting racist ideologies and altering racially oppressive arrangements.

Marx's dualistic framework captures both the voluntaristic role of human actions and the deterministic tendencies of economic structures (Gouldner 1982). This framework highlights those human actions designed to alter racially oppressive arrangements, to challenge racist culture and ideology, and to change racist laws and state policies. At the same time, it emphasizes the role of a racially oppressive economic structure in shaping the development of racist culture, personality types, and politics.

Second, Marx and Engels provide a powerful critical theory of Western economies. This theory is useful for examining the particular types of economic arrangements that sustain racial oppression. It focuses on the process of accumulating wealth. It maintains that oppression is perpetuated in an economic structure with the following features: (a) private ownership of the means of production, (b) the concentration of this ownership in the hands of a few, (c) inequity in the distribution of wealth, and (d) exploitative relations of production.

Third, Marx offers a philosophy of history most helpful in analyzing historical changes in forms of racism. This philosophy, *historical materialism,* a term invented by Marxists after the death of Marx, extends Marx's dialectical materialist paradigm into a theory of history based on three major premises: One, ideas and consciousness arise from the material conditions of human existence. Two, history progresses in stages distinguishable by changes in modes of production, relations of production, and levels of technology. Three, rationality varies from one epoch to another; that is, what appears rational in one milieu may become irrational in another. Thus historical materialism directs our attention to the material conditions out of which racism arises, to stages in the history of racism, and to the relative rationality of racism.

Historical materialism provides the umbrella framework for our eclectic analysis of racism in the United States. However, our approach remains eclectic as we include other frameworks under this umbrella.

Weberian Framework

Where appropriate, we use Weberian theory in our analysis. This framework is most useful for an examination of race in the areas of (a) social class, (b) bureaucracy and institutional practices, and (c) culture and economic base. Whereas some scholars see Weber's perspective as contradictory to Marx's, we see it as complementary.

Marx defines class in terms of a group's relationship to production and distribution; Weber defines class in terms of a group's status, power, and prestige, hierarchically arranged in society. Where Marxists look for class conflict, Weberians anticipate caste arrangements. Weber's model directs our attention to racial caste, institutional discrimination, and the culture of racism. Marx's framework directs us to the economic structure out of which caste, institutions, and culture emerge.

We maintain that race, class, and caste are interrelated in the United States in ways that cannot be adequately explained solely within either a Weberian or a Marxist framework. Both frameworks are required to decode this interrelationship.

Other Approaches

We use other approaches to analyze the various dimensions of racism. For example, we use the psychoanalytical approach for studying the psychological dimension of racism. We draw from the works of Adorno, Fromm, Kovel, Horney, Lasch, and others. We employ this approach because it provides a framework for understanding the psychocultural pathology of racism. It directs our attention to the irrational drives, repressed in the unconscious mind. It complements the Marxist and Weberian models. Whereas Marx and Weber direct our attention to economic and institutional arrangements and the social aspects of oppression, neo-Freudian theorists point to the psychological dynamics of culture and the mental aspects of repression.

We use contemporary political and neo-Marxist theories to examine the role of the state and politics in maintaining racially oppressive arrangements. We see this political dimension as important because it is the most indeterminate. Hence, we reject the classical Marxist perspective that trivializes this dimension by depicting the state as nothing more than the executive committee of the ruling class and by describing the political arena as a mask for class conflict. This is the most critical flaw of Marx's and Engel's writings, their neglect of the role of politics and the state. Politics involves more than just class conflict, and the state does more than just legitimize oppressive arrangements. Understanding race politics and the changing role of the state requires an investigation of the state and politics, quite apart from a study of the economy.

ORGANIZATION OF THE BOOK

We divide our discussion of racism into two parts. In the first part, we review the relevant literature, develop our model, and trace the evolution of racism. In Chapter 1, we examine theories of racism and race relations. We locate our model in the context of this literature. That is, we compare and contrast our model with others, noting areas of agreement and disagreement. We attempt to make a contribution to the resolution of some of the debates in the literature.

We develop our model of racism in Chapter 2. We examine each dimension separately and discuss how each one is related to the others.

In Chapter 3, we discuss the historical formation of racism. We locate the origins of racism in fundamental changes in the structure of the economy of Western Europe and subsequent changes in Western culture. These changes gave rise to an intense and dehumanizing drive to accumulate wealth. This drive was behind the Atlantic slave trade and the genocide of Native Americans. It undergirded modern racism.

In the second part of this book, we examine the historical development of racism and racial oppression in the United States. In Chapters 4 through 7, we apply our model to four historical stages corresponding to different modes of production and forms of racism: The plantation slavery mode of production corresponds to dominative racism; sharecropping, to dominative aversive racism; industrial capitalism, to aversive racism; and advanced capitalism, to meta-racism. Using historical data, primarily from secondary sources, we demonstrate the applicability of our model in explaining different forms of racism and in understanding the process through which racial oppression has been sustained throughout U.S. history.

In Chapter 4, we investigate the development of racism in North America. We underscore the connection between dehumanizing treatment of others and debasing views of them. We illustrate the association between plantation slavery and the formation of racism. Chapter 5 focuses on the post-Civil War era (after 1865) in the South until the civil rights era (before 1965). In this chapter, we demonstrate a relationship between the structure of the southern economy and the reformation of racist culture and ideology. Chapter 6 covers the period of industrial capitalism. This more intricate mode of production generated more complicated dynamics of racism. These dynamics involved labor movements, the interaction of race and class, and the formation of white identity among the white working class. Chapter 7 examines the post-civil rights era and advanced capitalism, the shift from Fordism to post-Fordism, and the emergence of meta-racism.

In every era, we focus on the connection between particular modes of production and particular forms of racism. Moreover, we pay careful attention to the role of the dominant class in developing a politics and culture of racial oppression.

In memory of Raya Dunayevskaya,
whose passion for human liberation lives on.

1

Theoretical Reflections

In this chapter, we examine select theories of race relations and racial oppression. Our discussion of the literature is not exhaustive. It focuses on a few authors and trends for the purposes of locating our model in the broader literature and of addressing some of the controversial issues in the literature. We briefly examine the assimilationist, pluralist, market, class conflict, Marxist, postmodernist, and Cress Welsing models.

ASSIMILATIONIST AND PLURALIST THEORIES

Assimilationist and pluralist theories focus on patterns of interaction among racial and ethnic groups. Assimilationists see racial and ethnic differences disappearing and racial conflicts evolving into patterns of racial integration. As pluralists see it, racial and ethnic differences persist, but conflicts are resolved in the political arena.

Assimilationists identify stages or cycles of interracial conflict, ending in assimilation. Park (1974), for example, identified the following stages:

Initial contact between racial or ethnic groups
Competition between these groups
Accommodation
Assimilation

He saw racial or ethnic conflict as only one stage of historical development, a stage that inevitably progresses toward accommodation and assimilation. Contentious racial groups become more tolerant and adjust to their differences in the accommodation stage. Finally, separate racial interests disappear, and a common identity arises in the assimilation stage. The cycle repeats itself with the introduction of new racial or ethnic groups.

Gordon (1964) divided assimilation into finer stages, which include the following:

Cultural assimilation; the acceptance of the dominant culture

Marital assimilation; interracial marriages occurring in large numbers

Prejudice-free assimilation; the disappearance of belief in racial or ethnic superiority

The final stage of assimilation, according to Gordon, is civic assimilation, which occurs when special racial or ethnic demands or interests disappear.

Nathan Glazer and Daniel Patrick Moynihan (1970) rejected the assimilationist thesis and set forth a theory of immigration, ascension, and group politics in its place. In their book, *Beyond the Melting Pot,* they examined racial and ethnic groups in New York City: Italians, Irish, Jews, Puerto Ricans, and African Americans. They suggested that African Americans will overcome prejudices against them and rise in social status just as the Italians, Irish, and Jews did in earlier periods. According to Glazer and Moynihan, blacks will not assimilate, but they will become more involved in pluralist politics.

The assimilationist and pluralist paradigms are fundamentally different from our model. These paradigms anticipate conflict and accommodation among groups and presuppose a natural process of ethnic ascension. That is, these paradigms assume that ethnic and racial groups that start at the bottom of the social ladder will naturally climb to the top over time. We reject this assumption because the social and historical experiences of blacks are fundamentally different from those of European ethnic groups. Whereas European immigrants faced discrimination, blacks have suffered exclusion. Whereas European immigrants struggled to move up the social ladder in the North, blacks remained trapped in slavery and debt peonage in the South. In the North, black city dwellers whose forefathers had lived in this country for centuries were excluded from the same skilled trade jobs open to first-generation immigrants (Pinderhughes 1987; Steinberg 1989). We do not assume that ethnic and racial groups naturally rise up the social ladder. The social and historical experiences of African Americans suggest this is not the case. Our model attempts to explain why blacks were subjugated so long in this country. It focuses on social, economic, and political processes that explain the persistence of racial oppression.

THE MARKET OR
NEOCONSERVATIVE APPROACH

The market or neoconservative approach assumes that individuals strive to maximize their self-interest, that racial discrimination results from a distaste for blacks, that government interference with the market causes more harm than good, and that competition drives discriminating companies out of business. This model focuses attention away from the institutional and societal forms of discrimination and away from links between the state and the economy.

Economist Thomas Sowell (1981) provided a concise summary of this position in *Markets and Minorities*. In this book, Sowell argued that in an open competitive market, the practice of racial discrimination is costly to both victims and discriminators. He contended that racially discriminatory firms, which refuse to hire highly productive and skillful black workers, pay a high price for their behavior: They pay a higher cost for a labor force that is less productive and less skillful than it would be in the absence of racial discrimination. These firms pay another price when their competitors hire the skillful and productive blacks they reject. Sowell (1981, p. 26) concluded, "Economic competition means that the less discriminatory transactors acquire a competitive advantage, forcing others either to reduce their discrimination or to risk losing profits, perhaps even being forced out of business." Thus within Sowell's framework, competitive markets impose enough costs on racially discriminatory firms to discourage this form of behavior.

According to this view, the market operates to eliminate discrimination while government works to promote it. Sowell (1981, p. 116) said,

> Historically, government has itself been a major promoter of residential segregation. A number of municipal governments made residential segregation official policy early in the 20th century, and the Federal Housing Administration required racial segregation as a precondition for federally insured loans on into the late 1940s.

George Gilder (1981), author of *Wealth and Poverty* and another proponent of the market view, claimed that racial discrimination has been eliminated and that social welfare and civil rights agencies harm African Americans. He found no valid data proving the existence of racial discrimination. He maintained that black and white income gaps all but disappear when one controls for region, education, and age. He attributed this gap not to racial discrimination, but "to earlier discrimination against their [blacks'] parents and to government-induced dependency and female-headed families" (p. 155).

We see several problems with the market model. First, if Sowell's (1981) model is correct, it has ominous implications for African Americans. If it is likely that racial discrimination will disappear from competitive markets but persist in monopolistic or oligopolistic markets, then African Americans face bleak prospects: fair treatment in the competitive sector, where wages tend to be lowest and unemployment highest; and racial discrimination in the oligopolistic sector, where wages tend to be relatively high and unemployment low. These arrangements create and perpetuate patterns of high unemployment and poverty among African Americans.

Second, the market paradigm focuses on atomized individual workers and firms motivated by self-interest. It tends to ignore the collective actions of firms and workers. It overlooks the prospect of white workers organizing to exclude blacks or firms using race to divide workers in order to reduce labor's bargaining power, especially over wages, and to increase profit margins.

Third, although this model directs attention to the racially discriminatory behavior of government, it ignores racially discriminatory behavior in the private sector and the political influence businesses and industries exercise over government. For example, Sowell (1981) recognized the racially discriminatory practices of the Federal Housing Administration (FHA), a government agency. At the same time, he ignored the political influence that the real estate industry exercises over the FHA. This private sector industry is the primary culprit in maintaining housing discrimination.

Finally, Sowell (1981) and Gilder (1981) offered an overly simplistic definition and measure of racial discrimination. They saw discrimination only as the direct action of a prejudiced individual to exclude blacks. They measured discrimination by comparing black/white wage disparities. This approach disregards the institutional dynamics of racial discrimination. Today, the major problem of racial discrimination is not inequality between the wages of blacks and whites employed in similar jobs, in the same region. The problem is that of unequal access to jobs and of the exclusion of blacks from job networks tied into firms with job openings. These aspects of racism are more pernicious than individual prejudices, and they are outside the purview of the market model.

CLASS CONFLICT THEORIES

Class conflict theories view racial strife as a form of struggle, either between the ruling class and the proletariat or between two classes of workers, black workers and white workers. In either case, racial conflict is reduced to a form of class conflict. In contrast, we see racial conflict as both similar to and distinct from class conflict. In our view, there are similarities between racial and class exploitation; but at the same time, racial oppression involves cultural forms and sociopsychological processes profoundly different from class dynamics.

Oliver Cox

Although Oliver Cox (1970) never explicitly linked his approach to a Marxist framework, he is often labeled an orthodox Marxist or class conflict theorist. He rejected the notion that blacks exist in a racial caste system in the United States. He maintained that racism is a function of capitalism and that racial oppression is a masked form of class oppression.

Arguing for a class conflict model of racism, Cox rejected the notion that blacks exist in a caste system. He claimed that caste systems are rigid in their treatment of lower caste members, that these members know their place, and that they are generally prohibited from marrying into the upper castes. He contended that a racial caste system does not exist in the United States because the system in this country is not rigid, blacks do not necessarily stay in their place, and marriages occur across racial caste lines.

Cox studied the Jim Crow system prior to the civil rights movement of the 1960s. In his study, he illustrated inconsistencies in U.S. segregation norms. For example, he noted that in some cities of the Deep South during this period, blacks entered and exited streetcars from the rear and sat at the back of the cars, whereas in other cities, they entered from the center or the front. He observed that in some cities, "white taxicabs compete for Negro passengers; in others they refuse Negro trade" (p. 451). On this basis, he concluded that the system is not rigid and therefore not a caste.

Cox added that the presence of racial tension in the United States demonstrates that blacks do not know their place; ergo, there is no caste. He conceded that laws and social customs in the United States oppose interracial marriages; but he claimed that the fact that a few interracial marriages have occurred and the fact that Americans have married foreigners demonstrate that blacks and whites in the United States do not belong to the endogamous groups that define caste systems.

Cox established a rigid definition of caste systems based on his study of India and applied this definition to race relations in the United States. The evidence presented in his study supports the conclusion that a caste system existed in the United States. Cox apparently rejected this conclusion because it was inconsistent with his class conflict framework. It did not occur to Cox that race relations might have aspects of both class and caste systems.

Cox insisted that racism is a product of capitalism and a form of class conflict, not a type of caste system. He said, "Here then are race relations; they are definitely not caste relations. They are labor capital-profit relations; therefore, race relations are proletarian bourgeois relations and hence political-class relations" (p. 336).

For Cox, the ruling capitalist class precipitates racism in order to suppress class conflict and divide white workers against black workers. Racism is an instrument used by the ruling capitalist class to control the working class and to extract more surplus value from them. Cox (p. 473) said, "both the Negroes and the poor whites are exploited by the white ruling class, and this has been done most effectively by the maintenance of antagonistic attitudes between the white and the colored masses."

Cox's theory is consistent with ours, insofar as he sees racism as a modern phenomenon that emerged with the fall of feudalism and the rise of capitalism. It diverges from ours insofar as he sees race relations simply as a form of class relations. We see race relations as having aspects of both class and caste arrangements. Of course, our perspective arises from an eclectic approach that combines the frameworks of Marx and Weber rather than seeing those approaches as mutually exclusive.

Paul Baron and Paul Sweezy

Paul Baron and Paul Sweezy (1968, p. 264) argued that race prejudice "was deliberately created and cultivated as a rationalization and justification for the enslavement and exploitation of colored labor." They maintained that this prejudice persists because it serves important social functions. Racism provides an outlet for frustrations generated by a class society. That is, the existence of a subordinate group, identifiable by race, provides a convenient scapegoat, a group others can feel superior to and release their frustrations on. Baron and Sweezy (pp. 265-66) claimed, "It thus happens that a special pariah group at the bottom acts as a kind of lightning rod for the frustrations and hostilities of all the higher groups, the more so the nearer they are to the bottom." They identified this pariah group as the black subproletariat.

Baron and Sweezy contended that a number of private interests benefit from the persistence of race prejudice and oppression. For example, they noted that employers benefit from racial divisions in the labor force because this division reduces labor force solidarity, erodes labor bargaining power, and improves profit margins. They added, "White workers benefit by being protected from Negro competition for the more desirable and higher paying jobs" (p. 264).

Michael Reich

Michael Reich (1977) offered a similar class conflict theory except that he emphasized that racism benefits the dominant white class and harms both white and black workers. On the one hand, he acknowledged that working-class whites, for psychological reasons, have participated in the exclusion and oppression of blacks. He said, "For example, the opportunity to participate in another's oppression compensates for one's own misery" (p. 188). On the other hand, he saw the dominant class as the primary force behind the maintenance of racial oppression and the primary beneficiary of racial inequality.

Reich's (1981, p. 219) historical information demonstrated that racism "hurt poor whites and benefited only planters and industrialists." He challenged C. Vann Woodward's thesis that poor whites played a prominent role in the disenfranchisement and subjugation of blacks. Reich pointed out that although poor whites participated in the Ku Klux Klan, members of the planter class dominated the leadership positions in this terrorist organization. The planter class incited racist hysteria in order to destroy the populist movement, which promoted racial coalitions between poor white and poor black farmers, Reich maintained. He added that planters instituted the debt peonage system, led the movement to disenfranchise blacks, retarded the economic development of the South, and contributed to the high rates of illiteracy and poverty in the South. Reich concluded that these arrangements hurt both poor whites and blacks. The industrial class also profited from racism. This class, Reich explained, used racism to divide workers and undermine their solidarity and bargaining power.

Split Labor Market

One variation of the class conflict model is split-labor market theory. As Edna Bonacich (1976, p. 36), a major proponent of this theory, described it, a split labor market began during slavery. This market is characterized by a lower price paid to black labor compared to the price paid to white labor, holding productivity and efficiency constant. Bonacich maintained that this price differential aggravates racial tensions. Moreover, capital exploits this differential by using blacks as strikebreakers or by substituting cheap black labor for more expensive white labor. Bonacich (p. 41) noted 24 instances, involving 14 different industries and several locations, in which blacks were used as strikebreakers between 1917 and 1929. Also, she discussed several cases in which employers replaced white workers with lower priced black workers.

Bonacich claimed that white workers responded to these efforts in two ways: They operated either to exclude blacks altogether or to maintain a racial caste system designed to prevent employers from substituting cheap black workers for more costly white workers. Both of these labor responses subordinate black labor and create a racial caste in labor.

Gordon, Edwards, and Reich (1982) and Piore (1977) set forth the segmented work or dual labor market theory, which ties the subordinate economic position of blacks to the structure of the post-World War II economy. We examine this theory more carefully in our section on industrial capitalism.

William Julius Wilson's Class Conflict Model

In *The Declining Significance of Race,* William J. Wilson (1980) examined changes in U.S. race relations from the antebellum period to the present. He identified three historical stages:

1. Slavery and plantation hegemony
2. Segregation and the rise of the white working class

3. Industrial expansion and dispersed racial conflict

He maintained that patterns of race relations in each stage were shaped by different systems of production and by state laws and policies. Wilson also tested class conflict theories of race relations as he investigated each stage.

In the first stage, the preindustrial period, the southern plantation economy allowed slave owners to emerge as a regional ruling elite, according to Wilson (1980). He added that this slaveholding class captured the state to protect its hegemony over southern society. He characterized this period as one of racial oppression and concluded that the Marxist model of upper-class rule applied here.

Wilson (1980) maintained that in the second stage, the Jim Crow period, power shifted from the slaveholding class to the white working class, primarily because of the economic decline of the plantation and the rise of industry. This view attributes the establishment of racial segregation and the disenfranchisement of blacks primarily to working-class and poor whites. Wilson (1980, pp. 145-46) said,

> Here a more industrial system of production enabled white workers to become more organized and physically concentrated than their southern counterparts. Following the abolition of slavery in the North, they used their superior resources to generate legal and informal practices of segregation that effectively prevented blacks from becoming serious economic competitors. . . . Their efforts to eliminate black competition helped to produced an elaborate system of Jim Crow segregation. Poor whites were aided not only by their numbers but also by the development of political resources which accompanied their greater involvement in the South's economy.

Wilson claimed that the split-labor market theory best applies to this stage of racial oppression.

The third stage, industrial expansion, began with racial conflicts overlapping with class conflicts, according to Wilson's model. This model sees employers in the 20th century ignoring norms of racial exclusion, using black labor to undercut white labor, and hiring blacks as strikebreakers or replacement for higher priced white labor. These practices forced labor unions to reverse their racial policies and to recruit black workers (Wilson 1980, p. 147). Wilson argued that the state intervened to promote racial equality, especially after World War II.

Wilson (1980, p. 151) concluded that in the advanced industrialized society, "access to the means of production is increasingly based on educational criteria." Hence, the life chances of blacks depend less on race and more on social class factors—skills, education, and so on.

Wilson (1987) extended his thesis in a more recent book, *The Truly Disadvantaged*. In this text, he argued that race could hardly be used to explain the increase of the so-called black urban underclass because of three historical factors: the passage, in the mid-1960s, of the most aggressive civil rights legislation in American history; the institution of affirmative action policies in the 1970s; and the dramatic growth of the black middle class. For Wilson, the decline of older industries and the low educational attainment of central city blacks, rather than the persistence of racial discrimination, best explains the growth of black poverty.

We see several problems with Wilson's (1980, 1987) model. First, Wilson overestimated the power of poor and working-class whites and underestimated the power of the economic elite. Although the working class and poor whites participated in the post-Reconstruction subjugation of blacks, the planter class played a much more decisive role than Wilson's model indicates. This class not only attempted to reestablish the plantation system after the Civil War, it played an instrumental role in instituting the sharecropping debt peonage system and in disenfranchising both blacks and poor whites.

Second, Wilson (1987) overestimated the extent to which civil rights policies have been implemented and the pervasiveness of affirmative action policies. Although these policies have eliminated the more direct and blatant forms of discrimination, they have had much less effect on institutional forms of discrimination. Racial discrimination within the housing market leaves blacks concentrated in the central cities, and discrimination in the labor market keeps black unemployment rates disproportionately higher than white rates, even among blacks and whites with the same levels of education.

Third, Wilson's concept of class shifted with each stage of history. He used a Marxist concept in the first, Weberian in the second, and a subjective definition in the third. For example, in the contemporary period, Wilson (1987) defined the urban underclass not by this group's relationship to production, not by its ascribed social status or power, but by its behavior: its lack of education, its dependence on welfare, its propensity for violence, and so on.

Sidney Willhelm

Sidney Willhelm (1970) associated the intensity of racism with the need for black labor. He suggested that racism recedes as the need for black labor increases and flares up as that need declines. He noted that racism intensified during the late 19th century and early 20th century, as immigrants satisfied the labor needs of an expanding industrial economic system. He claimed that racism declined during World War II because the need for black labor increased with the expanded war economy, with the decline of European immigration, and with the increased manpower demands of the war itself. He observed that industrial society has given way to a new technologically advanced society in which automation and bionics have reduced the need for a large blue-collar workforce. He concluded that black labor has become useless in this postindustrial society. In *Who Needs the Negro,* Willhelm suggested that the growing obsolescence of unskilled and semiskilled labor places blacks in a position similar to Native Americans; that is, blacks are vulnerable to genocide.

Although Willhelm (1970) was critical of the Marxist framework for reducing racism to a matter of class conflict, he ironically developed a technological deterministic model. For Willhelm, racism increases because of the growing inability of the technologically advanced society to absorb black labor. His model fails to account for the intense racism that arose in the antebellum South, at a time when black labor was well absorbed in the slave economy. We believe that a better model focuses not on technology per se but on the mode of production associated with the technology and the strength of the dominant class in determining the use of that technology.

RACE, CLASS, AND IDEOLOGY

A number of social scientists have treated race and racism in the context of ideology. Fields (1982), for example, described race and racism as purely ideological phenomena quite distinct from social classes. She said, "Class and race are concepts of a different order; they do not occupy the same analytical space, and thus cannot constitute explanatory alternatives to each other" (p. 150). For Fields, class refers to material circumstances, but race is nothing more than an ideological phenomenon. Class refers either to Weber's hierarchical arrangement of power, prestige, income, or occupational status or to Marx's concept of social relations to production.

We agree with Fields that race is an artificial social construct with absolutely no scientific basis, a view, championed by Cox (1970), that was well established among social scientists by the 1970s. We strongly disagree with Fields's position that race and class are so clearly separate and unrelated that they cannot occupy the same analytical space. We see class and race as both different and similar.

Indeed, there are profound differences between racial and class oppression. Racial subordination involves exclusionary practices and psychocultural dynamics far more pernicious than class exploitation. For example, whites in a skilled labor category may be exploited but enjoy average life chances. Racial oppression may involve the exclusion of African Americans from that category of labor, thereby condemning them to lower life chances. Racial oppression also involves a psychocultural process that dehumanizes African Americans and other racial minorities, thereby making possible the worst forms of human oppression and violence against them.

Racial and class oppression are similar because both racial and class exploitation occur within an economic context involving the appropriation of surplus value. Both involve hierarchical arrangements of status and power. The exploitation and subordination of African Americans involve both class and caste processes.

Roediger (1991) viewed race and class as both distinct and overlapping concepts. He demonstrated that the concept of white free labor developed simultaneously and in tandem with the idea of black slave labor. He showed that European workers in the United States developed their identity in reaction to the social position of black slaves. Because black slavery was the most wretched form of labor, European workers identified with the alternative, white free labor. Thus white *class* consciousness emerged concomitantly with white *race* consciousness.

Roediger (1991) concluded that race cannot be reduced to class, but that both race and class are located within social formations. He said, "To set race within social formations is absolutely necessary, but to reduce race to class is damaging" (p. 8).

This race/class paradox is not a new discovery. Du Bois (1969a) argued that race is different from class, but both are rooted in economic processes. For Du Bois, both class and race conflicts were founded on economic exploitation, but race was related to a folklore or a cultural form that distinguished it from class. He believed that race conflict was a more serious problem in the 20th century than class conflict.

The Cress Theory

Because of the controversy surrounding the Cress theory, we include it in our discussion of the literature. Psychiatrist Frances Cress Welsing (1970) originated this theory. Applying an Adlerian analysis, Welsing defined racism as a drive for superiority and supremacy among whites. This drive, she argued, arises out of deep and pervading feelings of inadequacy and inferiority derived from a biological origin: the inability of whites to produce melanin. She said, "The quality of whiteness is indeed a genetic inadequacy or a relative genetic deficiency state or disease based upon the genetic inability to produce the skin pigments of melanin which are responsible for all skin coloration" (p. 5). Beginning with a presumption of the biological deficiency of whites—their inability to produce melanin—Welsing identified a number of neurotic defense mechanisms that explain white racism. She maintained that whites created the myth of white genetic superiority and black genetic inferiority in reaction to whites' inferior genetic ability to produce melanin. Welsing (p. 7) said, "Being acutely aware of their lack of or inferior genetic ability to produce skin color, whites built the elaborate myth of white genetic superiority."

This theory is both popular and controversial. It is popular among African Americans because it says to them, the victims of racism, that they are not inferior and that the problem of race is not theirs. It says to them what they know intuitively: Racism is some sort of psychological pathology. This theory is popular among some neoconservatives because it gives them an easy target; that is, it provides a basis for arguing that theories of racism are groundless and a form of reverse racism. In the final analysis, this theory is flawed because it reduces racism to a single fictitious variable, one that is a product of racism itself: that Europeans are white people, devoid of blemish, color, or melanin.

RACISM AND THE POSTMODERN DEBATE

We would be remiss if we neglected to comment on the postmodern debate and underscore where we agree and where we disagree with postmodern approaches to analyzing racism. We find the postmodern approach valuable, and we draw insights from it. However, we see a much stronger role for economic structures and politics in shaping forms of racism than the postmodern literature permits.

In our estimation, the postmodern literature provides a powerful tool for analyzing the cultural and linguistic aspects of racism. This literature, with its roots in the works of Nietzsche, tends to reject global and systematic models of the world. It assails Enlightenment philosophy, with its model of man as rational and its view of knowledge as objective and progressive. It sees man as a prisoner of language, because language structures perception, shapes judgments, and circumscribes actions. It focuses on the manner in which discourse and knowledge reinforce patterns of domination (see Foucault 1972, 1980). It dissects academic and everyday discourse, identifying metaphors, uncovering the way important terms are defined with both synonyms and antonyms (see Derrida 1981).

Following the genealogical approach of Nietzsche and Foucault, West (1982) provided a postmodern analysis of the rise of racism. He examined the manner in which modern science and Enlightenment philosophy provided a discursive structure that bred racism. Discursive structures are formed by "the controlling metaphors, notions, categories, and norms that shape the predominant conceptions of truth and knowledge in the modern west" (West, p. 50). West demonstrated that the revolution in science and philosophy—associated with Newton, Descartes, Leibnitz, and others—introduced a new discursive structure. This new structure contained metaphors and categories that allowed for new forms of world domination. For example, the new metaphors in physics included a machine or mechanical model of the material world. This model provided the basis for manipulating and controlling the world. Also, it allowed for an easy rationalization of destructive actions against the world because it presumed that the world was already dead matter. The new language of biology spoke of the animal kingdom as if beings were arranged in order of superior to inferior. This discourse laid the groundwork for talking about racial superiority and inferiority.

West (1982, pp. 61-63) unveiled the racist assumptions of a number of Enlightenment thinkers. He noted Voltaire's endorsement of the idea of white supremacy. He quoted Hume saying that blacks are naturally inferior to whites. He exposed Kant equating blackness with stupidity. He indicted Montesquieu and Jefferson for accepting assumptions of black inferiority. He suggested that these racist assumptions arose out of the structure of modern discourse and operated to reinforce patterns of racial domination.

West (1982) rejected what he called vulgar Marxism because of its rigid economic determinism and its inability to see discursive structures as independent of any economic base. Nevertheless, he maintained it was possible to reconcile Marxism with postmodernism. He did not elaborate on how this reconciliation could occur.

Goldberg (1990) combined the postmodern approach with a neo-Marxist method. He examined the relationship between racist discursive structures and racist economic, institutional, social, and political practices.

Our approach is similar to the postmodernists' approach insofar as we examine the language and culture of racism. We differ from the postmodernists—especially with Foucault and Derrida—in a number of ways. We do not presume, as Foucault did, that power is fragmented, nor do we reject, as West did, the plausibility of elites maintaining patterns of racial oppression. We cannot a priori dismiss the possibility of racist discourse emerging out of oppressive economic structures. We believe that empirical evidence challenges many of these basic postmodernist assumptions. For example, power in the antebellum South was concentrated in the planter class, which operated to protect the institution of slavery and contributed to the formation of racist discourse and ideology.

2

The Model

Racism assumed different forms in different countries and historical periods. In the United States, it appeared with the establishment of a slave-based economy. It persisted throughout American history, and it changed forms in different stages of history. In this chapter, we develop a model designed to illustrate processes that sustain racial oppression and to identify changes in forms of racism. This model focuses on the economic, political, and cultural dimensions of racism. It examines each dimension separately and briefly explains how each interacts with the others.

The general view that emerges from this model is that racial oppression is sustained within an exploitative and oppressive economic structure. This structure shapes the formation of a racist culture that functions to reinforce patterns of racial oppression. The state, operating within this economic and cultural context, generally supports and legitimizes oppressive relations. However, its role is the most indeterminate because it is alterable by social movements, depressions, wars, technological changes, and international pressures.

We begin our analysis with a discussion of the economic dimension, then proceed to the political and cultural dimensions. We conclude with a discussion of how the three dimensions interact.

THE ECONOMIC BASIS OF RACISM

Economic factors play a primary role in producing and sustaining racism. These factors include the accumulation process, private property, and modes of production.

16

The Accumulation Process

Racism appeared after fundamental changes occurred in the economies of Western Europe. It emerged with a postfeudal economy, undergirded by a drive to accumulate wealth. This drive developed in stages, characterized by different ways of producing wealth or different modes of production.

The most primitive stage involved brute force, conquest, and plunder. This is the era when the Portuguese plundered the coastal cities of Africa for their riches and the Spaniards destroyed civilizations in the Americas for their gold. This period of plunder was primitive because those seeking wealth destroyed the source of wealth upon acquiring it. They destroyed the cities, the civilizations, and the people that produced the wealth.

Subsequent stages involved seizing land and forcing people to continuously extract wealth from the land. This required more than brute force. It required special ways of controlling the use of land and of organizing and sustaining labor. It required the development of special economic arrangements. Thus the perpetuation of the accumulation process and the maintenance of racial oppression required a particular economic structure.

Force, Accumulation, and Economic Structure

Friedrich Engels ([1877] 1975) made this point in his critique of Herr Duhring in *Anti-Duhring.* Duhring had argued that oppression was a function of direct force, as slaves were coerced into servitude. He used the example of Robinson Crusoe enslaving Friday. In this example, Crusoe, with sword in hand, enslaves Friday. Engels asked where did Crusoe get the sword? He argued that the presence of the sword presupposes a particular level of production and technology. Why doesn't Friday run away when Crusoe looks the other way? Engels maintained that Friday's state of servitude must be based on an arrangement in which Crusoe controls productive land, instruments of labor, and surplus resources. Engels's point is that oppression is sustained by more than force; it is perpetuated within the context of an oppressive economic structure.

Engels claimed that there are a number of economic prerequisites for the maintenance of slavery and other forms of oppression. He argued that the subjugation of a man or group is perpetuated only within an economic context with specific characteristics. Engels (1975, p. 192) said,

In order to be able to make use of a slave, one must possess two kinds of things: first, the instruments and material for his slave's labor; and second, the means of bare subsistence for him. Therefore, before slavery becomes possible, certain levels of production must already have been reached and a certain inequality of distribution must already have appeared. . . .

The subjugation of a man to make him do servile work, in all its forms, presupposes that the subjugator has at his disposal the instruments of labor with the help of which alone he is able to employ the person placed in bondage, and in the case of slavery, in addition, the means of subsistence which enables him to keep his slave alive. In all cases, therefore, it presupposes the possession of a certain amount of property, in excess of the average.

Private Property

Engels ([1877] 1975) added that private property is also required to sustain exploitative relations. He argued that in primitive societies based on common ownership of the land, "slavery either did not exist at all or played only a very subordinate role" (p. 193). According to Engels, slavery arose in the Greek and Roman societies when land ownership became concentrated in the hands of a small class of rich proprietors. In some areas of the ancient world, the slave population outnumbered freemen by a ratio of 10 to 1, Engels claimed. This oppressive system was not maintained by simple force, although force was involved. It was sustained within the context of an economic structure in which land ownership was concentrated in the hands of a few and in which society accepted the legitimacy of this arrangement.

Not only are oppression and accumulation sustained within an economic structure, this structure provides the skeletal frame for the form of that oppression. In other words, as this structure changes, so does the form of oppression. This structure consists of the dominant mode of production, the level of technology, and the sum total of relations of production (Marx [1859] 1959b, p. 42). The dominant mode of production plays the most important role in shaping the form of oppression.

Mode of Production and Exploitation

Gough (1985, p. 18) defined mode of production as "the way production is organized and the means by which the production and extraction of the surplus labor or surplus product takes place." We add that modes of production are distinguishable by the way production is organized, the manner in which wealth is created and labor exploited, and the dominant way in which goods are produced.

Marx ([1859] 1959b) suggested that since ancient times, the organization of production has involved a division between two groups: a dominant class that owns the means of production and a subordinate class that does not. Exploitation occurs when the dominant group appropriates surplus value from the subordinate class. This appropriation occurs, according to Gough (1985, p. 18), when the subordinate class

> produces a social product, part and only part of which is returned to or retained by that class in the form of consumption goods (food, shelter, clothing, fuel, etc.). . . . The remainder is appropriated by the dominant class whose members or agents may use it for a variety of purposes: enlarging the stock of means of production, building lavish temples, churches, or mansions, engaging in luxury consumption, furnishing large armies, or whatever.

Thus different modes of production are distinguishable by different ways the dominant class exploits the subordinate classes and accumulates wealth. Different modes of production are also identifiable by differences in the predominant type of productive activity. These modes of production shape forms of oppression. This proposition can easily be demonstrated by examining the eras of slavery and Jim Crow. The eras of industrial capitalism and late capitalism are more complicated and require more elaboration.

In the era of slavery, the predominant productive activity was agricultural production. A dominant class not only owned the means of production—land—it owned and controlled the bodies of the slave laborers who worked on the land. This mode of production created the arrangement of direct domination that characterizes this form of oppression.

In the period of Jim Crow segregation, agricultural production continued as the major economic activity, with industrial production emerging to overtake farming. Land ownership remained concentrated in a dominant class, but this class exploited labor in a different manner. The dominant class used tenant farmers and sharecroppers, who labored under threat of starvation, to produce for their own maintenance (necessary labor) and for rent (surplus labor). Because rent and debt absorbed maintenance production, this process of exploitation perpetuated and exacerbated the poverty and misery of the subordinate class. It also contributed to a hierarchy of poverty and status, with black sharecroppers on the bottom and white landowners at the top. The lowest class, blacks, were segregated from the other classes in a system of caste and class stratification. Thus this type of exploitation provided the framework for the Jim Crow form of racial oppression.

These examples demonstrate two points:

1. Racial oppression is grounded in exploitative and oppressive economic structures, in which a dominant class privately owns the means of production and in which wealth is concentrated in this class.
2. The form of racial oppression varies with modes of production.

POLITICAL FACTORS

The state (governments, laws, and public policies) and politics play the most indeterminate and paradoxical role in maintaining racially oppressive arrangements. On the one hand, there is a general tendency for the state to protect and legitimize oppressive relations. On the other hand, under special circumstances, it mobilizes resources to ameliorate oppression and to protect the interests of oppressed people.

On the negative side of the ledger, the state has protected oppressive relations throughout most of U.S. history. Prior to the Civil War, the state protected and legitimized the institution of slavery. Article IV of the U.S. Constitution required free states to return runaway slaves to their owners who lived in slave states. State laws of the Deep South, Black Codes, defined slaves as property and gave masters absolute and legally protected power over their subjects. The *Dred Scott v. Sandford* (1857) decision denied legal protection to slaves, affirmed their status as property, and denied citizenship to African Americans. *Plessy v. Ferguson* (1896) legitimized segregation with the "separate but equal" doctrine. Court support for private property and legal tolerance for private discrimination allowed for the development of a racial caste system in the era of industrial capitalism.

On the positive side of the ledger, the state has mobilized resources to provide some protection for African Americans during special periods in history: especially during the Reconstruction period and the civil rights era of the 1960s. Moreover, the role of the state has evolved in positive ways over time, particularly as the political power of African Americans has grown. In the past, the state reinforced the total and absolute control over enslaved African Americans, denied them any hint of human rights, and defined them as property. Today, African Americans play a minor role in shaping state policies, and the state provides limited civil rights protection, although racial discrimination persists in politics, labor markets, and other areas.

Theories of the state offer some explanations for its paradoxical role. Although a thorough examination of these theories goes well beyond the scope of our model of racism, we provide some explanations extrapolated from the literature. We organize our discussion into three parts: (1) traditional theories, (2) new political economy, and (3) ideology, politics, and social change.

Traditional Theories

Traditional theories of the state offer some explanations for the predisposition of the state to support racially oppressive relations. These theories can be divided into four categories: elitist, pluralist, systemic, and political party theories.

Elitism suggests that economic elites who benefit from racially oppressive arrangements dominate both politics and the state. They dominate politics because they tend to be well-endowed with resources, well-organized, clear about their goals, and articulate in expressing their interests. They tend to be disproportionately recruited into the state, either through election or appointment. Captains of plantations and industry are more likely to be selected into top-level governmental service because of their leadership skills and because their assistance is often needed to implement state policies, particularly those involving economic development. These elites played a dominant role in the construction of the U.S. Constitution. The Philadelphia constitutional convention was dominated by the planter class from the South and the merchant class from the North. According to elitist theory, the Constitution protected the institution of slavery precisely because plantation owners who had a stake in the maintenance of this institution played a dominant role in writing it (Beard 1941; Parenti 1988; Lowi and Ginsberg 1994; Dye and Ziegler 1996). The role of these elites exemplifies the general tendency of the state to support racially oppressive conditions.

Pluralist theory takes issue with the elitist explanation. Indeed, studies demonstrating the role of white working-class organizations in supporting racially exclusionary labor rules and state policies suggest an alternative to the elitist perspective (Woodward 1974; Wilson 1980; Foner 1981). The state supports racially oppressive arrangements because powerful interest groups pressure the state to do so, pluralist theory holds.

Systemic theorists argue that the state, for economic and political reasons, is predisposed to support upper stratum interest in society because this stratum generates the resources necessary for the maintenance of the state and because the state anticipates the political consequences of not supporting this stratum: formidable political opposition. Within this framework, the state is constrained by political and economic arrangements to protect the interest of the upper stratum (Lindblom 1977; Stone 1980).

Theories of political parties suggest that national party organizations in the United States must hold together a broad-based political coalition in order to win the presidency. This coalition is made up of diverse and sometimes contradictory political interests. Historically, racial ideology has functioned as a glue holding some of these coalitions together. Saxon (1990) demonstrated the role of this ideology in the Jacksonian, Whig, and Republican parties of the 19th century. Edsall and Edsall (1992) suggested that the old New Deal coalition fell apart after Johnson supported aggressive civil rights laws and that a new racial ideology emerged to hold a new conservative coalition together under the Reagan and Bush Republican party of the 1980s. This theory suggests that state support for racially oppressive arrangements results in part from the role of party coalitions held together by racial ideologies.

The New Political Economy

The contemporary Marxist literature offers additional explanations for the state's role in protecting oppressive arrangements. These explanations include the accumulation and legitimation functions of the state and the role of ideology.

Because of its dependency on the economy and its need for prosperity, the state is constrained to assist producers in their efforts to accumulate capital (O'Connor 1973). This accumulation process is required for economic expansion. The state assists in this process by building roads, harbors, railroads, and other instruments of commerce.

The state also functions to legitimize itself and the economic order within which it exists. It must operate to maintain law, order, stability, and social harmony. It accomplishes these tasks militarily, ideologically, and materially. It keeps a military presence, and it uses police powers to force compliance with oppressive laws and to suppress revolts or protests. It creates doctrines to justify slavery, racial segregation, and discrimination.

Ideology, Politics, and Social Change

Gramsci (1980) provides a dynamic framework for analyzing the changing role of the state. His model not only explains change, it explains how the dominant class is able to maintain its advantaged position despite grassroots opposition. His theory centers on the concept of hegemony. Summarizing Gramsci's concept of hegemony, Carnoy (1984, p. 87) said,

> In his doctrine of "hegemony," Gramsci saw that the dominant class did not have to rely solely on the coercive power of the state or even its direct economic power to rule; rather, through its hegemony, expressed in the civil society and the state, the ruled could be persuaded to accept the system of beliefs of the ruling class and to share its social, cultural, and moral values.

Within Gramsci's framework, political change or continuity are explained primarily by the crisis of hegemony, the war of position, and the war of maneuver. Explaining the problem of political change, Gramsci (1980, p. 235) said,

> The superstructures of civil society are like the trench systems of modern warfare. In war it would sometimes happen that a fierce artillery attack seemed to have destroyed the enemy's entire defensive system, whereas in fact it had only destroyed the outer perimeter; and at the moment of their advance and attack, the assailants would find themselves confronted by a line of defense which was still effective. The same thing happens in politics, during the great economic crises. A crisis cannot give the attacking forces the ability to organize with lightning speed in time and space.

Disruptive historical events, wars, economic upheavals, industrialization, urbanization, and international pressures precipitate hegemony crises. These crises are like artillery barrages. They weaken the defenses of the dominant class and create conditions ripe for social change. However, change does not occur automatically. It arises out of a *war of position* and a *war of maneuver.*

The war of position involves an ideological struggle between the subordinate and dominant classes. The subordinate groups—armed with new ways of thinking, new morality, and new ideas—challenge the ideology of the dominant class. The dominant class fights back with its ideology, its morality, its belief system, and its way of thinking. It uses existing culture and tradition to convince other social groups to accept the existing order as natural, rational, and legitimate. It depicts alternative orders as unnatural and irrational. It exploits the values, sensitivities, and identities of other groups in order to persuade them to support the present order. If their ideas are refuted and their political position weakened, they struggle to reformulate their ideology and reinforce their position. Some scholars have suggested that the eras following Reconstruction and the civil rights movement were periods of reformulation (Marable 1986; Omi and Winant 1990).

The war of maneuver is the assault on the trenches. It is a movement of oppressed groups to capture the state and to force the dominant class to relinquish power. Of course, for the most part, the upper class has maintained a superior position in the political arena and has dominated the state. Its hegemony arises from several sources. It emerges from the upper class's positional advantage, derived from its superior resources and from its control of production facilities. It comes from the dominant class's ability to persuade subordinate classes to accept its beliefs, values, and worldview. It also arises from the infrequency of social movements. Thus, although the political arena is the most indeterminate in explaining the maintenance of oppressive arrangements, the state has generally operated to protect these arrangements, especially when they favor the dominant class.

CULTURE

Whereas racial oppression is grounded in oppressive and exploitative economic arrangements and maintained by the state, culture plays a role in sustaining racism. That is, culture structures the way people think about and behave toward race in ways that perpetuate racial oppression. In order to demonstrate this function of culture, we need to answer three questions: What is culture? How does it shape the way people think about and behave toward race? How does it operate to sustain racial oppression?

What Is Culture?

Culture is a multifaceted phenomenon that provides the context out of which human consciousness develops. Culture embodies collective experiences, language, symbols, values, myths, and fantasies. It provides ways of resolving the universal dilemmas of human development—the crisis of separation from parents and of sibling rivalry (Lasch 1979). It constitutes worldviews. It contains models of the world, modes of explaining, and ways of interpreting reality. It harbors basic expectations and presuppositions about phenomena. It entails learned and shared patterns of behaving and thinking. It reflects the social character of society.

With culture, people do not have to learn from their experiences alone. They learn from the collective experiences of others, passed on from one generation to the next. With culture, people do not have to invent words and symbols for communications. Language already exists as part of culture, learned and shared by members of society and passed on from one generation to the next.

How Does Culture Shape the Way People Think?

Culture provides a framework for perception and judgment. Perception is not a matter of facts and events making impressions on a blank mind. Rather, facts and events acquire meaning within the context of a perceptual framework. This framework consists of language, symbols, images, myths, metaphors, and values. It also contains assumptions, expectations, and presuppositions about reality. These aspects of a perceptual framework interact. For example, metaphors and images embody expectations; definitions of words contain assumptions; symbols represent definitions and meanings. This framework operates like a special lens through which we view and interpret the world. This lens filters information and focuses attention. It tells us which facts are important, which to ignore, and which to take for granted. It influences our emotional reaction to the world.

Kuhn (1975) offered insights into the manner in which culture operates as a cognitive framework that shapes perception, although he focused on perceptual frameworks in the context of scientific epistemology. He referred to these frameworks as paradigms. He maintained that they are constructed out of collectively accepted sets of assumptions and expectations about the world and established ways of explaining and interpreting phenomena. He argued that scientific revolutions occur, not with the discovery of new facts, but with the construction of new paradigms that provide new ways of interpreting and perceiving phenomena.

Kuhn (1975) provided several examples of how paradigms shape perception. In one example, he compared the phlogiston paradigm with the oxidation one. When a block of burning wood is viewed through the lens of the phlogiston paradigm, this burning phenomenon is interpreted in terms of a substance, phlogiston, breaking away from a burning piece of material. This paradigm contains the expectation that the burning material will be lighter after it is burnt, as the phlogiston has left it. Weighing the material before and after burning confirms the phlogiston hypothesis. However, when the same phenomenon is viewed through a different paradigm, such as the oxidation framework, an entirely different process is observed. The oxidation paradigm assumes that burning is a process in which oxygen molecules combine with carbon and other molecules. The expectation of this paradigm is that burning will produce new molecules—carbon monoxide (CO), carbon dioxide (CO^2), and water (H_2O)—as oxygen molecules combine with carbon and hydrogen ones. People using the phlogiston paradigm perceive burning in ways profoundly different from those who operate within the oxidation paradigm. The paradigm structures perception.

Cultural perceptual frameworks operate the same way as these two scientific paradigms. Explaining the nature of the cultural perceptual framework, Hall (1981, p. 85) said,

> One of the functions of culture is to provide a highly selective screen between man and the outside world. In its many forms, culture therefore designates what we pay attention to and what we ignore. This screening function provides structure for the world and protects the nervous system from "information overload."

Hall suggested that culture contains models that give meaning to the world and provide the context for understanding and judging events and phenomena. He added, "Myths, philosophical systems, and science represent different types of models of what the social scientists call cognitive systems" (p. 13).

This view of culture suggests that race and racial differences do not exist out there in the real world. Rather, race and racial differences are cultural constructs, products of a cultural perceptual framework. This framework shapes perception of differences and ascribes meaning to those differences. Illustrating this point, Fields (1982) recounted an interview between an American journalist and the late Papa Doc Duvalier of Haiti. In the interview, Papa Doc claimed that 98% of the Haitian population was white. The perplexed interviewer asked Papa Doc how Haitians determine who is white, whereupon Papa Doc asked how Americans determine who is black. Fields (p. 146) said, "Receiving the explanation that in the United States anyone with any black blood was considered black, Duvalier nodded and said, 'Well, that's the way we define white in my country.' " The creation of the terms *white* and *black,* the meanings ascribed to these categories, the determination of who is placed in which category, expectations about the behavior of whites and blacks—all these are functions and products of the cultural perceptual framework. These frameworks arose in the modern period. They vary from one country to another and from one milieu to another.

How Does Culture Operate to Sustain Racial Oppression?

The dominant American cultural paradigm has historically operated to sustain racial oppression. To understand this function, we must examine various aspects of this culture, especially language, symbols, images, and values. We must also analyze the basic assumptions, expectations, and views of the world contained in this dominant culture.

For example, consider the word *race* itself. This word arises from a cultural perceptual framework based on particular assumptions about human difference. These assumptions are the following:

1. Differences in skin color and other physical characteristics among people represent different subspecies of humankind.
2. These subspecies are substantially different from each other.
3. These subspecies are hierarchically arranged from superior to inferior in intelligence, virtue, and other capabilities.
4. The term race is meaningful in interpreting and explaining variations in human behavior and potentials.

The word race arises from a racist paradigm; that is, one that explains perceived differences in human behavior and potentials—especially differences in levels of intelligence and virtue—in terms of differences in races or biological species or subspecies of humankind.

For another example, consider the word *mongrel.* This word makes sense only in a racist paradigm. It implies that the mixing of superior with inferior races would destroy or corrupt the superior race. This term was common in American racist culture, especially before the 1960s, not only among extremist groups but also in established institutions, such as the judicial system. A 1955 Virginia Appeals Court decision, *Naim v. Naim,* illustrates this point. This case involved a state law prohibiting interracial marriage, enacted allegedly to protect the physical and moral well-being of the citizens. The court maintained that the State of Virginia had a right to protect the racial integrity of the people of Virginia and to prevent the mongrelization of the white race. Specifically, the court said,

> We are unable to read in the Fourteenth Amendment to the Constitution, or in any other provision of that great document, any words or any intendment which prohibits the state from enacting legislation to preserve the racial integrity of its citizens, or which denies the power of the state to regulate the marriage relations so that it shall not have a mongrel breed of citizens. (quoted in Bosmajian 1983, p. 42)

The use of the phrase *mongrel breed* makes sense only within a racist paradigm. It embodies the assumptions of this paradigm. At the same time, this paradigm structures the way its proponents think and talk about human relations. It reinforces racist ways of thinking and talking about the world.

Not just the words, but the manner in which words are defined within paradigms, supports racist ways of thinking. Consider the words white and black for example. White is defined as Caucasian, pure, innocent, free from blemishes, not intending harm. Black is defined as "pertaining to a dark-skinned race; soiled; stained; foreboding; devoid of light or goodness; deadly, malignant or morbid" (*Webster's New World Dictionary,* 1976). Black is the antithesis of white. Black is bad and dirty; white is good and clean. Black is evil and ugly. White is righteous and beautiful.

Some words not only contain derogatory notions of blacks, they also symbolize something debased and trigger enraging or revolting emotions. For example, the word *nigger* symbolizes the lowest of the lowest class and race in American society. It not only debases blacks, it triggers enraging and revolting emotions against them.

Today, the urban underclass symbolizes the lowest class made up of violent men, street criminals, drug addicts, immoral women, welfare dependents, and the homeless. This term evokes feelings of fear and revulsion. It is a more polite version of the term nigger, but it serves the same purpose.

Dehumanizing images of the black character have been part of the American cultural paradigm since slavery, although they have changed from epoch to epoch. During the era of slavery, these images included pictures of happy, lazy, dumb, chicken-stealing black men and of over-weight, talkative, brainless black women. They included figures like Little Black Sambo, Aunt Jemima, and Stepin Fetchit. Today these images include pictures of large, bull-like, dangerous black men on drugs and of overweight, welfare-dependent black women. These dehumanizing images are transmitted through television, newspapers, movies, and literature. They function to reinforce racial oppression.

Freedom, Equality, and Justice in American Culture

Other terms within the American cultural framework operate to support racially oppressive arrangements, although they were not intended to serve this function. Consider the terms *equality* and *freedom*. These terms, prevalent in American culture, appear anathema to racism. The notion that all men are created equal is inconsistent with the belief in the inferiority of blacks. Freedom is contrary to slavery. It would seem that the belief in equality and freedom would create pressures to eliminate racial oppression. It did not.

These terms failed to ameliorate racial oppression for two main reasons. First, they were suppressed by racist perspectives. In the racist mind, the "we the people" in the Constitution included whites only, not blacks. The idea that whites were superior to blacks superseded the notion that all people were created equal.

Second, Americans conceptualize freedom and equality in ways most tolerant of racial oppression. Freedom within the American political tradition has been negative freedom rather than positive freedom. Positive freedom involves the creation of conditions conducive to human growth and the development and realization of human potentials. It requires a downward redistribution of resources. Negative freedom is freedom from restraints and from government intrusion. It is the freedom to live, to work, and to associate with others as one pleases. In the antebellum South, negative freedom meant the freedom to own slaves and the freedom from federal intervention in slavery. Myrdal ([1948] 1975) and other social scientists (Dollard 1949) have long recognized the manner in which racists have used this notion of negative freedom to justify segregation. Apologists for racial discrimination and segregation have argued that people should have the freedom to hire, associate with, live next door to, or send their children to school with whomever they please, even if the outcome is racial exclusion or segregation. This negative concept of freedom explains why most Americans appear to be nonracists, claim to abhor racial discrimination, and yet oppose government action to eliminate racial discrimination, root and branch (Jaynes and Williams 1989).

Americans have a similar problem with their concept of equality. They prefer the restrictive *equal treatment* definition over the expansive *equitable outcomes* definition. Equal treatment means treating all people the same and judging them on their merit, regardless of their background. Adherents to this definition resist efforts to redistribute resources to give more to those who have less in order to equalize chances of success in life (Ryan 1982). They see inequality arising out of differences in levels of talent, effort, intelligence, and ingenuity, exercised in an open system that treats all people the same. Although this view is not inherently racist, it allows for the easy explanation that blacks occupy a subordinate position in this society because they lack talent, intelligence, and motivation. This equal treatment definition is more tolerant of racist explanations of black subordination.

Bellah et al. (1986), in *Habits of the Heart,* pointed out that the American political tradition encourages Americans to think about justice in terms of fair treatment and equal opportunity. The problem with this concept of justice is that it is devoid of a vision of a fair distribution of societal resources. Bellah et al. (p. 26) concluded, "Unfortunately, our available moral traditions do not give us nearly as many resources for thinking about distributive justice as about procedural justice and even fewer for thinking about substantive justice."

This adherence to the equal treatment definition of equality and this absence of a concept of distributive or substantive justice partially explain the historical tolerance of American political institutions for racial injustice. For example, between *Plessy v. Ferguson* (1896) and *Brown v. Board of Education* (1954), the U.S. Supreme Court permitted states to segregate blacks in the worst schools, to deny them the right to vote, to prohibit interracial marriages, to bar blacks from public facilities, to allow the execution of blacks at a rate of about 10 blacks to every 1 white executed for rape (figures estimated from Bell 1973, p. 949)—all on grounds that procedures and treatment appeared fair and equal. The Court permitted segregation so long as it appeared that black and white schools were treated equally. It allowed states to deny blacks the right to vote so long as the denial was not based directly on race and so long as the standards used for denial—poll taxes or literacy tests—appeared to apply to all people. It permitted, and still permits today, states to execute a disproportionately greater number of blacks than whites, so long as it appears that the same law is applied equally to each person who commits a capital crime. In almost every case, the Court focused on the issue of same or equal treatment. The Court disregarded racial inequalities in outcomes and lacked a vision of substantive justice.

Segregation and racial oppression were not threatened until the Court shifted from an equal treatment framework to a just outcome one. Progress against segregation did not occur in the courts until the justice system began to look at outcomes.

Racism, Culture, and Social Character

Whereas language, symbols, and political terms affect the way Americans think about racial issues and operate to sustain racial oppression, there is another dimension of culture that serves these functions: social character and the collective unconscious.

Fromm (1965) suggested a relationship between economic production and distribution, on the one hand, and the formation of dominant character types, on the other. For example, he noted that early capitalism's dependency on savings to accumulate wealth contributed to the development of the hoarding character type, especially in the 18th and early 19th centuries. He also observed that industrial capitalism's emphasis on exploitation encouraged the development of the oral exploitative character, especially in the late 19th and early 20th centuries.

Kovel (1984) argued that racism is associated with particular social character types, and it involves the repression of specific drives and fantasies in the collective unconscious. He associated the anal character with the aversive racism of Jim Crow segregation. Oral exploitative and narcissistic character types can be associated with contemporary forms of racism. These dominant social characters are driven to maintain patterns of racial oppression. The anal character is driven to maintain the separation of races; the oral exploitative type is driven to exploit the powerless races.

These drives can be traced to emotions and fantasies repressed in the collective or social unconscious. The social unconscious, Fromm (1971, p. 88) said, refers

> to those areas of repression which are common to most members of a society; these commonly repressed elements are those contents which a given society cannot permit its members to be aware of if the society with its specific contradictions is to operate successfully.

Kovel (1984, p. 104) defined the collective unconscious "as the summation, on a mass level, of the unconscious mental processes of the people in a social group." He related it to the Cultural Id and concluded that the Western Cultural Id embodies intense drives to accumulate wealth, drives to separate the world between the dirty and the pure, drives to dominate people and nature. These drives undergird racism. They are irrational and powerful forces. The maintenance of civilization and rationality requires their repression in the collective unconscious.

These drives fuel racial oppression and racial violence. They have been the energy behind the genocide against Native Americans, the African slave trade, the institution of slavery, Jim Crow segregation, and industrial caste systems. The interaction of these drives with race has contributed to the construction of racist images and fantasies, such as the image of the happy and lazy slave; fantasies of sexually promiscuous blacks; pictures of savagely violent and primitive blacks; fantasies of feces representing repulsive people. They support racial oppression and encourage racial violence.

Racial violence is seen here, not as a psychological aberration found in an individual out of touch with reality, but as the surfacing of culturally repressed drives and fantasies about race. As Kovel (1984, p. 52) said, "After all, the bigot is the man who applies the blow that society prepares for the racially oppressed." He added,

> At the far end of normality, the bigot may present himself as tolerant and rational, and may hold his racist belief in a remote attic-room of his consciousness; may have, under impetus of moral censure, driven it from consciousness into a latent zone that is not activated until a black attempts to move next door. (p. 52)

ECONOMIC BASE AND POLITICAL AND CULTURAL SUPERSTRUCTURES

We have drawn from a broad literature in an attempt to build a model for explaining the formation and perpetuation of racism in the United States. We construct our model in the historical materialist framework. That is, we reject the idealist notion that racism and racial differences are merely attitudes or images that are voluntarily created by the mind. We eschew the materialist view that racism is caused by inexorable economic forces. Our historical materialist framework is based on the assumption that racism emerged during a particular stage in history, under particular material conditions, and in dynamic ways. We focus on the economic base of racial oppression, which contributes directly to political and cultural aspects of racism. We see the relationship between base and superstructure as dynamic and interactive. Moreover, we see politics as an indeterminate factor.

In developing this eclectic model, we combine several different but complementary perspectives. Each perspective focuses on different aspects of the relationship between base and superstructure. These perspectives include the Marxist-Gramscian, the radical psychoanalytical, and the neo-Weberian models.

Marxist-Gramscian Approach

Economic base is a broad Marxist term that refers to the primary mode of production, instruments of production, social relations of production, the way in which people are treated in the process of producing goods and services, the manner in which wealth is generated and distributed, and other economic processes and arrangements. In a racially oppressive society the important elements of this base include the following:

1. Wealth, concentrated in the hands of a few
2. Private ownership of the primary means of production
3. An exploitative accumulation process
4. Alienating and dehumanizing modes of production
5. Hierarchical relations in production

In this model, racial oppression is understood as arising out of an exploitative accumulation process in which wealth is concentrated in the hands of a few. Racial oppression is grounded in this economic base, which in turn sustains racial oppression.

This economic base, with its concentrated wealth, produces a dominant class that maintains its hegemony and protects these oppressive arrangements in several ways. It captures or pressures the state to use state power to protect these arrangements. It creates a racial ideology to convince members of all classes that these arrangements are legitimate and natural and that more equitable arrangements will be disastrous. Persuading members of other classes to accept inequitable and oppressive arrangements is a more powerful way of sustaining oppression than the use of state power. This persuasion occurs more readily with the construction of racist culture.

Although culture is constructed in many ways and on both individual and social levels, the dominant class plays a major role in the initial construction of racist culture. Members of this class generate racist discourse in their everyday conversations about the oppressed. This process was most evident in the antebellum South, as planters talked about their slaves and the legitimacy of slavery. This culture arises as members of this dominant class become active socially and politically. Members of the dominant class are disproportionately represented among political leaders. They are in key positions to disseminate their ideas. Their worldview becomes well-known throughout society as they or their sympathizers articulate it in state legislatures, in the U.S. Congress, in courtrooms, in administrative offices, on political campaign trails—train stops, convention halls, and so on—and in the newspapers, magazines, theaters, and other media sources. Members of this class often own local newspapers or are able to influence the editorial boards, especially when newspapers depend on advertising revenues from this class. Members of the dominant class have the resources and the connections to make their views known to a wide audience. They make substantial contributions to major universities. They often influence universities that train people for other institutions, such as schools, churches, courts, businesses, and industries.

Once racist culture is established and permeates the major institutions of society, it functions to perpetuate racial oppression. It influences people of all classes, including white workers, to accept racially oppressive arrangements as natural, rational, and legitimate.

Gramsci's (1980) model of the relationship between economic base and politics and culture is dynamic in the sense that it accounts for political conflict. This model considers the possibility of social movements. In these movements, efficacious oppressed groups are able to capture parts of the state for use in ameliorating oppressive conditions and challenging racist culture by underscoring its irrational and oppressive features and by articulating an alternative worldview. The possibility of social movements makes the outcome of political struggles uncertain and indeterminate. It makes the construction and reconstruction of culture dynamic.

Radical Psychoanalytical Approach

The radical psychoanalytical approach associates oppressive modes of production and relations of production with psychological processes that explain the formation of oppressive social character types and cultural forms. For example, this framework sees a strong association between the slave mode of production and the formation of the sadistic character type. This mode of production required the master to exercise intense, direct, and incessant control over the slave. The sadistic character type was most successful in operating a slave plantation. Hence, it emerged as the dominant social character associated with the slave mode of production.

The psychoanalytical approach also connects the formation of racial images to particular psychological needs and processes. For example, the image of blacks as sexually promiscuous is connected to the process of repression/projection; the white racist mind represses its own sexual impulses and projects them onto blacks. The image of the black cannibal is connected to whites' intense fear of those blacks who are unrestrained by white society. The image of the childlike Black Sambo is related to the white racist mind's need to see the controlled black slave as innocuous.

The psychoanalytical approach associates the formation of racist discourse and images with the fulfillment of ego needs. For example, in order for the slave master to live with himself and to see himself as a good, decent Christian after brutalizing the slave, the master had to dehumanize the slave. The master's ego, his image of himself as a decent human being, required that he see the slave as less than human, as a subspecies, like an ape or a monkey. His ego needed ideas and discourse that justify slavery as a natural, rational, and legitimate arrangement.

Weberian Approach

The Weberian approach focuses on hierarchical arrangements and cultural processes. There are several ways in which these arrangements are associated with the formation of racist culture. Within a class/caste society, identification with the dominant white group yielded special privileges and higher status. This arrangement encouraged lower status ethnic groups to define themselves as white. White identity deflected discriminatory treatment and gave esteem to the lowest class white worker. This arrangement also allowed higher strata workers, especially skilled laborers, to identify with the dominant class. These higher strata workers had a greater stake in the preservation of existing arrangements. They tended to join the dominant class in justifying these arrangements. When these arrangements involved racial oppression, higher skilled white workers often played a major role in justifying racial exclusion.

In our analysis of racism, we draw from this approach. It is like a special lens, sharpening our focus on the dynamics of racial oppression. We use it to help us explain the origins of racism in Chapter 3 and the nature of racism in four historical stages in Chapters 4 through 7.

3

The Historical Origins of Racism

Racism is a modern historical phenomenon, grounded in alienating, exploitative, and oppressive economic arrangements. It arose in a particular stage in history, after the dissolution of feudalism, after the Protestant Reformation, and with the rise of a new economic order undergirded by an intense drive to accumulate wealth. This drive was both a creative and a liberating force. At the same time, it was destructive, dehumanizing, and exploitative. On the one hand, it contributed to the growth of Western culture and civilization. On the other, it fueled the genocide against Native Americans and propelled the Atlantic slave trade. Modern racism emerged out of slavery and colonialism. These economic institutions created clear demarcation lines between the oppressed and the oppressor, which overlapped with color lines. The oppressed were not only separated from the oppressors, the oppressed were primarily people of color. The notion that people of color were of a different species and were inferior to the oppressors functions to legitimize the oppressive arrangement and to desensitize the dominant group to the plight of the oppressed.

RACISM AND ANCIENT CIVILIZATION

A number of scholars who have examined the history of the concept of race and race prejudice suggest that there are few examples of race prejudice in ancient civilizations. Du Bois presents evidence of race prejudice emerging in India about 5,000 years ago, after the light-skinned Aryans conquered the darker-skinned inhabitants. The lighter-skinned people despised the darker-skinned ones. However, Du Bois (1969a, p. 177) concluded, "The whites long held the conquered blacks in caste servitude, but eventually the color line disappeared before commerce and industry, intermarriage, and defense against enemies from without." Underscoring Du Bois's view, Gossett (1971, p. 7) said, "If race ever was the original basis of caste in India it did not remain so."

Although the Greeks were aware of differences in skin color, these differences did not have the same connotation they have in modern society. The Greeks, for example, referred to Africa as the land of the burnt faces, but they never attached a stigma to darker skin color (Du Bois 1969b).

The Greeks were suspicious of foreigners, and they were chauvinistic, but they treated foreigners who became part of their society, including Africans, much as they treated their own people. Although the Greeks divided people into Greeks and barbarians, this division was nonracial. It was based on membership in society rather than racial or ethnic origin. Arguing this point more succinctly, Cox (1970, p. 323) said,

> The Greeks knew that they had a superior culture to those of the barbarians, but they included Europeans, Africans, and Asiatics in the concept Hellas as these peoples acquired a working knowledge of the Greek culture. . . . The experience of the later Hellenistic empire of Alexander tended to be the direct contrary of modern racial antagonism.

The Greek myth of Phaëthon, the son of the god Helios, illustrates the point that Greek culture explains differences in skin color as a function of different levels of exposure to the sun. According to this legend, Phaëthon convinced his father to allow him to pilot the sun chariot across the sky. Phaëthon lost control of the chariot and drove it "too close to the earth in some regions, burning the people there black, and drove it too far from the earth in other regions, whose inhabitants turned pale from the cold" (Gossett 1971, p. 6). In Greek culture, darker skin meant closer exposure to the sun and little else.

The Greek philosopher Aristotle wrote about slavery and race. Although his writings were used to justify black slavery in 19th-century United States, his views are profoundly different from those of modern racists. In the early 1800s, supporters of slavery in the United States interpreted Aristotle as saying that some races are naturally suited for slavery. Indeed, in his *Politics,* Aristotle (1969, p. 11) said, "For there is one rule exercised over subjects who are by nature free, another over subjects who are by nature slaves." He added, "The master is not called a master because he has science, but because he is of a certain character, and the same remark applies to the slave and the freeman" (p. 12).

Although Aristotle justified slavery, he offered some criticisms. He conceded that it is possible for powerful nations to engage in unjust wars and make slaves of the nobility of the conquered nations. He intimated that slavery should not be a permanent state and that slaves should be rewarded with liberty (Aristotle 1969, p. 191). Moreover, he suggested that constitutional governments, which rule by law rather than by nature, are inconsistent with slavery (pp. 11-12).

Aristotle maintained that racial differences are products of climatic and environmental differences and that slaves taken in war are often more intelligent than their captors. Specifically he said,

> Those who live in a cold climate and in Europe are full of spirit, but wanting in intelligence and skill; and there they retain comparative freedom, but have no political organization, and are incapable of ruling over others. Whereas the natives of Asia are intelligent and inventive, but they are wanting in spirit, and therefore they are always in a state of subjection and slavery. But the Hellenic race, which is situated between them, is likewise intermediate in character, being high-spirited and also intelligent. Hence it continues free, and is the best-governed of any nation, and if it could be formed into one state, would be able to rule the world. (Aristotle's *Politics,* quoted in Gossett 1971, p. 6)

Aristotle did not see slaves as less intelligent, less virtuous, or less human than others. In contrast, modern racism stigmatizes oppressed racial groups as less intelligent, less virtuous, and less human than the dominant racial groups.

Like the Greeks, the Romans were chauvinistic but not racist. Commenting on the Romans, Cox (1970, p. 324) said,

> In this civilization also we do not find racial antagonism, for the norm of superiority in the Roman system remained a cultural-class attribute. . . . Sometimes the slaves, especially the Greeks, were the teachers of their masters; indeed, very much of the cultural enlightenment of the Romans came through slaves from the East. Because slavery did not carry a racial stigma, educated freedmen, who were granted citizenship upon emancipation, might rise to high positions in government or industry. There were no interracial laws governing the relationship of the great mass of obscure common people of different origin.

A number of historians corroborate Cox's contention that the type of color prejudice found in modern America and in Western society simply did not exist in the ancient world. For example, Snowden (1983, p. 63) said,

> Yet nothing comparable to the virulent color prejudice found in modern times existed in the ancient world. This is the view of most scholars who have examined the evidence and who have come to conclusions much as these: the ancients did not fall into the error of biological racism; black skin color was not a sign of inferiority, Greeks and Romans did not establish color as an obstacle to integration in society; and ancient society was one that, for all its faults and failures, never made color the basis for judging a man.

Snowden concluded that Greek and Roman culture portrayed a favorable image of blacks. This favorable image is evident in the works of Greek and Roman artists, historians, philosophers, poets, and writers, including Ovid and Homer. Commenting on the integration of African characters into Greek and Roman mythology, Snowden (1983, p. 94) said that Zeus, "called the Ethiopian by the inhabitants of Chios, may have been the black- or dark-faced stranger in the Inachus of Sophocles (c. 496-406 B.C.) and may have appeared as a Negro in the dramatist's satyr-play." Other black figures include Delphos, the founder of the Delphi, whose name means the Black Woman, and Andromeda, wife of Perseus, who was the daughter of an Ethiopian king. Although these figures were depicted as black, their images have been positive and well-integrated in Greek culture.

Color for the Greeks and Romans did not have the same connotation that it had for the Western world after the 17th century. For example, Africans intermarried with Greeks and Romans and held prominent positions in these societies. In contrast, during the 19th and 20th centuries, U.S. laws prohibited interracial marriages, black skin was a stigma of inferiority, and slavery or sharecropping were fixed social stations.

For the most part, incorporation and accommodation followed conquest in ancient societies. When the Greeks conquered the Egyptians, they incorporated Egyptian culture—science, mathematics, philosophy, and technology—and advanced Greek culture well beyond its preconquest state. The Romans advanced their culture after conquering, incorporating, and accommodating the Greeks. Both Romans and Greeks struggled to maintain cultural unity in the midst of color diversity. This pattern began to break down in late feudalism, especially during the Crusades.

THE FEUDAL ERA: CHRISTIANITY, THE CRUSADES, AND RACISM

Prior to the Crusades, the Christian Church was a powerful force promoting the unity of people. According to the New Testament, Jesus came not to save a chosen few, but all of humankind. St. Paul (Acts 24-26, King James Version) said, "God that made the world and all things therein. . . . And hath made of one blood all nations of men for to dwell on all the face of the earth." St. Augustine argued that all people—regardless of color, language, movement, or physical appearance—are of the same origin (Gossett 1971, p. 9). Early Christians believed that all people of all nations were of the same blood. The doctrine of the early church was the antithesis of racism.

The role of the church in promoting the unity of man ended during the Crusades, when the church called for Christians to wrench the Holy Land from the hands of infidels. The Crusades ignited flames of hatred toward non-Christians, primarily Muslims and Jews. Apparently, hatred toward Muslims generated by the Crusades was turned on the Jews.

Pope Urban II lit the fuse of this hatred in a sermon he delivered before the Council of Clermont, on November 26, 1095 A.D. This sermon incited a religious frenzy to avenge the blood of Christ and to attack the opponents of Christianity. Six months after the pope's sermon, Crusaders began to assault Jews. They attacked several synagogues and Jewish communities along the Rhine valley. At Worms, with the cooperation of the local burghers, the Crusaders massacred a Jewish community (Gossett 1971, p. 10; Roth 1972, pp. 180-81).

These events signaled the beginning of a series of brutal assaults on Jews that continued throughout history. Horrendous myths emerged to rationalize the atrocious treatment of the Jews. These myths and brutal treatment define anti-Semitism, a form of racism. Jews were said to belong to a different race, to have contaminated blood, to engage in ritual child murder, to practice sorcery, and to oppose Christ.

THE ORIGIN OF MODERN RACISM

The dynamics of anti-Semitism were similar to the dynamics of white racism. Both involved the brutal oppression of a group identified by race and a system of ideas and myths that rationalized the oppression.

However, white racism did not emerge until after the dissolution of feudalism. Racism ascended with the rise of modern Western Europe. It grew out of the same historical forces that elevated Western Europe to world domination. It emerged after the Protestant Reformation, after the discovery of the Americas, after the decline of feudalism, and after the development of new economic forces of production and exchange. These historical events were both liberating and enslaving, both creative and destructive. They provided the foundation for freer social relations, democratic political institutions, new technology—in short, they were the basis of the growth of Western culture. At the same time, these events were the fertile ground in which the seeds of modern racism were planted.

Although the organization of feudalism varied in different parts of Europe, feudal society tended to be rigidly structured with a hierarchical social order. Members of this society were chained to their social position and to their geographical area with little chance of moving up the social ladder or relocating to other parts of the country. Their behavior and economic activities were governed by strict rules. Artisans were obligated to sell their products at a fixed place for a fixed price. Members of guilds were forbidden to share trade secrets with nonmembers (Fromm 1965).

Both the feudal landlord and the peasant farmer were tied to the land in a system of mutual obligation. The peasant was obligated to work the land, pay duty to the lord, and sell his produce at the designated market. The lord was required to provide protection for his subjects.

Although this class structure was rigid and paternalistic, it gave its members a sense of belonging, community, and security. People were identified by their class, peasant, artisan, or lord. They found support among their peers. They were members of a local community, in the village. Lords provided security both from external threats and internal strife. The concept of *noblesse oblige,* the obligations of the members of the upper classes to those of the lower classes, emerged out of this system (Fromm 1965).

Feudal society began to weaken as early as the 13th century, after the Crusades and after the discovery of markets in China following the journeys of Marco Polo. By the end of the 15th century, the feudal order was dissolving, and new money and merchant classes were developing. With the growth of cities and new modes of production, peasant and artisan classes were dislocated. The sense of belonging and security found in the feudal system was disappearing.

Merchants, bankers, and small manufacturers emerged as prominent classes with the decline of feudalism and the rise of mercantilism.

These new classes were no longer tied to local markets, no longer restricted by feudal laws or rules of mutual obligation. They became free to make the entire world a market and to transform anything and everything in it into a commodity, a thing of value to be sold on the market for profit.

Alienation, Accumulation, Religion, and Racism

The dissolution of feudalism and the rise of mercantilism and capitalism did two things related to the rise of racism. First, these conditions generated a heightened sense of human alienation from community, labor, production, and self. That is, the new, postfeudal people became alienated from community, as they became dislocated from the land and as people became more transient. They became alienated from their own labor, as labor became a commodity to be sold on the market. Labor alienation became more complete with industrial production as workers lost control over the production process. That is, unlike artisans of the feudal period, industrial workers neither designed nor produced the entire product. They functioned as cogs in the larger machinery of production. They no longer realized their human potential in the process of production. They became alienated from their own potential, and thus, from themselves. This alienation made possible deeper levels of dehumanization, a detachment from self and from others that made it easier to eliminate other selves in wars of extermination.

The move from feudalism to mercantilism and capitalism also released new passions and new drives: the passion for profit and the drive to dominate the world market. The desire for profit is an insatiable form of greed. Kovel (1984) maintained that greed, which has been around as long as man, is the desire to have the most or to take from others. However, he added, "The desire for profit . . . is an extended form of greed, a rationalized abstract pursuit which aims at the progressive accumulation of the medium of exchange" (p. 114). Under feudalism, greed was constrained by a sense of mutual obligation, by notions of community, by the social virtues of charity and cooperation. With the fall of feudalism, Kovel (p. 114) observed, "Giving was no longer proof of virtue; taking became its replacement." What emerged with the new order was an unrestrained desire for wealth. In greed, the desire was for the object to be obtained and enjoyed. In the drive for profit, the passion was not for the object but for the process itself—the process of accumulating more and more wealth.

This passion for profits subordinated everything, including human life, to the quest to extract value, exchange commodities, and accumulate wealth.

The change from feudalism to mercantilism and capitalism was also accompanied by the Protestant Reformation, which introduced a new but dehumanized view of man. Fromm (1965, p. 92) argued that whereas the medieval church stressed the dignity, equality, and brotherhood of man, Protestantism was based on a pervasive and intense hostility toward man. Fromm (p. 115) said,

> The most striking expression of this hostility is found in their concept of God, especially in Calvin's doctrine. Although we are all familiar with this concept, we often do not fully realize what it means to conceive of God as being as arbitrary and merciless as Calvin's God, who destined part of mankind to eternal damnation without any justification or reason except that this act was an expression of God's power.

This new religion was based on a belief that only a chosen few would be saved, while the great masses of humankind would be damned to eternal hell fire. This religious belief, as Fromm (1965) suggested, embodied a deep contempt and hostility toward humanity. No doubt this contempt and hostility stood behind the cruelty toward non-Europeans during the colonial era. Smedley (1993) demonstrated that this cruelty was mitigated by the Catholic Church in areas controlled by Spain, but unmitigated in areas controlled by Protestant England. The god of the new Protestant religions was more arbitrary, more merciless, more vengeful, and more likely to damn a greater part of humankind than the Catholic god.

In addition to a new religion, a new science emerged that also paved the way for domination and destruction driven by the passion for wealth. This new science introduced a new paradigm, depicting the world as dead matter or a large machine. This new view of the world provided an established rationale for destroying the world for the sake of wealth—the world was already dead matter, and matter can neither be created nor destroyed, just transformed into a different form. This science stimulated the drive to dominate the world, as the world was seen as a vast machine needing to be controlled.

The Age of Exploration

By the end of the 15th century, the Western character was more alienated and more driven to accumulate wealth. Both this alienation and this drive have been behind the tendency of Western culture to reduce the entire world, including human beings, into lifeless things to be used to create wealth, to be exchanged for wealth, or to be disposed of if they stood in the way of acquiring wealth. This drive and this alienation were behind the African slave trade, the rise of the plantation system, and the extermination of Native Americans.

Columbus expressed this drive for wealth and contempt for man in his description of the Native Americans he encountered. He said,

> They [Native Americans] are the best people in the world and above all the gentlest—without knowledge of what is evil—nor do they murder or steal. They are very simple and honest . . . none of them refusing anything he may possess when he is asked for it. They exhibit great love toward all others in preference to themselves. They would make fine servants. With 50 men we could subjugate them all and make them do whatever we want. (quoted in Phillips and Phillips 1992, p. 166)

In pursuit of wealth, Columbus and his men enslaved, tortured, mutilated, and massacred Native Americans. In 1495, he and his forces captured 1,500 Native Americans, packing 500 of them on his ships to send to Spain for sale. Two hundred died en route (Zinn 1990, p. 4). On Haiti, Columbus and his men forced natives to collect gold. Those who refused had their hands cut off, and they bled to death. In 2 years, as a result of murder, massacre, mutilation, or suicide, half the native population of Haiti was dead (Zinn, p. 4).

Commenting on the depopulation of Haiti, Cuba, San Juan, and Jamaica, Father Bartholome De las Casas, an eyewitness to the carnage, said,

> And Spaniards have behaved in no other way during the past forty years, down to the present time, for they are still acting like ravening beasts, killing, terrorizing, afflicting, torturing and destroying the native peoples, doing all this with the strangest and most varied new methods of cruelty, never seen or heard of before, and to such a degree that this Island of Hispaniola, once so populous (Having a population that I estimated to be more than three million), has now a population of barely two hundred persons. The island of Cuba is nearly as long as the distance between Valladolid and Rome; it is now almost completely depopulated. San Juan and Jamaica are two of the largest, most productive, and attractive islands; both are now deserted and devastated. (quoted in Bradley 1991, p. xvii)

Spanish explorers and conquerors, in their passion for seizing wealth, decimated Native American populations and destroyed whole civilizations. Most notable among the Spanish conquistadores were Cortez, who massacred the Aztec in Mexico, destroying their civilization for their gold, and Pizarro, who slaughtered natives in Peru for the same purpose—gold.

After seizing land in the Americas, Spanish conquerors and colonists needed labor to extract wealth from the land. When they failed to attract sufficient numbers of European laborers—and after they decimated the Native American population with disease, overwork, and violence—they turned to the African slave trade, which had already begun on a small scale several years before Columbus sailed to the Americas.

The passion to accumulate wealth and a deep sense of human alienation were behind the genocide of Native Americans and the enslavement of Africans. These passions emerged out of changes that occurred in Western Europe's economic structure, social organizations, culture, and patterns of human interaction. As feudalism gave way to mercantilism and capitalism, the social chains of feudalism—with their social and community obligations—were broken, thus creating a greater sense of alienation and releasing new social classes with an unrestrained passion to accumulate wealth.

These changes in Western Europe did not cause racism. Rather, they provided the fertile ground out of which racism grew. These were the seeds of racism: slavery and colonialism, drawn along a color line, with an uncommonly high level of brutality and exploitation. The passion for wealth drove particular European nations to subjugate and enslave people of other worlds. Racism emerged with the brutal and dehumanizing treatment of people of color. This racism was not present at the beginning of the age of exploration. It emerged with the African slave trade, with colonialism, and with the oppression and dehumanization of people who appeared different from their oppressors. Two cases best illustrate this relationship between oppressive and dehumanizing treatment of a people and the production of dehumanizing images of and attitudes toward them: Spain and England. We examine the first case in this chapter and the second in the next.

The case of Spain illustrates the relationship between the African slave trade and racism. Spain had a long history of interaction with Africa dating back to the time of Hannibal and the second Punic War, 218 to 201 B.C. (Du Bois 1969b, p. 141). Like most occupying armies, Carthaginian soldiers commonly intermarried with European women, especially in

Spain and Italy. Hannibal married a Spanish woman (Du Bois 1969b, p. 142). Africans invaded Spain again in the 11th century A.D. The Almoravids, black Africans from west Africa who were also known as Moors, conquered Morocco. From Morocco, they invaded and conquered Spain, dominating this country until 1492. The point is that Africans were in Europe before the African slave trade. They were with Columbus when he journeyed across the Atlantic. Apparently, an African was the captain of one of his ships (Bennett 1970, p. 35). African Spanish explorers, most notably Estanvanico, led a number of expeditions in the Americas. African Spanish were with Cortez in Mexico and Pizarro in Peru.

Before the establishment of slavery in the Americas, dark-skinned Africans freely intermingled and intermarried with light-skinned Europeans. There was little evidence of the type of race and color prejudice that plagues the modern and postmodern eras. Even during the early period of the African slave trade, the Portuguese pillaging of the coastal cities of Africa, and the Spanish ravaging of the civilizations of the Americas, there was little evidence of the type of racism found in the 18th, 19th, and 20th centuries. This racism emerged as more Africans were imported to the Americas to work the mines and plantations of the Caribbean and South and Central America.

Color prejudice emerged with a new world order. This order involved a new division of the world between dominant European nations and people of color in other parts of the globe. Among the dominant class in Europe, it entailed a passionate drive to accumulate wealth. This drive propelled dominant European nations on a path of savage destruction and brutal subjugation of other people. This accumulation drive was the force behind the Atlantic slave trade, the destruction of the Aztec and Mayan civilizations, the reduction of the Native American population, and the establishment of the plantation system. In other words, it was not racism that produced the enslavement of people of color. It was the accumulation drive that led to the enslavement that produced the racism—the notion that people of color constitute a subspecies of humanity or a species below humankind.

4

The Origins and Maintenance of Slavery and Dominative Racism in North America

Modern England emerged in ways similar to modern Spain. A new class, driven to accumulate wealth, arose in England, especially by the 17th century. This class led the British charge to colonize the world—to conquer other people to use them to create wealth for England. The formation of these colonies involved the subjugation of people in foreign regions, most of whom had darker skins. This conquest and subjugation produced a new world order divided along a color line and a new worldview. This new view characterized dominant Europeans as superior and portrayed subjugated people as inferior.

ORIGINS

It is not coincidental that the word *race*—meaning different human species—appeared in the English language at precisely the time Britain began to colonize other lands (Jordan 1968; Smedley 1993, p. 37). The early history of color prejudice and the racial worldview illustrates a strong association between the brutal treatment of a people and the formation of dehumanizing views of them. This association was evident in Great Britain even before the colonial period. It was especially evident in Britain's treatment of its own poor and of the Irish.

The Case of Britain's Indigent

With the expansion of industrial production and the dislocation of agricultural workers and peasants, the number of poor people increased in England in the late 16th and 17th centuries. In response to this increase and to the need for cheap labor, England passed a series of poor laws. Poor houses were constructed and administered in ways punitive to able-bodied men. Charity was attacked for promoting indolence. Contempt for the poor intensified (Morgan 1975, p. 321). The poor in England were not only seen as different from others, they were perceived as lazy, diseased, immoral, dangerous, and ignorant. They were viewed almost as sub-human. The stereotypes of the poor in 17th-century England were similar to those developing of black slaves in the colonies. Historian Edmund Morgan (1975, p. 325) said,

> The stereotypes of the poor expressed as often in England during the late seventeenth and eighteenth centuries were often identical with the descriptions of blacks expressed in colonies dependent on slave labor, even to the extent of intimating the subhumanity of both: the poor were a vile and brutish part of mankind; the black were "a brutish sort of people."

The Irish

The British conquest of Ireland further illustrates this connection between the brutal treatment of a people and the construction of denigrating views of them. Starting in the late 12th century, England attempted to crush Irish resistance and colonize Ireland. The 16th and 17th centuries witnessed efforts to subjugate the Irish so brutal that some historians accuse the English of genocide (Quinn 1965; Liggio 1976; Smedley 1993, p. 57). Liggio (1976, p. 28) described Oliver Cromwell's campaign of the mid-17th century as a war of extermination:

> Cromwell's army in Ireland, often New England Puritan-led or -inspired, carried out the most complete devastation that Ireland experienced until that time. Extermination became a policy. Massacres were carried out. Prisoners of war were transported to servitude in the new English colonies in the West Indies. . . . Lord Clarendon observed that the Cromwellian policy was to act without "any humanity to the Irish nation, and more especially to those of the old native extraction, the whole race whereof they had upon the matter sworn an utter extirpation." (quoted in Smedley 1993, p. 58)

Cromwell's forces confiscated land, killed women and children, and enslaved many of the survivors.

The English viewed the Irish as a separate race of savages, an image similar to the racist portrayal of Native Americans and Africans. English literature of this period denigrated the Irish. Authors, politicians, and religious leaders of this period referred to the Irish as wild, beastly, cannibalistic, promiscuous, uncivilized, immoral, lazy, and unclean (Smedley 1993, pp. 57-59).

Smedley (1993) claimed that in the 17th century, the British transported large numbers of Irish to work on sugar plantations in the British colonies of the West Indies. This enslavement of the Irish was accompanied by the construction of images of them as subhuman.

Black Slavery and White Racism

Initially, plantation laborers were integrated. During the first three quarters of the 17th century, most plantations laborers in the British colonies were European indentured servants. Few were African slaves. Historian Kenneth Stampp (1956, pp. 21-22) observed,

> Moreover, the Negro and white servants of the seventeenth century seemed to be remarkably unconcerned about their visible physical differences. They toiled together in the fields, fraternized during leisure hours, and, in and out of wedlock, collaborated in siring a numerous progeny. Though the first southern white settlers were quite familiar with rigid class lines, they were as unfamiliar with a caste system as they were with chattel slavery.

Color prejudice against Africans was rare in the first two thirds of the 17th century. Legal distinctions between black slaves and white servants did not appear until the 1660s (Stampp 1956, p. 22).

At first, the plantation owners relied more on European indentured servants than African slaves. The high mortality rates for both slaves and servants made it more profitable to invest in a short-term servant than a lifetime slave (Morgan 1975, p. 297). Moreover, profits on cash crops were not high enough to allow massive investment in slaves.

Initially, attitudes and behavior toward the African slave differed little from those toward the European servant, except that the servant served for a short term, usually 7 years, and the slave generally, but not always, served for life. Franklin (1969, p. 71) noted that some early census records listed African slaves as servants rather than slaves. Of course, other historians argue that blacks were servants on paper but lifetime slaves in fact (Jordan 1968). However, Franklin (1969, p. 71) maintained that up until 1651, some of these black slaves were assigned land after their terms expired in the same manner as white indentured servants.

Jordan (1968) challenged Stampp's historical materialist view of racism: that racism did not arise until the late 17th century. He cited the Hugh Davis case as an example of racism existing in Virginia as early as 1630. In this case, the state of Virginia had Davis, a white male, whipped "before an assembly of Negroes for abusing himself to the dishonor of God and shame of Christians, by defiling his body in lying with a negro" (quoted in Morgan 1975, p. 333). However, Morgan supported Stampp's perspective with a detailed examination of slavery and racism in Virginia and a reassessment of the Hugh Davis case. Morgan (p. 333) argued that court records show that whipping was a common punishment for fornication or sodomy, regardless of the color of the accused man or woman. Morgan maintained that Davis was whipped for fornicating, period. The race of the woman he slept with was incidental to the case. Morgan asserted that the court ordered Davis to be whipped before an assembly of blacks because the court wanted to impress Christian morals on non-Christian blacks. The order was a function of religion, not race. Furthermore, Morgan demonstrated that interracial marriages were common in the first half of the 17th century and that at this time, they provoked little or no reaction. Christian status and Christian morals were important. Race was not.

The Great Transformation

The color of plantation laborers changed from white to black during the last quarter of the 17th century and the first half of the 18th century. African slaves began to pour into southern colonies in large numbers, throughout the late 17th and the 18th centuries. Between 1700 and 1750, roughly 45,000 African slaves were imported to Virginia alone. The African population in this colony increased from about 9,000 to more than 100,000 (Morgan 1975, p. 301). In the Carolinas, the African slave population equaled the European population by 1708 and exceeded this population by 1724. By 1765, the African population was about 90,000 compared to a European population of about 40,000 (Franklin 1969, p. 79).

In the first half of the 18th century, the slave population increased dramatically in almost every colony, including northern ones. For example, the African slave population in New York increased from 2,170 in 1698 to 6,171 in 1723, and to 19,883 by 1771, when blacks accounted for more than 10% of the colony's total population (Franklin, p. 90).

As the number of imported African slaves increased, the number of imported indentured servants declined (Morgan 1975). A clear shift occurred from a reliance on indentured servants to a dependency on black slave labor.

Several factors contributed to this shift. First, mortality rates declined, and life expectancy increased. This change made investment in slave labor more attractive. Second, expanded agricultural production increased the demand for labor at the very time the supply of indentured servants was declining. No doubt the declining costs of transportation across the Atlantic, the growing unpopularity of indentured servitude status, and the increase in the demand for unskilled labor in England's expanding industries all contributed to the decline in the supply of indentured servants. Moreover, capital accumulated in the colonies during the 17th century provided resources to purchase large numbers of slaves.

Third, rebellion and discontent among freed indentured servants and the tendency of African slaves to escape with indentured servants made social control in the racially mixed plantation system problematic. Moreover, as more indentured servants completed their terms of service, more were freed. These freed people expected land and a decent life in an area in which land ownership was concentrated in the hands of a few. This concentration of land ownership, prevalent in the southern colonies, limited opportunities for freed servants to own land. Frustrated and angry, these freed servants rebelled. The Bacon revolt in Virginia in 1676 was one of the largest such rebellions in colonial history (Morgan 1975, p. 308).

Black slavery had advantages in the area of social control. Black slaves were easier to identify, distinguishable especially by skin color. They were unarmed and easily confined to a small area, the plantation. They were rendered hopeless and had no expectations of freedom and land ownership (Morgan 1975, p. 309).

Finally, black slavery was more productive than indentured servitude. The system of slavery allowed for much greater and more direct control over laborers. There was no limit to the amount of work the master could extract from the slave, except the time necessary for the slave to eat and sleep (Morgan 1975, p. 309). Slavery was also more productive for demographic reasons. Under slavery, black women and their children worked in the fields. Servant women rarely worked the fields and their children were free (Morgan, p. 310).

For these reasons, the complexion and treatment of the lowest level of plantation labor changed in the late 17th century. The black skin became the stigma of slavery and wretchedness. The treatment of the slave degenerated to the lowest level of brutality. The image of the African became associated with savagery, paganism, immorality, ignorance, and primitiveness. In short, racism materialized.

Slavery, Public Policies, and Racism

The change in the color of plantation labor did not magically cause racism to appear. Rather, local public policies reflected and promoted this racism. Morgan (1975, p. 331) maintained that Virginia's legislative body "deliberately did what it could to foster the contempt of whites for blacks and Indians." He noted, "In 1680 it prescribed thirty lashes on the bare back 'if any negroe or other slave shall presume to lift up his hand in opposition against any christian' " (p. 331). This law subordinated the black slave to the white Christian indentured servant. It allowed the servant to harass or assault the slave with little fear of reprisal. A 1705 law mandated the dismemberment of unruly slaves but, at the same time, prohibited masters from whipping white Christian servants naked, without a court order (Morgan 1975, p. 331). Laws protected the property of servants but denied slaves any right to property.

These laws made clear distinctions between the status of black slaves and white servants. They made the black slave subordinate to the white servant. They denied all human rights to slaves; placed them in the lowest possible social position imaginable; defined them as beasts of burden, pieces of property, owned totally and absolutely by the master, and forced to do the most dreadful work in society. At the same time, these laws elevated indentured servants, gave them some powers over black slaves, protected their property rights, recognized some of their human rights, and afforded them some social privileges.

Contempt for subordinated groups now focused on black slaves. A deeper, more profound subordination produced a deeper and more profound level of contempt. Although the images of black slaves were similar to some of those of poor whites, the fear, contempt, and hatred for blacks was much deeper than anything exhibited toward poor whites. This deeper contempt is reflected in laws enacted by the colonial legislatures mandating the castration of slaves guilty of assaulting their masters or of habitually escaping. Of these laws, Jordan (1968, p. 155) said,

It was sometimes prescribed for such offenses as striking a white person or running away; until 1722 South Carolina legally required masters of slaves running away for the fourth time to have them castrated and in 1697 the Assembly ordered castration of three Negros who had attempted to abscond to the Spanish in St. Augustine.

Until the 1760s, North Carolina paid jailers to perform official castrations, reimbursing masters if their slave died (Jordan, p. 155).

State-mandated castration of black slaves found guilty of habitually running away or of striking a white person was one of the most powerful political expressions of the racism of this era. This policy symbolized the absolute power of white masters over black slaves and the total emasculation of slaves. It symbolized the slave's relegation to the level of the bull or workhorse, other animals that faced castration for the purpose of control. It reflected a deep contempt and a controlled hatred for black slaves. It was one of the most sadistic and inhuman laws in world history.

Racism, Slavery, and Economic Determinism

Slavery did not cause racism. Rather, slavery provided the material basis for racism. Several conscious human decisions helped form and shape racism: the decision to shift from the use of European indentured servants to African slaves; the decision to increase the level of control and brutality toward African slaves; the decision to deny all rights to African slaves but grant some rights to the lowest class of Europeans; the decision to subordinate all Africans to all Europeans—all of these decisions contributed to a clear dichotomy, at the lowest level of society, between black slaves and white free persons.

The black slave became the most undesirable thing to be. Even the lowest class worker was better off than the black slaves. In fact, as Roediger (1991) demonstrated, European laborers developed their identity as free white workers in contrast to black slaves. Even the Irish, who were once treated no differently than African slaves, identified with white labor.

Black slavery made white liberty possible (Morgan 1975; Cooper 1983; Bell 1987). Cooper (1983, p. 38) made this point cogently when he said, "The whites, all of whom stood above the slaves economically and socially, joined together in a hymn of liberty that gave thanks for the enslaved blacks, who made white harmony and republicanism, thus liberty possible." The social acceptance of Africans as belonging to the slave class allowed for greater solidarity among other European classes. That is, black slavery facilitated white unity. No matter how low their social rank, no matter how poverty-stricken they might be, Europeans could always identify with other whites and stand above blacks. To be white is to be free. To be black is to be a slave.

SLAVERY, RACISM, AND REVOLUTION

White consciousness and white racism were well established before the American Revolution. Racism was quite congruent with the old worldview in which some men were born to rule whereas others were born to serve. This old worldview was accepted as natural, ordained by God, a world of kings and subjects, of lords and peasants, of masters and slaves, of superior people and inferior people. This old worldview supported British rule, slavery, and white racism.

The American Revolution was Gramsci's (1980) war of position and war of maneuvers. It assaulted the old worldview along with British rule. The Revolution gave birth to a new worldview and it murdered the old. The new worldview underscored natural rights, social contracts, and human equality. The ideas of the American Revolution not only condemned British rule and advocated Revolution, they challenged the morality of slavery.

According to John Locke ([1670] 1980), whose ideas inspired the Revolution, governments are established under a social contract to protect these natural rights of man: life, liberty, and property. When a government violates this contract, fails to protect these rights, or abuses them, then men have a right to revolt, sever their ties with that government, and create a new one. These ideas justified the colonists severing their ties with Great Britain. The ideology also condemned slavery, as this institution is the antithesis of notions of the natural law of liberty and equality. As Montesquieu said, "Slavery not only violates the Laws of Nature, and of civil Society, it also wounds the best Forms of Government; in a Democracy, where all Men are equal Slavery is contrary to the Spirit of the Constitution" (quoted in Nash 1990, p. 44).

These ideas inspired efforts to enlist slaves into the Revolution. Indeed, a few northern states recruited slaves and reimbursed owners for their slave's service in the war and freedom after the Revolution. In 1779, the Continental Congress offered to pay owners up to $1,000 for each slave they allowed to enlist (Franklin 1969, p. 136). About 5,000 blacks served with the Revolutionary forces, with distinction.

Revolutionary ideas also spawned the abolitionist movement. Abolitionist societies proliferated during and just after the Revolution, between 1775 and 1787. The first abolitionist society was formed by the Quakers in 1775. In this same year, John Jay, one of the principal authors of the Federalist Papers and the first Chief Justice of the United States, served as president of the New York Society for Promoting Manumission. By the late 1780s most states had such societies.

Several states passed laws to prohibit the slave trade, and a few passed laws to gradually abolish slavery. Virginia forbade the importation of slaves in 1774. Maryland prohibited the importation of slaves in 1783 (Franklin 1969, p. 140). The same year, the Massachusetts Supreme Court found slavery in violation of its state constitution (Franklin, p. 140; Nash 1990, p. 19). In 1780, Pennsylvania became the first colony to pass a law to eliminate slavery over a period of two generations (Nash, p. 112). In 1784, Connecticut and Rhode Island passed abolitionist laws similar to Pennsylvania's. In 1786, New York and New Jersey passed laws allowing for manumission (Franklin, p. 141).

The northern movement to end slavery contrasted sharply with southern efforts to protect this institution. Although the southern plantation economy suffered during the war and although slave production appeared unproductive, the South had invested too much money in and had become too dependent on slave labor to permit its abolition. The South supported slavery during the Revolution. It exhibited this support several ways.

First, a number of southern states used slaves to support the war effort. In the South, wealth was in land and in slaves. Georgia, South Carolina, North Carolina, and Virginia promised and awarded slaves along with land to encourage enlistment and to reward soldiers for honorable service (Cooper 1983, p. 35).

Second, all the southern states, except Maryland, refused to enlist slaves (Cooper 1983, p. 37). Virginia allowed free blacks to enlist, but it required them to present papers certified by a justice of the peace that they were free. It did not allow slaves to enlist, even at the urging of northern colonies and leaders of the Revolution. These southern states adamantly opposed enlisting slaves, even when they faced possible military defeat in 1780. They were afraid of the prospect of having large numbers of armed ex-slaves in their state (Cooper, p. 37).

Third, planters vehemently denounced the British for offering freedom to slaves in exchange for military service in the royal army. In 1775, the governor of Virginia, loyal to the British monarch, offered freedom to slaves who would join the British forces and serve the king of England. Planters denounced the governor for "diabolical schemes against good people that threatened lives and property with 'the very scum of the country' " (Cooper 1983, p. 36). Planters opposed freeing slaves under any circumstances.

Thus the American Revolution was limited to a war of independence from Great Britain, as the Declaration of Independence was limited to white males. The Revolution never expanded into a struggle for human liberation. Although the rhetoric of the Revolution spoke of freedom and although this rhetoric precipitated abolitionist sentiments, economic dependency on slavery functioned as a profound constraint on efforts to turn the Revolution into a struggle for human liberation.

Even the most passionate and sincere supporters of freedom were constrained by this economic dependency on slavery. For example, leaders of the Revolution such as Patrick Henry ("give me liberty or give me death") and Thomas Jefferson both supported the idea of freeing the slaves in theory, but they were constrained by economic interest from implementing this idea in actual practice. Henry, writing to an antislavery Quaker, explained,

> Would any one believe that I am Master of Slaves of my own purchase! I am drawn along by ye general inconvenience of living without them; I will not, I cannot justify it. However culpable my conduct, I will so far pay my devoir to virtue as to own the excellence and rectitude of her precepts and to lament my want of conformity to them . . . we can not reduce this wished for reformation to practice. (quoted in Cooper 1983, p. 33)

Henry was saying that while he cannot justify slavery, he is trapped in the slave business because of the disadvantage of doing without it.

Jefferson faced the same dilemma. Although he drafted bills in the Virginia state legislature for the gradual emancipation of slaves, he never campaigned for the freedom of slaves. He opposed slavery, but he too could not stand the financial loss of liberating his own slaves. The only slaves he freed were his own children, and he freed them on his death bed, leaving Sally Hemings, the mother of his children, enslaved (Smedley 1993).

Most planters who supported the Revolution did not share even Henry and Jefferson's support for the abstract idea that slaves should be free. Most believed in their own liberty, not the liberty of the slave. Most associated their liberty with their freedom to maintain the institution of slavery. Most developed a sense of white consciousness in which white freedom was based on black subjugation. Thus not only did slavery emerge intact out of the ashes of the Revolution, but white racism arose and accommodated itself to liberal political thought.

The planters also played a role in reformulating revolutionary ideology to protect the institution of slavery. Revolutionary ideology emphasized natural rights and limited government. Planters seized the natural right to property issue. Defining slaves as property, they maintained that they had a natural right to their property in slaves. Moreover, planters equated freedom with limited government; that is, a government that did not interfere with their right to own slaves. Thus planters adapted revolutionary ideas of freedom to accommodate slavery. Cooper (1983, p. 136) made this point cogently:

> At least since the Revolution, most white southerners had equated their own liberty with their right to decide the fate of their section's black slaves. To white southerners, controlling slavery was simply a part of controlling local institutions that signified liberty.

SLAVERY AND DOMINATIVE RACISM FROM 1787 TO 1865

How do we explain the persistence of slavery and racial oppression after the Revolution? The answer lies in the structure of the economy, the role of politics and the state, and the presence of a racist culture. These factors interacted to produce and sustain dominative racism, a form of racial oppression based on society's total direct domination and control of blacks.

We begin our analysis with politics and the state, because this is where the Revolution ended: the Revolution that promised to abolish slavery. In this new nation, both the national government—Congress, presidents, and the Supreme Court—and state governments operated to protect the institution of slavery, primarily because a slave aristocracy defended this institution in the political arena and because the national economy depended on the southern slave economy. Moreover, the slave mode of production required a high level of direct control and brutality to function profitably. It encouraged the development of the sadistic social character that functioned to maintain slavery. It stimulated the formation of a culture grounded on repressed fears and sadistic drives.

POLITICS AND THE STATE

The planter class protected slavery during the Revolution, changed revolutionary rhetoric to defend this institution, and with other economic elite, dominated the Constitutional Convention and created a government that legitimized and protected this institution. The Constitution, presidents, Congresses, national political parties, and state governments all operated to protect slavery and to maintain dominative racism throughout this entire period, 1787 to 1865.

Wealthy men of property dominated the Constitutional Convention in Philadelphia in 1787 (Beard 1941; Prewitt and Stone 1973; Parenti 1988; Lowi and Ginsberg 1994; Dye and Ziegler 1996). These men were as concerned with protecting property as they were with forging a new nation. Parenti (1988, p. 56) described these men as wealthy young planters, financially successful merchants, and creditors with years of service in government and the military. Dye and Ziegler surmised that about 80% of the delegates to this convention held public securities or bonds, about 25% earned wealth from real estate and land speculation; 20% earned wealth from mercantile, manufacturing, and shipping business; 44% earned from lending and investment practices; and 27% were planters and slaveholders (calculated from Dye and Ziegler, pp. 32-33). These men expressed anxiety about revolts and fear of leveling movements to equalize wealth. As Beard (1941, p. 30) said, "The Southern planter was as much concerned in maintaining order against slave revolts as the creditor in Massachusetts was concerned in putting down Shays' 'desperate debtors.' "

This property elite created a Constitution that legitimized and protected the institution of slavery. Although this document emerged out of a spirit of compromise, it did not compromise the institution of slavery. The three fifths compromise, which counted the slave as three fifths of a person, dehumanized the slave and presupposed that slavery would continue. This provision compromised the power of southern states. It did not compromise the institution of slavery nor did it provide any human rights protection for the slave.

The 1808 compromise posed no threat to the institution of slavery, although abolitionists vehemently advocated banning the international slave trade. In fact, older slaveholding states such as Virginia and South Carolina benefited from such a ban. With a surplus of slaves and a willingness to sell slaves to planters in the newer areas, a ban on international slave trade meant they would dominate the domestic market.

The Constitution provided direct support for the institution of slavery. This support is found in Article IV, section two, which reads, "No Person held to Service or Labor in one State, under the Laws thereof, escaping into another, shall, in consequence of any Law or Regulation therein, be discharged from such Service or Labor, but shall be delivered up on Claim of the Party to whom such Service or Labor may be due." This Constitutional provision required free states to return runaway slaves to their owners in slave states. It legitimized and protected the institution of slavery. Also, the Fifth Amendment protects slavery, insofar as the judicial system recognized slaves as property and the Fifth Amendment protected property from arbitrary government seizures.

At the Constitutional Convention, planters, especially from the lower southern states, were adamant and uncompromising on the issue of slavery. They would not support a national government that might abolish slavery. For example, South Carolina's representative to the Convention, Thomas Lynch, claimed that his state would not be part of any national government that even debated "whether their slaves are their property" (quoted in Nash 1990, p. 27). Also, John Rutledge, South Carolina's delegate to the Constitutional Convention, exploded during a debate over taxing imported slaves. Rutledge said the resolution of the issue would determine whether the southern states would be part of the union (Nash, p. 27). Representatives from the Deep South even opposed federal regulation of slavery.

The First Test of the Constitutionality of Slavery: The Foster Report

After its ratification, some ambiguity remained about what the Constitution said about slavery. When abolitionists besieged Congress over the slave issue, Congress created a special committee headed by Abiel Foster from New Hampshire to investigate and report on the Constitution and the slavery issue.

The original Foster Committee report claimed that after 1808 Congress might be free to regulate slavery as well as abolish the slave trade. This report precipitated a ferocious reaction from representatives from the lower southern states (Cooper 1983; Nash 1990). These representatives defended the slave trade as a humanitarian act that saved Africans from savagery (Nash, p. 41). They condemned the abolitionists as dangerous extremists.

Madison, ameliorating the report, added an amendment stati⸺ Congress has no authority to interfere with the treatment of slaves ... the South nor the power to emancipate the slaves (Cooper 1983, p. 72; Nash 1990, p. 41). The final report claimed that Congress may prohibit the importation of African slaves after 1808, but it may neither regulate nor abolish slavery.

The Dred Scott Decision

In keeping with the Foster report, Congress passed a law in 1808 prohibiting the importation of slaves. It also restricted the expansion of slavery in new territories. It did not interfere with the treatment of slaves in the South nor did it attempt to emancipate slaves until after the Civil War.

The U.S. Supreme Court became involved in the slavery issue in the infamous *Dred Scott v. Sandford* decision of 1857. Dred Scott, a slave, born in Missouri, initiated this case when he sued for his freedom on grounds that he had become a citizen in states that prohibited slavery. In 1834, his master, an army physician, took him from the slave state of Missouri to Illinois and then to Wisconsin Territory, areas in which slavery was forbidden.

In this case, Chief Justice Taney raised two questions:

1. Is Dred Scott a citizen with the right to initiate this suit?
2. Is he entitled to his freedom by virtue of living in a territory that prohibits slavery?

In answering these questions, the Chief Justice reached a number of strong conclusions about blacks, slavery, and the Constitution. He concluded that blacks were not citizens; that they were not members of the "people" mentioned in the Preamble of the Constitution; that the framers of the Constitution had no intention of including them in the Constitution; that these framers saw blacks as an inferior and subjugated class of beings with no rights or privileges; and finally, that the Constitution recognized slaves as property and protected this property as it protected any other form of property. He argued that the general opinion at the time of the construction of the Constitution was that whites might justly enslave blacks for the good of blacks. He added that slaves were property protected by the Constitution. He concluded that the provision of the

Northwest Ordinance that freed slaves violated the Constitution's protection of private property. Specifically he said,

> They [blacks] had for more than a century before been regarded as beings of an inferior order; and altogether unfit to associate with the white race, either in social or political relations; and so far inferior that they had no rights which the white man was bound to respect and that the negro might justly and lawfully be reduced to slavery for his benefit. (*Dred Scott v. Sandford,* 1857)

The Role of the National Government and National Political Parties

Despite a laissez faire appearance, the national government and the major political parties in Congress, throughout the entire period of slavery, played a critical role in promoting a system of racial oppression. Congresses and presidents, from Washington to Lincoln, promoted what Saxon (1990) called the white republic. Various presidents were involved in protecting the institution of slavery, removing Native Americans east of the Mississippi, and legitimizing patterns of wide disparities in the distribution of wealth. Although presidents and national parties differed on many issues—democracy, growth of national governmental powers, the establishment of a national bank, protective tariffs, the expansion of slavery in new territories, and even the morality of slavery—they all tended to support the institution of slavery, the expansion of territory, the removal of Native Americans, and the maintenance of inequality in the distribution of wealth.

Historical data provide substantial evidence of this role of presidents and major political parties. Even those presidents with reputations for supporting democracy and equality are guilty of promoting a racially oppressive regime. For examples, consider Thomas Jefferson and Andrew Jackson.

Jefferson's Presidency

Jefferson ran for president in 1796. In this election, William Smith, a Federalist candidate for president or vice president—at this time the second-place candidate for president became vice president—accused Democratic Republican candidate Thomas Jefferson of being friendly toward blacks and unfriendly toward slavery. Smith had won previous elections for Congress using this tactic (Cooper 1983, p. 97). Smith's tactic placed Jefferson on the defensive. In addition, John Adams, a Federalist and a front-runner, branded Jefferson a leveler. Responding to the slave issue, Jefferson focused his campaign on Adams. Jefferson's supporters pointed out that Jefferson owned slaves whereas Adams did not and that Jefferson believed that the Constitution protected the institution of slavery from federal regulation and interference. Jefferson, who owned more than 200 slaves and who had once agonized over slavery, exploited the slave issue in his campaign for president (Cooper 1983, pp. 97-100). Arguing this point, historian Cooper (pp. 97-98) said,

> Eager for the supposedly doubtful electoral votes of South Carolina, Jefferson in 1800 authorized his leading spokesman there to declare in his name, "that the Constitution has not empowered the federal legislature to touch in the remotest degree the question respecting the condition of property of slaves in any of the States, and that any attempt of that sort would be unconstitutional."

Jefferson was elected president in 1800. His administration expanded U.S. territory immensely with the Louisiana Purchase, protected slavery in this territory with the Louisiana treaty, and allowed the expansion of slavery in the new states of Kentucky and Tennessee (Cooper 1983). While president, Jefferson did nothing to redistribute land or wealth in more equitable ways. He opposed leveling. He was the first president to suggest that Native Americans should be forcibly removed from their land east of the Mississippi (Smedley 1993, p. 180). His policies facilitated the expansion of plantation slavery.

Andrew Jackson and the Jacksonian Democratic Party

The case of Andrew Jackson and his party offers another example of a president with a reputation for supporting democracy and equality and a practice of promoting racial oppression. There are two sides of Jackson. On the one hand, Jackson appealed to the common man, expanded voting rights, destroyed the national bank, attacked the northern banking establishment, supported the small farmer, and identified with the frontiersman. On the other hand, Jackson supported slavery, advocated the removal of Native Americans residing east of the Mississippi, and justified inequalities in the distribution of wealth. This president and his party supported the Indian Removal Act of 1830, which expatriated all Native Americans who lived east of the Mississippi, forcing them to migrate west. He verbally attacked abolitionists. His administration used the Post Office to ban the distribution of abolitionist literature in the South (McDonald, Decker, and Govan, 1972, p. 440; Cooper 1983, p. 190).

Although the Jacksonian party had the reputation of being a democratic party committed to egalitarian principles, it supported the institution of slavery and legitimized inequality (Hofstadter 1948; McDonald et al. 1972; Saxon 1990; Smedley 1993). Although Jackson and his party opposed the government's granting of special or exclusive privileges to the very rich, they supported the government, protecting the wealth and property of all classes, especially the very rich. Jackson himself identified with the southern slave aristocracy. He tended to justify concentrated wealth on grounds that more wealth should go to those who are superior in industry and virtue. Commenting on Jackson's veto message of the bill to recharter the national bank, Hofstadter (1948, p. 62) said,

> Certainly this is not a philosophy of a radical leveling movement that proposes to uproot property or to reconstruct society along drastically different lines. It proceeds upon no utopian premises—full equality is impossible, "distinctions will always exist" and reward should rightly go to "superior industry, economy, and virtue." What is demanded is only the classic bourgeois ideal, equality before the law, the restriction of government to equal protection of its citizens.

John Calhoun, vice president under Jackson, provided one of the clearest examples of this support for both slavery and inequality. Calhoun was a passionate champion of the institution of slavery. In a speech delivered January 10, 1838, he argued that this institution was the foundation of a free and stable society (McKitrick 1963, p. 19). Illustrating Calhoun's support for both slavery and inequality, Hofstadter (1948, p. 68) quoted Calhoun:

> It would be well for those interested to reflect whether there now exists, or ever has existed, a wealthy and civilized community in which one portion did not live on the labor of another; and whether the form in which slavery exists in the south is not but one modification of this universal condition.

Calhoun was a white supremacist and a white nationalist who viewed the United States as a white nation (Fredrickson 1971). Fredrickson (p. 136) also quoted Calhoun:

[The United States has never] incorporated into the Union any but the Caucasian race. . . . Ours is a government of the white man . . . in the whole history of man . . . there is no instance whatever of any civilized colored race, of any shade, being found equal to the establishment and maintenance of free government.

Fredrickson argued that this view was pervasive and held by both Democrats and Republicans at the end of the 1850s.

The Jacksonian Democratic party dominated national politics from 1828 to 1860. This party played a major role in legitimizing patterns of racial opposition. Even the last Jacksonian Democrat, Buchanan, participated in this legitimizing process, evidenced in his reaction to the Dred Scott decision. Buchanan, president at the time of the decision, responded with a statement arguing that the slave issue was now solved and beyond the reach of fanatic and irrational abolitionists (McDonald et al. 1972, p. 499). Incidentally, Taney, the author of this decision, was appointed Chief Justice by Andrew Jackson.

Opposition Parties

The opposition party, the Whigs, which held the presidency during the 1841 to 1845 and 1849 to 1853 terms, offered little alternative to the Democratic party's position on slavery, Native American removal, acquisition of territory, and inequality of wealth. Whig president Harrison, senator from Ohio, born in an aristocratic, slave-owning Virginia family, was famous for assaulting and destroying the Native American village of Tippecanoe. Whig president Zachary Taylor, a Louisiana planter who owned about 300 slaves, was noted as the head of U.S. forces during the Mexican American war. His vice president and successor, Millard Fillmore, opposed slavery. However, once Fillmore became president he supported slavery, particularly by signing and implementing the Fugitive Slave Act of 1850, one of the most aggressive of such laws in history. Other leaders of the Whig party who never became president but who played central roles in Congress, such as Henry Clay, supported slavery, Indian removal, and territorial expansion.

One explanation for the role of the federal government in supporting slavery is that this role was part of the government's accumulation and legitimation functions. The national government generally supported efforts to accumulate private wealth. This accumulation process entailed the acquisition of new territory, especially through the Louisiana purchase, through the removal of Native Americans from their land, and through the seizure of land from Mexico. The national government supported the institution of slavery and the expansion of slavery into new territories because a large part of the wealth of the nation was derived from slave labor. The state operated to legitimize the institution of slavery through the passage of fugitive slave laws and through public statements justifying slavery and inequality. In addition to its direct support for racially oppressive arrangements, the national government gave the southern states complete freedom to control the institution of slavery. It did this through the Foster Report and through the notion of state rights.

The Role of the State Governments

The slave state governments provided complete and total protection for the institution of slavery, creating a totalitarian state for slaves and abolitionists. These governments provided this protection through state statutes and military support.

State Slave Laws

Slave codes were designed to sustain a social order based on slavery and racial subordination. With all the power and authority of the state, these laws held blacks in their subordinate position and maintained a system of racial oppression.

Although there was some variations among the states, the general focus of these codes was the same. The laws defined slaves as property and protected the owners of this property as other laws protected the owners of any other form of property. These codes prescribed slave behavior. They restricted the movement and possessions of the slave. They generally prohibited slaves from leaving their plantations without written permission from the master. They forbade slaves from having firearms, from assembling with other slaves without the presence of a white supervisor, and from buying or selling goods. In most states, the property of the slave belonged to the master who owned the slave. A few states allowed slaves to own some personal property. States barred slaves from testifying against whites and from entering into contracts.

Although state laws defined slaves as property, they held slaves responsible for certain forms of behavior punishable by whipping, imprisonment, or death. A few states made it a capital offense for a slave to strike his master or a member of the master's family, causing a laceration or contusion (Stampp 1956, p. 211). Other capital offenses included arson, conspiracy to rebel, or the rape of a white woman (Franklin 1969). Some states outlawed habitual runaways; that is, they authorized any white person to kill a fugitive slave with a history of running away.

Slave codes also prescribed white behavior, not to protect the slave but to safeguard the institution of slavery. Codes prohibited whites, including slave owners, from teaching slaves to read or from freeing their own slaves, unless the slaves left the state. Laws forbade interracial marriage, even between free adult blacks and whites.

During the 1830s, the Deep South states passed laws prohibiting anyone, black or white, from selling, distributing, or possessing abolitionist literature. By 1849, Virginia laws prohibited people from saying that masters had no right to own slaves as property (Stampp 1956, p. 211). Louisiana prescribed the death penalty for anyone found guilty of speaking in a bar, pulpit, stage, or any other public place in a way that might incite insubordination among slaves.

Slave codes also repressed free blacks. In reaction to the Denmark Vessey rebellion in 1822, South Carolina passed a law requiring the imprisonment of free black sailors. Arkansas expelled free blacks from the state in 1859 and authorized the reenslavement of those blacks who refused to leave (Stampp 1956). In the decade before the Civil War, most southern states passed laws authorizing the voluntary reenslavement of blacks and allowing blacks to choose their own masters (Stampp). Virginia allowed counties to sell into permanent slavery those free blacks convicted of crimes punishable by imprisonment. Florida prescribed the same penalty but included vagrancy among those crimes that allowed the reenslavement of free blacks. A number of states required free blacks to post bond or leave the state. Most states denied free blacks the right to vote.

State slave statutes appeared, on the surface, to mitigate the unrestrained barbarity of slavery and to provide some minimum protection for the slave. These laws prohibited the malicious mutilation, dismemberment, or murder of slaves. States had repealed laws mandating castration. Kentucky authorized counties to take and sell those slaves who were treated cruelly by their masters. Nevertheless, these laws provided only the bare minimum protection for the slave. States accepted as legal a range of circumstances that justified the killing of a slave. For example, they considered it legal to kill a slave who resisted arrest or acted rebellious. Also, states considered the death of a slave resulting from a reasonable beating to be an accident, not a murder. Definitions of a reasonable beating gave masters a great deal of latitude to kill slaves legally. Moreover, all slave states prohibited slaves from testifying against whites. When a white overseer maliciously murdered a slave, the only witnesses against him generally were slaves who were prohibited from testifying against whites. These codes did much to give the appearance of a more civilized form of slavery. In reality, they provided the slave with little to no protection from violent overseers.

The Slave Patrol

Slave patrols enforced the slave codes and maintained a system of race control. These patrols were not incidental or extralegal vigilante groups. They were an important aspect of southern society and an integral part of the state militia.

Every state in the South had a state militia in which every able-bodied white male was required to enroll. The subdivisions of the state militia corresponded to political subdivisions. Each county in the state was subdivided into villages, parishes, or beats. Each beat, the most common subdivision, contributed companies to the county, and the county contributed regiments to the state militia (Williamson 1986).

Slave patrols operated within the beat and were generally organized by the county sheriff or court (Franklin 1969; Williamson 1986). However, officers in the militia supervised the beat patrol. For example, the militia captain also served as the beat patrol captain. Those who served in the beat patrol also served in the militia, under the same officers. Thus the entire southern society was organized in a military fashion to maintain a system of race control, to stand ready to crush slave revolts before they were conceived, to keep blacks in their subordinate position, and to preempt white support for the freedom of slaves (Williamson).

These patrols had authority over all blacks, free or enslaved, and over whites suspected of violating the slave codes. Patrols were authorized to stop any black person on the road and arrest those who lacked either free papers or a pass to leave the plantation. Patrols enforced the slave codes by breaking up groups of blacks, by searching slave cabins for weapons or stolen goods. They also enforced laws prohibiting the circulation of abolitionist literature or concealing or aiding runaway slaves. They were authorized to kill slaves who were away from the plantation, who failed to present proper papers, and who resisted apprehension.

ECONOMIC FACTORS

On the one hand, state protection of slavery was not caused by the structure of the economy. The role of the state was somewhat indeterminate as state governments had the opportunity to abolish slavery. For example, in the early 1830s the state legislature of Virginia narrowly missed the opportunity to abolish its slave system by a vote of 65 for slavery and 58 against it (Williamson 1986, p. 6). Slavery might have died in Virginia had four representatives voted against it instead of for it. Here politics, political decision making, and the inclinations of individual political leaders determined the future of slavery in Virginia, not the structure of its economy.

On the other hand, politics, political decision making, and the inclinations of political leaders do not arise in a vacuum. They emerge under particular historical circumstances and are influenced by their socioeconomic environment. Often they are shaped by the economic structure out of which they arise. Several features of the slave economy explained the role of the state in protecting this institution: (a) the slave economy's concentration of wealth, (b) its profitability, (c) its level of integration with the national and international economies, and (d) its particular mode of production.

Concentrated Wealth and the Planter Class

Plantation slavery was anchored in an economic system that concentrated land, wealth, and slave ownership in the hands of a few. During the era of slavery, wealth and land ownership tended to be more unequally distributed in the South and most concentrated in the plantation areas. In the pre-Revolutionary South, especially in Virginia and South Carolina, strongholds of the plantation system, it was not uncommon for less than 5% of the population to own an average of 1,000 acres of land and more than 25 slaves (Main 1965, p. 48). In some counties of the commercial farm areas of South Carolina, the richest 10% of the population owned about half of all the slaves and the land (Main, p. 58). This concentration of wealth in plantation regions produced some of the wealthiest counties in the United States. By 1860, the 12 richest counties in the United States were located in the Deep South (Oakes 1982, p. 39). At the same time, about 7% of the southern population owned about 3 million out of the total of 3,953,696 slaves (Du Bois 1969a, p. 32).

This concentration of wealth produced a powerful planter class with the resources and resolve to protect slavery. This class dominated southern regional politics and strongly influenced national politics.

The political power of this class was based on its wealth, its positional advantage in society, and the nature of southern politics. Members of this class used wealth and prestige to either run for office or support pro-slavery candidates. This class enjoyed political advantages because it generated wealth that contributed to a stable and prosperous economy. Initially, this class dominated state politics through land or property owning requirements. As these requirements were abolished just prior to the Civil War, other techniques of political control emerged. Although they were numerically a minority, they were able to control state government by controlling the county. Summarizing the political devices used by the planters to secure their power, Spero and Harris (1931, p. 7) argued,

> Tradition, property qualifications for suffrage, the counting of the slave population for the purposes of legislative apportionment, the gerrymandering of legislative districts, to the detriment of poor whites, or as in South Carolina, qualifications which barred office to all but slave holders made it easy for the master class to control the state and block all unfavorable legislation. (quoted in Wilson 1980, p. 26)

Profitability and the Slave Mode of Production

As prosperous as the South and this planter class were, a number of historians argue that slavery was unprofitable. For example, Genovese (1989, p. 43) maintained that slavery was irrational, less productive than free labor, wasteful during economic downturns, saddled with enormous administrative costs, obstructive to industry, and inflationary to free labor. He argued that slaves, lacking the incentive of wages, tended to be careless, wasteful, and lazy. Genovese concluded that the South sustained this institution, not because it was profitable, but because slavery had become a part of southern society, a way of life southerners wanted to preserve.

We see slavery as a stage in the accumulation process, preceding industrial capitalism. Indeed, slavery generated the accumulated capital required to build the newly forming industries in the North just prior to the Civil War. If production in the North appeared more productive than slave labor, it was not because free men worked harder than slaves. It was because machines were more productive than men. Stampp (1956, p. 85) made this point succinctly:

> Black slavery in the South was the most productive and profitable mode of production of this era. Free white labor avoided the plantation because the work was too hard and the rewards too few. Black slaves in the South performed those tasks that free white labor found too back-breaking or too dangerous. White workers often claimed they would rather be dead than a black slave on a big plantation.

Because slaves made their own clothes, grew their own food, and maintained their own quarters, on their own time, after sundown and on Sundays, maintenance costs for the slave did not detract from surplus value and profits as it did for the free laborer. Because slaves worked all year long, harvesting at least twice a year; processing cotton or sugar; clearing new ground; repairing buildings, tools, and fences; canning fruits and vegetables; salting meats and vegetables; fertilizing the field; and preparing the ground for a new crop during the winter months, slaves were never idle (Stampp 1956, pp. 44-47). Planters compensated for declines in the price of cash crops by increasing production, making the slave work harder, faster, and longer hours.

Using econometric data further challenging Genovese's position, Fogel and Engerman (1974) claimed that southern plantations were about 40% more efficient than the northern farm and that per capita income grew 30% faster in the South than it did in the North. Shugg ([1939] 1968, p. 89) demonstrated that a planter who employs 300 workers saves $79,140 per year by using slave labor instead of free labor. Of course, this figure does not account for an initial investment of $300,000 for 300 slaves. However, the planter earns back this initial investment in 4 years and continues to accumulate more than $79,000 annually in labor cost savings alone.

There are other intuitive reasons why slave labor was more profitable than free labor. There were fewer restraints on slave labor than free labor. The free worker was protected by laws and customs; he could quit, move to another region, or strike. In contrast, the slave was a captive, forced to remain on the plantation and denied the legal protection given to the free worker. The amount of work a master could extract from a slave was limited only by the life of the slave. Although the willingness of a master to work a slave to death appeared limited by the cost of the slave, the drive for immediate profits often overruled the master's concern for the slave's life. Moreover, overseers, believing they were evaluated by their ability to produce a high crop yield, commonly disregarded the welfare of slaves (Stampp 1956). Often planters, even those who expressed concerns for the welfare of their slaves, would set crop yield standards that could only be achieved by overworking slaves.

A medical doctor, quoted by Stampp (1956, p. 84), complained that even with the high cost of slaves, masters still regarded "their sole interest to consist in large crops, leaving out of view altogether the value of Negro property and its possible deterioration." Slaves, even when their costs were high, worked at a level intolerable for free labor. Clearly, planters were able to extract a higher level of work output from slaves than they could from free laborers.

Slavery and the International and National Economy

Slavery was part of a larger national and international economic system. This institution had already contributed to the rapid growth of the British economy during the 18th century, a process well documented by Williams (1966).

Slavery was also a critical part of the national economy. In fact, by the early 19th century more than 80% of the overseas trade from the United States was in goods produced by slave labor (Smedley 1993, p. 195). Cotton alone made up 50% "of the total American exports during the antebellum period" (Billings 1979, p. 25). Trade in southern plantation cash crops benefited commercial and manufacturing interest in the New England states, stimulating ship building, road construction, banking, manufacturing, and other enterprises, especially in the North. Thus the national government had a stake in protecting the institution of slavery because the national economy depended on this institution.

CULTURE: THE SLAVE MODE OF PRODUCTION AND THE SADISTIC SOCIAL CHARACTER

The slave economy facilitated the development of a culture that functioned to maintain racially oppressive relations. An important aspect of this economy, the slave mode of production and its institutional supports, encouraged the formation of the sadistic character type.

In analytical and clinical psychology, the sadistic character is driven— by an unbearable sense of aloneness, by fear, and by feelings of insignificance—to control, exploit, hurt, and humiliate others (Fromm 1965,

p. 165). The southern slave system of the antebellum period fits this definition of sadism. In this system, slaves were denied all human rights, transformed into things, pieces of property, owned totally and absolutely by the master, to be used to generate profit. This was a controlling, humiliating, exploitative, in short, a sadistic relationship. Moreover, the extraction of greater profits in the system of slavery required more control, more humiliating treatment, and more painful experiences. In other words, increasing profits in this system required increasing the level of sadistic control over the slave. However, the greater brutality of this system required additional support from state and quasi-state institutions, enlisting slave patrolmen and private citizens in an intense system of race control.

Of course, a number of scholars have rejected this view of slavery as a sadistic system. Instead, they see it as a paternalistic institution (Wilson 1980; Genovese 1989). No doubt paternalism existed, particularly on the small farms and between the master and the house slaves. Stampp (1956) and Genovese discuss cases in which masters rewarded slaves, for example, with a ham on Christmas and Easter, with words of praise and encouragement, and with genuine expressions of care and concern. Masters occasionally referred to their slaves as their children, suggesting a form of paternalism.

Nevertheless, masters on large plantations saw their slaves as a sub-human species, as property, an investment, calculated to generate wealth. Generating this wealth required breaking the spirit of the slave; whipping, humiliating, terrorizing, hurting, and cajoling slaves, all for the sake of controlling them as absolutely as possible; exploiting them, forcing them to work 15 hours a day, seven days a week, during harvest season. It required sadistic treatment, not paternalism.

This system of labor generated an intense fear that undergirded southern society and drove southerners to establish a sadistic system of race control. Slave revolts, especially Toussaint-Louverture's revolt in Haiti and Nat Turner's revolt in Virginia, and rumors of slaves butchering whites, struck terror in the minds of whites connected with slavery. These fears created a need for a system of racial control to preempt any possibility of a revolt. This system of racial control encouraged sadistic public treatment of blacks. It involved the slave patrols that had the power to kill blacks who refused to show free papers and who resisted arrest. It also entailed the power of private citizens to chastise blacks for not showing proper deference to whites, not looking down to avoid eye contact, not addressing whites as "sir" or "miss."

The southern slave society encouraged the development of the sadistic character and provided socially accepted outlets for sadistic tendencies. In turn, the sadistic personality operated to maintain racial oppression.

Images: The Sambo and the Savage

In addition to shaping the sadistic character that maintained the system of racial oppression, slavery also generated images that functioned to perpetuate this institution. One image produced by slavery is that of the Sambo, the stereotypical childlike slave, with downcast eyes, shuffling feet, and soft voice. Williamson (1986, p. 16) argued that blacks played the role of Sambo in order to survive the holocaust of white racist hysteria and that whites needed the Sambo to feed their egos and mask their terror of slave revolts. Thus the Sambo image functioned in southern society to reinforce whites' view of themselves as Christian and civilized and their perspective of the slave as happy and childlike. Whites had to see the slave as Sambo, or they would have been driven to the brink of insanity by their fear of the slave and by their inhumanity.

The image of Sambo contrasted with that of the African savage. The savage is the incarnation of unrestrained passions, uncontrolled rage and sexuality. The savage is a cannibal, a horrifying and brutal beast. To some extent this image arose from repressed white passions projected onto the black African—repressed fear of slave revolts, repressed sexuality, repressed drives to dominate and to destroy.

Within the white mind, the Sambo becomes the savage if improperly cared for outside the white family or if freed from the civilizing influence of slavery. This view justified slavery. It dehumanized Africans and allowed unrestrained violence toward those who would revolt. It permitted Europeans to treat Africans atrociously on the one hand and to see themselves as decent, civilized human beings on the other.

Ideological and Scientific Racism

In the late 18th and early 19th centuries, two books had a major influence on race thinking. The first is Thomas Jefferson's *Notes on Virginia* (1787/1955). In this volume, Jefferson maintained that blacks are inferior in mental capabilities, in mathematics, science, and abstract reasoning. Jefferson (p. 143) added, "Blacks, whether originally a distinct race or made distinct by time and circumstance, are inferior to the whites in the endowment both of body and mind." Historian John Hope Franklin

(1969) argued that southerners used Jefferson's work to contend that blacks were an inferior race.

The second book is Edward Long's (1972) *History of Jamaica.* In this book, Long described Africans in animal-like terms, having bestial hair, fetid smell, and lice. He placed Africans on the same level as the orangutan and below the human species. He claimed that Hottentot women sometimes mated with the orangutan (quoted in Smedley 1993, pp. 182-83). He also suggested that Africans' uncontrollable sexuality made them most like beasts. These descriptions of blacks contributed to the construction of subhuman cultural images of blacks. These images, reproduced and distributed in other media forms—newspapers, art, everyday conversation—functioned to justify slavery and inhuman treatment of blacks.

Scientific and systematic writings on race emerged in the 1830s and 1840s, primarily in reaction to abolitionist assaults on slavery (Fredrickson 1971; Smedley 1993). Polygenists' theories were popular during this period. One noted polygenist was Dr. Samuel Morton, a physician and anatomy teacher. Morton measured the sizes, shapes, angles, and other features of human skulls and concluded that there were five races with varying levels of brain size and capacity, beginning with the large-brained Caucasoid and ending with the small-brained Negroid. In *Crania Aegyptiaca,* Morton argued that the Egyptians were not Negroid but Caucasoid. When confronted with pictures of dark-skinned Egyptians, Morton concluded that they were merely dark-skinned Caucasoids. This racist view that black Africans were too inferior to have built the Egyptian civilization remained popular in the United States into the 20th century.

Other polygenists included Dr. Josiah Nott of Mobile, Alabama. In addition to claiming that blacks belonged to a separate subhuman species, he also said that mulattoes were hybrids, analogous to mules. He described blacks as childlike, needing care, direction, and control. He maintained that blacks would perish if freed because they were incapable of enduring the hazards of freedom. These views contributed to the formation of racial ideologies used to justify slavery. The science behind these perspectives gave them a heightened sense of objectivity and authority, although they were connected to proslavery advocates (Fredrickson 1971; Smedley 1993, p. 239).

Racist theorists were well connected with proslavery forces in the South who were fully aware of the implications of these theories for slavery (Fredrickson 1971). For example, Morton corresponded with John Calhoun, in the hope that Calhoun could use scientific information to counter British and French opposition to the U.S. annexation of Texas as a slave state (Fredrickson, p. 77).

Value Systems

Two value systems prevalent in the South functioned to maintain both the institution of slavery and the slave aristocracy. Southerners either ascribed to a Herrenvolk democracy—that is, democracy for whites only and slavery for blacks—or to a slave aristocracy that vehemently rejected any form of democracy or equality in favor of a racial caste system of superior white masters, inferior slaves, and other classes in between. Andrew Jackson best represented Herrenvolk democracy. He envisioned a democracy in which Native Americans were banished, blacks subjugated, white males enjoyed political freedom, and the slave aristocracy prospered. John Calhoun represented the slave aristocracy. He rejected democracy altogether in favor of a slave aristocracy governed by rich white planters, with other whites in the middle and blacks subjugated at the bottom. Both systems of values operated to sustain slavery.

Dominative Racism

Out of this era of slavery emerged a particular form of racism, dominative racism (Kovel 1984). This form of racism involved the direct, sadistic control and domination of blacks by whites in the institution of slavery. This racism was the bottom side of a culture that on the surface appeared civilized, genteel, rational, opulent, paternalistic, chivalrous, and virtuous. Underneath the surface, this culture was full of fantasies, images, worldviews, and character types that all interacted and functioned to maintain a system of intense race control. It was filled with images of the Sambo and the savage. It was undergirded by fantasies of blacks as bestial, savage, animalistic, unrestrained, uninhibited, and promiscuous. It was dominated by a scientific paradigm that saw blacks as an inferior species, well below the superior Caucasoid and on the level of the orangutan. It was governed by views of blacks as property, things, chattel. This rational culture exalted productivity and property rights over human rights. It rested on intense repressed fears. It was ruled by a sadistic character type that took pleasure in controlling, hurting, and humiliating others.

Dominative racism emerged out of a particular economic structure, one based on a slave mode of production and a concentration of wealth and land ownership in the hands of a few. This mode of production shaped the development of a sadistic personality type committed to the maintenance of the institution of slavery. The maintenance of plantation slavery encouraged the development of the sadistic character not only in the master, the overseers, and the slave patrolmen, but also in the average citizen who also operated to control blacks. The level of control required in this society could only be maintained with deep forms of sadism and with the complete dehumanization of blacks. This process generated a science of race, dedicated to proving the subhuman, inferior status of blacks. It contributed to the formation of a sadistic and dehumanizing racist culture that sustained slavery.

Plantation slavery concentrated wealth in a way that produced a dominant planter class. This class possessed the resources and the will to use both the state and the national governments to protect this institution. Moreover, because the national economy depended on the southern plantation economy, the national government was already predisposed to protect slavery. Hence, presidents, congresses, and the Supreme Court acted in ways to legitimate slavery. The national government supported slavery because the national economy depended on this institution and because the planter class mobilized to use the national government for this purpose. This class also dominated southern regional and state politics and used the state government to suppress freedoms of speech, assembly, and press, in order to protect slavery.

5

Debt Peonage and Dominative Aversive Racism (1865-1965)

The Civil War ended with the abolition of slavery, although the war did not begin with this goal. The war began for the South, intent on preserving and expanding slavery, as a war for independence. It began for the North as a war to preserve the Union. It was not a war to end slavery. Lincoln himself had said that he would protect the institution of slavery if necessary to preserve the Union. Nevertheless, by the end of the war, the scope of the conflict had expanded to include the struggle of African Americans for their freedom.

The war ended with the participation of African American troops and the emancipation of the slaves. This end emerged both as a military necessity and a moral imperative. The assistance of 300,000 black laborers and spies and the participation of 200,000 black soldiers fighting for their freedom and the freedom of their families—and fighting with an enthusiasm unmatched by other soldiers—made it possible for the North to win the war (Du Bois 1969a, pp. 80, 238). Emancipation emerged as the best moral justification for the carnage and destruction caused by the war. The war ended with the real possibility of freedom for African Americans.

The Civil War was a social upheaval analogous to what Gramsci (1980) referred to as a fierce artillery attack on an enemy's entrenched position. On the surface, the bombardment appeared to have destroyed the enemy's entire defensive system, but instead it left the enemy well fortified inside the trenches. That is, the war had a heavy impact on the dominant class in the South—the planter class, an upper-class family that owned more than 1,000 acres of land and more than 50 slaves. The war destroyed crops, buildings, and farm equipment. It eliminated the wealth planters held in slaves. It imposed economic hardship on the South and caused some planters to sell their land. However, the oppressed classes and their supporters never stormed the trenches; that is, they never seized the state long enough to force the planters to completely relinquish their power or to redistribute land in favor of ex-slaves. Thus they left the power base of the landed aristocracy intact. The lowest classes remained powerless and vulnerable. Consequently, the planter class survived the war and emerged with a vengeance to dominate the region and to resubjugate African Americans. This landlord class used all of its power and skills— economic, political, and physical; it used its control of land, jobs, wealth, its dominance of political institutions; it used violence and racist demagogy—to secure its hegemony over the region and over its laborers. This class was the major force in the construction of a new form of racial oppression—dominative aversive racism.

This new form of oppression involved new ways of organizing and exploiting plantation labor: sharecropping, tenant farming, and debt peonage systems. It involved a racial caste system that relegated African Americans to the lowest rung of society. Protected and legitimized by all levels of government, this caste system entailed both direct control of blacks and their segregation from whites, hence, dominative aversive racism.

In this chapter, we examine the formation and perpetuation of this form of racism. Because our class analysis of this period contradicts the orthodox view of postbellum southern history, we briefly reexamine this view and summarize recent studies that support our alternative paradigm. We then proceed to discuss the Reconstruction period, which promised freedom to African Americans but failed to institute land reforms. We analyze the era of reaction and reunion between the Hayes and Hoover administrations and review the role of the national government in legitimizing the new racial order. We discuss the rise of the planter class to a position of hegemony over the South. Finally, we analyze both the political economy and cultural formation of dominative aversive racism.

THE OLD ORTHODOXY

The orthodox view of this period of southern history maintains that the planter class died after the Civil War, that the middle class emerged to modernize the southern economy, and that the white masses, especially poor farmers, disenfranchised blacks and created the system of racial segregation that plagued the South until the middle of the 20th century. This orthodox view or some version of it has been held by most progressive American historians.

C. Vann Woodward (1951), a prominent proponent of this view, argued that segregation became more pronounced in the late 1890s, after the dissolution of the planter class, after the Populists seized control of state governments, and after blacks and whites came into closer contact with each other and competed for the same jobs. He suggested that one of the ironies of this period is that Jim Crow and the disenfranchisement of blacks were the products of the rise of southern democracy. Specifically he said, "It is one of the paradoxes of Southern history that political democracy for the white man and racial discrimination for the black were often products of the same dynamics" (p. 211). He argued that "barriers of racial discrimination mounted in direct ratio with the tide of political democracy among whites" (p. 211). Woodward also blamed Jim Crow on lower-class whites. He said,

> As the Negroes invaded the new mining and industrial towns of the uplands in greater numbers, and the hill-country, whites were driven into more frequent and closer association with them, and as the two races were brought into rivalry for subsistence wages in the cotton fields, mines, and wharves, the lower-class white man's demand for Jim Crow laws became more insistent. (p. 211)

Educator and writer W. E. B. Du Bois (1969a) also pronounced the planter class dead and attributed the repression of blacks to the efforts of the entire white society of the South. Of the planter class, Du Bois (p. 54) said,

> With the Civil War, the planters died as a class. We still talk as though the dominant social class in the South persisted after the war. But it did not. It disappeared. . . . Of the names of prominent southern families in Congress in 1860, only two appear in 1870, five in 1880. . . . The disaster of war decimated the planters.

Of course, Du Bois conceded that no scientific study of the postwar planter class had been conducted at the time of his study.

Wilson (1980) blamed white workers for establishing Jim Crow. He said,

> White working-class efforts to eliminate black competition generated an elaborate system of Jim Crow segregation that was reinforced by an ideology of biological racism. . . . The white working class was aided not only by its numerical size but also by its increasing accumulation of political resources that accompanied changes in its relations to the means of production. (p. 61)

Wilson argued that the planter class dominated the antebellum South, but the white working class dominated the postbellum South. He explained this shift in class hegemony in term of changes in systems of production. He noted that the slave mode of production, which required a concentration of landownership, produced the slave aristocracy. With its tremendous economic power, this class easily controlled the political system and dominated the South. However, Wilson indicated that this old system of production in the South changed after the Civil War from plantation slavery to industrial capitalism, thus eroding the power base of the planter class and facilitating the rise of the working class, the group responsible for segregation.

A few Marxist scholars subscribe to a variation of this orthodox paradigm. For example, Camejo (1976) blamed Jim Crow on the rising southern bourgeoisie and the northern capitalists who dominated the South after the death of the planter class.

Paradigm Problems

This orthodox paradigm suffers from a number of problems and anomalies. First, the "white working class did it" thesis appears counterintuitive. The white working class did not seem powerful enough to secure the passage of Jim Crow and disenfranchising laws. In the late 19th and early 20th centuries southern labor unions were weak in general, practically nonexistent in the growing industries, and ineffective in state politics. Moreover, the same state legislatures that disenfranchised blacks took away the vote from a large proportion of poor whites and passed the most repressive labor laws in the United States. The notion that poor whites would disenfranchise themselves and that white workers would repress labor organizations runs counter to intuitive reasoning.

Second, the conclusion that the planter class died after the war is based largely on speculation. It is not derived from an empirical study of this class. It is drawn from a variety of indirect sources: newspapers, autobiographies, correspondence, travel logs, and secondary sources. It is based on two a priori and fallacious assumptions: (1) that the devastation of the war and emancipation destroyed this class, and (2) that substantial changes in its membership signaled the death of this class.

The New Paradigm: The Hegemony of the Landed Aristocracy

John W. Cell (1982), operating in the new paradigm, offered a strong critique of the assumptions underlying the orthodox view. He argued that a social class is like a bus: "Exchanges of riders go on constantly and are easily mistaken for the end of a journey" (p. 107). Put another way: planter classes and buses do not suddenly cease to exist merely because members or riders today are different from those of yesterday.

Cell (1982) contended that not only did the planter class survive the war and Reconstruction, it emerged as a well-entrenched and powerful class by the end of the 19th century. He argued that emancipation meant a substantial loss of property and investment for the planters, but it did not spell the end of this class. It did not require planters to pay direct cash outlays nor did it eliminate their source of labor. After emancipation, planters continued to own and control the primary means of production: land, mules, and plows. Cell argued that a redistribution of land in favor of the ex-slaves would have crippled the planter class. However, this redistribution never occurred. Thus emancipation without land reforms left landownership concentrated in the former slavocracy and the ex-slaves at the mercy of the planters. Cell (p. 108) concluded, "contrary to what was once supposed, the period after 1865 probably saw an increase in the concentration of economic wealth and power in southern agriculture."

Other studies support the view that the planter class survived the war. In one example, Wayne (1983) examined planters residing in counties in Mississippi and Louisiana. He discovered that in the few years immediately following the war, some planters lost their land in foreclosure, some sold land, some migrated north, some went to South America, some attempted to recruit Chinese laborers to replace blacks, and some rented land to northerners. However, Wayne concluded that by 1868, planters dominated agricultural production in the South. He noted that in some black belt counties, planters owned more than 75% of the land (see also Rabinowitz 1992).

In another example, Wiener (1978) demonstrated that membership in the planter class had never been entirely fixed or permanent. That is, there had always been some exchange of members in the upper class with those of the lower classes. Wiener's data indicated that this rate of exchange for the postbellum period was not much different from the rate for the antebellum period. He suggested that most of the antebellum planters not only survived, they emerged to dominate the postbellum south. He concluded, "the new class that emerged from war and Reconstruction owning the land and controlling the labor force included a surprisingly large proportion of the antebellum cotton families, while the structural basis of their wealth and power had been altered" (p. 5).

In another example, Billings (1979) demonstrated that the planter class played a dominant role in the growth of industry in the South and in the formation of the economic basis of the southern racial caste system. He focused on the rise of the textile industry in North Carolina. In this state, capital investment in cotton mills alone increased 60% between 1865 and 1884 (p. 62). Textile manufacturing increased by over 1,100% from 1880 to 1900 (p. 42).

Billings (1979) investigated a total of 78 cotton mills that operated between 1865 and 1884. Out of this total, 18 or 23% were owned and operated by planters, people whose names appeared in the Branson's North Carolina Business Directory as prominent farmers owning between 1,188 and 3,000 or more acres of land (p. 63). An additional 26 or 34% of these mills were owned or partially owned by planters (p. 64). Thus 57% of the mills were either owned or partially owned by planters (p. 64); and this was a conservative estimate, because eight of the nonplanter owners had the same family name as other prominent farmers.

For a closer examination of the mills, Billings (1979) focused on Richmond County. Seven mills operated in this county between 1865 and 1884. Out of this seven, two were owned by planters owning more than 3,000 acres; two were owned by relatives of planters; one was jointly owned by planters; one went out of business; and one was not identified. In other words, out of the total number of mills that remained in business in Richmond County, whose owners were known, 100% were owned completely or jointly by planters or their relatives.

A number of earlier studies of this era corroborate Billings's research and confirm the dominant role of the planter class. Mitchell and Mitchell (1930) demonstrated that most of the new industrialists of the South in the late 19th century were former slave owners who were accustomed to giving orders and being obeyed. They simply transferred their plantation customs to the factory. Cash (1941) argued that progress in the South occurred completely within the plantation framework. McLaurin (1971, pp. 38-39; quoted in Billings 1979, p. 104), describing mill towns as plantation villages, added that managers "exerted a substantial influence over where the operatives lived, shopped, studied, played, and worshipped." Reich (1981, p. 249) confirmed that blacks tended to be excluded from employment in the textile mills until the 1960s, with the exception of a few of the dirtiest mill jobs. Kousser (1974), in a meticulous study of southern politics, provided direct evidence of the dominance of the planter class in state politics. Lester Salamon, in a study of Mississippi, attributed the underdevelopment of this state to the hegemony of a landed upper class that depended on a docile and disciplined labor force. This class promoted state policies that repressed labor and discouraged education. Specifically, Salamon said,

> The result has been a regime that is essentially hostile to democracy, that had little incentive to provide public education or to introduce labor-saving improvements, that had little real interest in rapid industrialization, but was willing to support limited industrial growth geared to the needs of the cotton plantation and respectful of plantation-inspired labor policies. In short, the result has been economic backwardness, the "closed society," and limited economic development. (quoted in Billings 1979, p. 37)

Social and Political Consequences of Planter-Led Industrialization

This industrialization role of the southern landed aristocracy has two major social implications for the new paradigm. The first implication is that planters were in the strongest position for reorganizing labor in the South in ways that formed the economic foundation of the southern racial caste system. Planter-led industrialization meant that planters controlled labor both on the land and in the mills. Through this dual control, they were able to tie blacks to the land through a debt peonage system and exclude them from the mills. One purpose of blocking blacks' opportunities in the mills and tying them to the land was to maintain a cheap, docile, and stable labor force on the plantations. Mill owners also tightened their influence and control over white mill workers by giving them special privileges over blacks, by building mill towns, and by using blacks as a weapon against organized labor. Not only did owners create mill jobs for whites, they built houses, supported churches, and contributed to charity. At the same time, they used blacks to threaten whites who complained about conditions in the mills. Workers were told that if they did not behave, they would be replaced by black workers. Through this process, planters/mill owners cemented their relationship with poor whites and precipitated tensions between poor whites and poor blacks. The outcome of this process was the formation of a stratified order with blacks concentrated at the lowest strata on the land and poor whites above blacks in the mills. Billings (1979, p. 92) concluded, "Although sociologists often describe prejudice as a lower-class personality trait, it was actually a cultural construct of the landed upper class. The labor needs of the plantation were reflected in a white supremacist ideology."

The second social implication of planter-driven industrialization is that this process created social conditions that undermined the development of democracy. Drawing primarily from the works of Barrington Moore (1966), Billings (1979) argued that developing societies are more likely to evolve into democracies when the power of the landed aristocracy is balanced by a strong urban middle class and an independent bourgeoisie. Democracies are less likely to arise in societies in which a landed aristocracy is powerful and its powers are enhanced by its direct involvement in industrialization and by the absence or weakness of an urban middle class. These societies tend to produce antidemocratic regimes. These were precisely the conditions that characterized the postbellum South.

NEW MODES OF RACIAL OPPRESSION

A new system of racial oppression emerged after the abolition of slavery, as planters were forced to develop new ways of exploiting labor on their plantations. This system involved a complicated hierarchical structure in which racial oppression overlapped with class and caste arrangements. We provide a simplified version of this structure, focusing on landownership, tenant farming and sharecropping, direct supervision, credit systems, crop share arrangements, the convict lease programs, and debt peonage.

Landownership

Out of a total of 1,393,000 black agricultural workers, only 13% were landowners, according to 1930 Census Tract data reported by Myrdal ([1948] 1975). This figure compared to 42.4% of a total white agricultural workforce of 2,945,000.

Black landowners tended to be more marginal than white owners, as the average size of black-owned farms was a fraction of the size of white-owned farms. Myrdal ([1948] 1975, p. 240) concluded that "the average size of Negro owner-operated farms (60.4 acres) is about the same as for white sharecroppers (58.9 acres)." Extreme poverty and the hostility of whites to black landownership contributed to the marginal position of black-owned farms (Du Bois 1969a; Reich 1981; Mandle 1992).

Tenant Farming and Sharecropping

In the South, there were three types of tenant farmers: cash tenants, share tenants, and sharecroppers. Cash tenants were at the top of the hierarchy of tenant farmers. They were entrepreneurs who rented land in cash. Some cash tenants were better off than most landowners. Few blacks fell in this class.

Share tenants were next in this hierarchy. They were below cash tenants but above the sharecroppers. Because they often lacked cash for rent, share tenants paid their rent as a percentage of their crop. However, they owned their own tools and work animals.

Sharecroppers were at the bottom of the hierarchy. They had nothing, not even their own tools. They paid rent as a percentage of their crop and borrowed their tools and work animals from the planter. Because they had nothing, they were the most exploited. They existed in a system of perpetual poverty.

Race, class, and geography overlapped in this system. Although most sharecroppers were white, a greater proportion of the black population (28.2%), compared to the white population (13.0%), were sharecroppers (1930 U.S. Department of Commerce Census data cited in Myrdal [1948] 1975, p. 236). In the black belt region of the South, where laborers faced more oppressive working conditions and suffered higher rates of poverty, over half of the sharecroppers were black (Mandle 1992, p. 36).

Several features of the sharecropping and tenant farming system contributed to its exploitative and oppressive nature: the credit system, crop share, and direct supervision.

The Credit System

In the credit system, the planter either advanced loans or provided supplies on credit to tenants or croppers, using the crop as collateral. Mandle (1992) reported that 82% of croppers (tenant and share) received cash advances from planters and were charged an average interest rate of 21%. Myrdal ([1948] 1975, p. 247) suggested that by the 1930s this rate ranged between 10% and 37%, depending on the duration of the loan—whether a couple of months or a year.

According to Mandle (1992, p. 42), about 60% of the croppers received household supplies on credit with an interest rate of about 53%. The price of goods from planter-owned stores was exorbitant (Myrdal [1948] 1975). Moreover, credit interest rates charged to croppers for these goods were two to three times the credit interest rates charged to planters by their creditors. Furthermore, Mandle (p. 42) contended that in areas devoid of plantation stores, merchants allowed croppers to purchase supplies on credit if the planter guaranteed the loan. Interest rates on these loans averaged 71%.

Because sharecroppers had nothing to begin with, they were the most victimized by this system of inflated prices and usury interest rates. This system, along with the crop share program, kept sharecroppers in perpetual poverty.

Crop Share

The crop share system was a method of paying rent as a percentage of the crop yield, set at the beginning of the growing season, usually at 50%. In this arrangement, a cropper worked throughout the year on a fraction of the planter's land to produce a crop. The planter expropriated this crop because he owned the land and the instruments of production and because state power supported him. The planter also decided how much the cropper owed him and how much to subtract from the cropper's share. If the cropper felt cheated, he had no recourse, except to move to another plantation, providing both the old and the new planters allowed it. It was not necessary for the planter to cheat the cropper. Under the fairest conditions, the croppering system enriched the planter and impoverished the cropper (Mandle 1992).

Croppers often received little or no money after the planter deducted credit and interest from earnings (Mandle 1992, p. 43). Thus black poverty in the South during this period was structural. It was deeply rooted in the postbellum mode of agricultural production (Mandle, p. 43).

Although this mode of production was sufficient to impoverish blacks without force or dishonesty, the literature on this system abounds with examples of habitual cheating of croppers and violence toward them. Dollard (1949, p. 121) offered this example:

A tenant may make ten bales of cotton, worth $750, for which his share would be $375, less his advances. The Negro has kept accounts and knows the advances to be, say $100. The landlord or his overseer calls in the tenant and tells him he did very well this year: he made $10. If the Negro offers a mild challenge, he is told, "Do you mean to call me a liar?" This settles the discussion because to call a white man a liar is extremely dangerous for a Negro.

Elsewhere Dollard (pp. 122-23) added,

Some owners, not all, juggle the accounts to keep the cropper in debt and thus hold him on the land. This is apparently another device for stabilizing the labor force; the man who is in debt has to leave all his goods if he tries to move. Informants said that the cropper is called to the accounting, the boss man sits at the desk, a .45 revolver beside him, roughly asks what the tenant wants. The tenant says he wants a settlement. "Yes," says the boss man, "you made fifteen dollars last year." The tenant cannot argue or dispute or the boss will grasp the gun and ask him if he is going to argue. If he does, "boom-boom." (Only white juries sit on such cases, or any other cases for the most part; provocative behavior, such as an argument by the Negro, is considered as an adequate extenuating circumstance.)

Direct Supervision

For the most part, planters rigidly supervised their plantations. The level of supervision tended to correspond with the hierarchy of labor. Black sharecroppers were most closely supervised, white cash tenants the least. Planters managed labor, especially the labor of black sharecroppers, in ways similar to the old authoritarian slave system. Often work on these plantations began with the sounding of a predawn bell, followed by a sunrise bell calling the croppers to work (Mandle 1992, pp. 40-41). In many cases, planters hired plantation supervisors and taskmasters and worked black sharecroppers in gang-labor arrangements like those of the slave era. Planters often used force to control labor, to extract higher levels of production, to quash labor organizing efforts, and to prevent the loss of good workers. This force was almost always supported by the local sheriff (Dollard 1949).

Convict Lease

The new southern mode of production was repressive and exploitative even without peonage. Convict lease and debt peonage added a dimension to this system comparable to the worst horrors of slavery.

In the convict lease system planters, mine owners, railroad construction companies, and other employers would bid on state contracts to employ large numbers of convicts on chain gangs for a few pennies a day per prisoner (Camejo 1976, p. 203).

Du Bois provided vivid descriptions of this system:

A Southern white woman writes:

"In some states where convict labor is sold to the highest bidder, the cruel treatment of the helpless human chattel in the hands of guards is such as no tongue can tell nor pen picture. Prison inspectors find convicts herded together, irrespective of age; confined at night in shackles; housed sometimes, as has been found, in old box cars; packed almost as closely as sardines in a box. During the day all are worked under armed guards, who stand ready to shoot down any who may attempt to escape from this hell . . . "

George W. Cable protested in 1883 and wrote: "If anything may be inferred from the mortal results of the Lease System in other States, the year's death rate of the convict camps of Louisiana must exceed that of any pestilence that ever fell upon Europe in the Middle Ages." (Du Bois 1969a, pp. 698-99)

Convict laborers suffered high morbidity and mortality rates in this system. The annual mortality rate for these laborers during the 1880s was one out of nine in Mississippi and one out of four in Arkansas (Camejo 1976, p. 203). Apparently, this system died out by the 1940s.

Debt Peonage

By the beginning of the 20th century, almost every southern state had laws that defined the act of leaving a plantation without paying back advances or debts as a form of labor fraud punishable by imprisonment in convict lease systems with their high mortality rates. These laws allowed employers to engage in forced labor (Daniel 1972; Camejo 1976). Although the U.S. Supreme Court struck down some of these laws in the early 20th century, forms of state-supported debt peonage continued in the South until the 1960s (*Clyatt v. United States* 1905; Daniel 1972).

There is a great deal of debate in the literature over the extent and duration of peonage. Most studies suggest that peonage was incidental and short-lived, ending before the Great Depression (Myrdal [1948] 1975;

Mandle 1992). However, the Department of Justice studies and the case law presented by Daniel (1972) indicate that this system was more than incidental, that its maintenance entailed state-supported violence, and that cases continued up until the 1960s.

POLITICS

On the one hand, the economic structure of the South favored the rise of both antidemocratic politics and the planter class. This class created a state that operated to support and legitimize racially oppressive and exploitative economic arrangements.

On the other hand, before the planter class could completely subjugate blacks in the economic realm, it had to dominate the political arena, defeating African Americans and their supporters politically. This outcome—planter hegemony and black subjugation—was not automatically determined by the southern economic structure. It resulted from a fierce and protracted political struggle.

This struggle can be divided into three stages: (1) Reconstruction and planter subordination, (2) hegemony crisis and planter counterrevolution, (3) populist revolt and consolidated planter rule. Historians identify two phases of Reconstruction. The first phase is the period of presidential Reconstruction. In this period, the president sympathized with the planters and allowed them to reassert themselves. The second phase is one of congressional dominance. In this phase, the U.S. Congress, acting against the will of the president, subordinated the planter class for a brief moment.

Presidential Reconstruction

Presidential Reconstruction was conservative and conciliatory toward the former Confederates. As the war was fought to maintain the Union and not to free the slaves, reunion and reconciliation took precedence over the liberation of the slaves in the Reconstruction programs of Presidents Abraham Lincoln and Andrew Johnson. These presidents opposed equal rights for blacks and favored incremental progress toward freeing African Americans (Stampp 1965; Du Bois 1969a; Fredrickson 1982).

Andrew Johnson opposed civil rights and voting rights for blacks. He believed that only whites should have political power in the South; that without white rule, blacks would relapse into barbarism; and that nature may assign blacks to an inferior social status. In his third annual message to Congress, Johnson said,

> It must be acknowledged that in the progress of nations, negroes have shown less capacity for government than any other race of people. No independent government of any form has ever been successful in their hands. On the contrary, wherever they have been left to their own devices they have shown a constant tendency to relapse into barbarism. . . . The great difference between the two races in physical, mental, and moral characteristics will prevent an amalgamation or fusion of them together in one homogeneous mass. (quoted in Stampp 1965, p. 87)

In 1864, in response to a question on whether he supported emancipation, Johnson said, "As for the Negro I am for setting him free but at the same time I assert that this is a white man's government" (quoted in Du Bois 1969a, p. 244).

Johnson moved quickly to forgive the South and restore the Union. In May 1865, he issued two Restoration proclamations. The first required southerners to take an oath of allegiance to the Union. Amnesty, pardon, and citizenship rights would be given to those taking this oath. Although ex-Confederate civil and military officials would be barred from these benefits, the president would make special exceptions. The second proclamation established the process of forming new governments in the South. Only those who voted in 1860 were allowed to vote in 1865, a process that effectively disenfranchised blacks. Also, only those granted amnesty would be eligible to run for public office. Johnson informally required the ex-Confederate states to denounce their secession ordinances, repudiate Confederate debt, and ratify the 13th Amendment.

The old Confederate leadership moved quickly to exploit Johnson's offer. Many ex-Confederate generals and public officials converged on Johnson for special presidential pardons. Many refused to take the loyalty oath. Many were elected to state offices and to the U.S. Congress. For example, Alexander H. Stephens, the former Confederate vice president, was elected to the U.S. Senate from Georgia; Benjamin G. Humphreys, former Confederate brigadier general, was elected governor of Mississippi (Stampp 1965, p. 67). The majority of the new leaders of the South elected to state and federal offices were planters and former leaders of the Confederacy (Stampp 1965; Du Bois 1969a).

Ex-Confederate states halfheartedly followed Johnson's restoration guidelines. Several states repealed their secession bills without denouncing them. South Carolina did not repudiate its war debt, and Mississippi refused to ratify the 13th Amendment (Stampp 1965).

Reenslavement of Blacks

Johnson's restoration program left the ex-slaves at the mercy of their former masters and left the masters in power. It left blacks defenseless against violent attacks from defeated and embittered rebels. It allowed the planters to reemerge and reestablish their hegemony over the region and to reenslave blacks by force and by state laws.

The New Black Codes

With the ex-Confederate leaders in control of state governments, southern states passed Black Codes designed to reenslave blacks. These codes denied blacks the right to vote, barred blacks from public education, prohibited interracial marriages, excluded blacks from juries, and reenacted some of the antebellum slave codes. South Carolina codes forbade blacks from working in areas other than agriculture without a special state license. Mississippi codes prevented blacks from owning or leasing land. Louisiana laws prohibited blacks from leaving plantations without permission, once they signed labor contracts. Most states enacted vagrancy laws that allowed counties to arrest unemployed blacks as vagrants and force them to work on plantations (Stampp 1965, p. 80; Camejo 1976, p. 58). Some state laws gave employers the right to whip employees. Other laws excluded blacks from towns (Latham 1969, p. 28).

Congressional Reconstruction

Initially, Johnson's restoration program was supported by Congress, with the exception of the Radical Republicans who were in a minority. However, several factors provoked congressional opposition to Johnson and precipitated support for the Radical Republicans' Reconstruction program. First, on the opening session of the 39th Congress, northern Republicans were confronted by ex-rebel leaders elected to Congress from the former Confederate states. Many of these ex-rebels, in defiance of Johnson's restoration proclamations, refused to take any loyalty oath. Republicans were confronted with the real possibility of the defeated and defiant rebels dominating the national government. Second, the passage of the Black Codes, the reenslavement of blacks, and the high level of violence in the South shocked even the conservative Republicans into believing that a more radical approach to Reconstruction was required.

Third, Johnson's abrasive style and his opposition to the most moderate Reconstruction Acts turned Congress against him. He had vetoed the Freedman's Bureau Reauthorization Act and the 1866 Civil Rights Act. He campaigned against the 14th Amendment and accused the Radical Republicans of treason.

Congress responded vigorously to the president. It expelled the ex-Confederates, disbanded the southern governments, and divided the South into four military districts. The purpose of military rule was to enforce the peace until legitimate, loyal governments could be established. The military commander of each district was responsible for maintaining law and order; registering people, including blacks, to vote; overseeing the construction of new state governments; and supervising free elections.

Congress provided extensive civil rights protection for blacks, especially with the Civil Rights Act of 1866, the Enforcer Acts of 1870 and 1871, the Civil Rights Act of 1875, and the 14th and 15th Amendments. The 1866 Civil Rights Act, designed to repeal the Black Codes, protected blacks' rights to own property, to vote, to make contracts, to sue, to testify in court, to buy and sell real estate, and to be citizens of the United States (Stampp 1965, p. 136). The Enforcer Acts prohibited Ku Klux Klan violence. The Civil Rights Act of 1875 forbade racial discrimination and segregation in public accommodations. It also protected blacks' rights to serve on juries (Latham 1969, p. 51). The 14th Amendment overturned the Dred Scott decision, granting citizenship to all people born or naturalized in the United States and prohibiting state governments from taking life, liberty, or property from individuals without due process of the law. It also mandated state governments to provide all citizens with equal protection of the law. The 15th Amendment said that state governments must not deny individuals the right to vote on account of race, color, or previous conditions of servitude.

Radical Republicans advocated land reform programs, a policy direction essential to black liberation but unacceptable to the majority of Congressmen. For example, Thaddeus Stevens sought to confiscate the land of the top 70,000 planters and ex-Confederate leaders, who collectively owned about 400 million acres of land. Moreover, Stevens proposed to redistribute this land to the ex-slaves, giving each family 40 acres. The implementation of this proposal would have destroyed the planter class and secured the freedom of ex-slaves.

Land reform failed for several reasons. It violated principles of private property and of the Protestant ethic, deeply ingrained in American political culture. It threatened the interest of Republican party supporters, particularly northern industrialists, who saw propertyless blacks as a potential source of cheap labor, and northern land speculators, who desired to purchase cheap southern land (Stampp 1965, pp. 130-31). The failure of any land reform program left the economic power base of the planters intact and left blacks totally at the mercy of the landowners.

Hegemony Crisis and Planter Counterrevolution

The Reconstruction Acts altered the balance of political power in the South. They barred ex-Confederate leaders from holding office. These Acts temporarily shifted political power from the planters to the lower classes and allowed blacks to participate in the political process. The result was a more progressive regime, one that created public education for all children, black and white; that extended voting rights to women; that expanded welfare programs for the needy; and that created special programs to repair war-damaged roads, ports, and bridges.

At no time did blacks dominate state governments. Although blacks constituted a majority of the population in South Carolina and Mississippi, although they constituted a majority of the electorate in Alabama, Florida, and Louisiana, and although they dominated a few state constitutional conventions, they never dominated any state government. They constituted a minority in every state legislature except North Carolina's, where they were a majority only in the lower house. The Reconstruction Act of 1867 disenfranchised only about 10% of the white ex-Confederate population, affecting primarily the upper class. No black was ever elected governor. One black, former Lieutenant-Governor P. B. S. Pinchback, became governor of Louisiana, after the impeachment of Governor Warmoth (Du Bois 1969a, p. 470). A few blacks were sent to Congress.

Although the antebellum ruling class was suppressed during Reconstruction, this class swiftly reemerged after the passage of the 1872 Amnesty Act. Its rapid ascendancy was aided by its superior economic position, its control of land and jobs, its command of personal resources—money, education, and leadership experience. This class was also aided by the absence of an autonomous industrial class and a strong middle class. The Southern culture of violence, inherited from the slave system, also helped the plantation class forcibly overthrow the state Reconstruction regimes. Although the shape of this counterrevolutionary movement varied from state to state, the Mississippi and South Carolina coups provide good examples.

The Mississippi Coup

In the early 1870s, terrorist attacks against Radical Reconstructionists and blacks were common in Mississippi, as they were throughout the South. The state response to this terrorism was ineffective, primarily because of the reluctance of both the governor of Mississippi and the president of the United States to use force against southern whites to protect blacks.

The Meridian massacre in Mississippi illustrates this problem of white violence and ineffective state response. Alabama planters initiated this atrocity. These planters pursued black laborers, escaping from forced labor contracts, and their white radical supporters. When they first caught up with them in Meridian, Mississippi, the planters were repelled by organized blacks. Later the Alabamians joined local Meridian property owners in demanding that the town expel the fugitives from Alabama. Both groups—Alabama planters with the support of Meridian property owners and black croppers with the support of white Republicans—appealed to the Republican Governor, James L. Alcorn, an antebellum Whig leader and a former slaver owner. He refused to take sides or to call the state militia to protect Meridian. Encouraged by the governor's neutrality, over 300 well-armed and well-organized whites, mostly from Alabama, attacked Meridian, shooting and killing a white Republican judge and several black leaders, burning a black church and the home of a white Radical leader, and lynching four blacks (Camejo 1976, p. 147). This massacre was a preview to the violence that carried over into the electoral process.

White Mississippians used a variety of means to overthrow the Radical Republicans. Employers would include in labor contracts provisions requiring their workers to vote against the Republicans (Stampp 1965, p. 204; Camejo 1976, p. 153). It became common practice to fire those who voted Republican and hire those who voted for Democrats. Camejo (p. 154) added, "Blacks who supported the Democrats were given badges to wear, which they were told would protect them from possible beatings by Democratic party detachments."

Opponents of Republican Reconstruction were willing to employ any tactic necessary to overthrow Reconstruction regimes. Some used labor contracts to require workers to vote against Republicans (Stampp 1965). Some employed violence. In Vicksburg, between 40 and 80 blacks who resisted the assaults were murdered on July 5, 1875. Massacres occurred in several counties throughout the state. Eventually, the Republican governor of Mississippi, Adelbert Ames, asked President Grant for assistance. Grant refused to send additional troops. He said, "The whole public are tired out with these autumnal outbreaks in the South, and the great majority are ready now to condemn any interference on the part of the Government" (quoted in Camejo 1976, p. 154). The governor ordered the armed groups to disband and declared that legitimate governments in Yazoo and Hinds counties had been illegally overthrown. With great reluctance, Ames activated a small state militia unit. Grant sent a negotiator to arrange for Ames and the state Democratic leader, James George, to meet and work out a compromise. Ames agreed to disband Mississippi's black militia in exchange for George's agreement to stop the violence. The black militia was disbanded, but the violence continued. As a result of violence, threats of job loss, assaults at the polls, fraud, and other extralegal devices, the Democrats were victorious.

The South Carolina Coup

South Carolina followed Mississippi's example. An ex-Confederate commander, Martin W. Gary, headed the Democratic party's campaign to depose the Republicans in this state. Gary organized both political and military clubs. He mapped out a broad strategy of intimidation, bribery, deceit, propaganda, and terror to retake the state from the Republicans. Gary outlined his strategies in a communiqué to local Democratic organizations. The following is an excerpt:

> 3. . . . That the Democratic Military Clubs are to be armed with rifles and pistols and such other arms as they command. They are to be divided into two companies, one of the old men, the other of the young men; an experienced captain or commander to be placed over each of them. That each company is to have a first and second organization. That each captain is to see that his men are well armed and provided with at least thirty rounds of ammunition. That the Captain of the young men is to provide a Baggage Wagon, in which three days rations for the men are to be stored on the day before the election in order that they may be prepared at a moment's notice to move to any point in the County when ordered by the Chairman of the Executive committee. . . .

> 12. Every Democrat must feel honor bound to control the vote of at least one Negro, by intimidation, purchase, keeping him away or as each individual may determine, how he may best accomplish it.

13. . . . Democrats must go in as large numbers as they can get together, and well armed, behave at first with great courtesy and assure the ignorant Negroes that you mean them no harm and so soon as their leaders or speakers begin to speak and make false statements of facts, tell them then and there to their faces, that they are liars. . . .

15. Let it be generally known that if any blood is shed, houses burnt, votes repeated, ballot boxes stuffed, false counting of votes, or any acts on their part that are in violation of Law and Order! that we will hold the leaders of the Radical Party personally responsible whether they were present at the time of the commission of the offense crime or not. . . .

16. *Never threaten a man individually. If he deserves to be threatened, the necessities of the times require that he should die* [italics added]. A dead Radical is very harmless—a threatened Radical or one driven off by threats from the scene of his operations is often very troublesome. . . .

20. Every club must be uniformed in a red shirt and they must be sure and wear it upon all public meetings and particularly on the day of election. (quoted in Camejo 1976, pp. 160-61)

Camejo (1976) compared the Red Shirts of the Democratic organization to Hitler's Brown Shirts. In the 1876 gubernatorial election, this organization mobilized behind Democrat Wade Hampton, who opposed incumbent Republican Daniel H. Chamberlain. During this election, Red Shirt units and other armed Democrats harassed and assaulted Radical Republican candidates throughout South Carolina. Rather than using the state militia to suppress the violence, Governor Chamberlain disbanded the black militia and asked President Grant for assistance. Prior to this disbanding, on July 8, 1876, the Red Shirts, well armed with Winchester rifles and cannons and led by General M. C. Butler, attacked the all-black town of Hamburg, South Carolina, massacring a small black militia force and killing town leaders (Williamson 1965; Camejo 1976, pp. 161-62). President Grant ordered the Red Shirts to disband shortly after this attack. Officially, this group complied with the order. Unofficially, it reorganized under different names such as The Hampton and Tilden Musical Club and the First Baptist Church Sewing Circle. The harassment and assaults continued (Williamson 1965; Camejo, p. 166).

Fraud was rampant in this 1876 gubernatorial election. In some counties, the number of votes casted exceeded the population. Both sides claimed victory. Two separate governments were created. The outcome was settled by the new Republican president, Rutherford B. Hayes, who withdrew federal troops from the South and recognized the Hampton regime (Williamson 1965; Camejo 1976, pp. 167-68). The Red Shirt units disbanded. Many of their members transferred to the newly formed state militia. Hampton assured President Hayes and the public that the rights of blacks would be respected. By 1877, the last Radical Republican regime had been overthrown.

Du Bois (1969a, p. 412) offered a more detailed analysis of this election and the role of the Democratic party. He suggested that Hampton represented a moderate faction of this party and the Red Shirts represented the radical right wing, which feared a revolution by poor whites joined by blacks. Nevertheless, planters played a major role in the emergence of the southern Democratic party. Hampton was a planter and a former member of the antebellum slavocracy.

The demise of the Radical Republicans was not entirely inevitable. It arose out of the failure to redistribute land and to destroy the economic power base of the planter class. It resulted from the well-organized and violent Democratic offensive, led by ex-Confederate officers, most of whom were of the planter class. Indeed leaders of the Ku Klux Klan came disproportionately from this class (Stampp 1965, p. 196; Trelease 1971, pp. 296, 354, 363; Reich 1981, p. 226). The indecision of Republican governors and their reluctance to maintain state militias, especially with black members, also contributed to the fall of Reconstruction regimes. Moreover, this fall was made possible by the substantial removal of federal troops from the South well before the Hayes administration. The number of federal troops in the South declined from 200,000 in 1865 to 20,000 in 1867 (Camejo 1976). By 1870 there were only 7,000 troops in the South, a figure woefully inadequate to maintain peace, to guarantee free elections, and to protect the rights of blacks and Radical Republicans. Finally, the Radical Republicans disappeared from the national political arena, through death, retirement, or political defeat (Stampp 1965, p. 189).

Populist Revolt and Planter Consolidation

Although the Democratic party dominated southern politics after the overthrow of Reconstruction regimes, it failed to completely vanquish the Republicans and to totally control the black vote. In the early 1890s, the Populist movement momentarily united poor white farmers with black farmers and threatened to overthrow the Democratic party, which counterattacked again, this time completely disenfranchising blacks and barring large numbers of poor whites from the polls.

The Populist movement, supported by the lower classes, advocated racial equality, assaulted corporate and financial interests, promoted progressive public policies, and demanded the vote for all people, including the illiterate. One of the best known Populist leaders, Tom Watson, argued passionately that racism divided poor blacks and poor whites, making it easier for financial interests to exploit both groups. Watson said,

> You are made to hate each other because upon that hatred is rested the keystone of the arch of financial despotism which enslaves you both. You are deceived and blinded that you may not see how this race antagonism perpetuates a monetary system which beggars you both. (quoted in Bloom 1987, p. 40)

The Populist party made every effort to promote racial harmony among its members throughout the South. It elected blacks to leadership positions in state party organizations. It nominated blacks to run for state and local offices. It held integrated parties and conferences. It protected black Populist leaders from white violence. For example, in Georgia, 2,000 white farmers and Populists came to the defense of a black preacher and ardent Populist leader when he was threatened by a lynch mob (Bloom 1987, p. 40).

The Populist party supported progressive policies. In general this party supported public ownership of railroads, lower interest rates on loans, the abolition of convict and child labor, and an increase in state support for public schools. In Texas, Populists demanded an 8-hour working day and the abolition of vagrancy laws that punished the unemployed (Bloom 1987). The Populist legislature in North Carolina secured the passage of laws lowering the legal interest rate to 6% and allowing local elections of local officials.

For a third party, the Populists enjoyed substantial support. A Populist was elected governor of Tennessee in 1890 and governor of Louisiana in 1892. In 1896, Populists dominated North Carolina politics, holding the majority in the state senate, sharing control of the lower house with Republicans, and providing eight out of nine U.S. representatives and both U.S. senators (Bloom 1987, p. 41). In the early 1890s, half of the congressmen from Virginia were Populists, as were 2 out of 7 from Mississippi and 4 out of 11 from Kentucky (Bloom 1987, p. 41). In 1892,

despite massive voter fraud in Georgia, the Populists' gubernatorial candidate obtained 44.5% of the popular vote.

Although Democrats remained in a dominant position during this
tumultuous period, the Populists posed a serious threat to planter and
Democratic party hegemony. The reaction to this threat followed a
familiar pattern. The Red Shirts reappeared, especially in those states
dominated by the Populist party. Groups associated with the Democratic
party harassed and assaulted Populist candidates and their supporters.
Voter fraud and intimidation were rampant. Democrats used racist
demagoguery to divide black and white farmers and to defeat Populist
candidates.

Although this offensive against the Populists was moderately successful, this party declined for other reasons. It suffered from the disadvantage
of being a third party, based on a grassroots movement. Support waned
with time. Voters split their votes between Populist and Republican
candidates, giving Democrats enough of a plurality of votes to win the
election. White supremacist rhetoric undermined black and white
solidarity and diminished support for the Populist party.

Finally, planters began to assume leadership positions in the Populist
party, a strategy they had used against the Republicans as well. Billings (1979) suggested that the rise of racism and conservatism in
this party is associated with both the Democratic offensive and the infiltration of planters into the Populist party. A prime example of this
infiltration is the case of Ben Tillman. Tillman was a Populist leader who
campaigned as a poor farmer, who emerged as a racist demagogue, and
who later switched to the Democratic party and became governor of South
Carolina. Tillman's father was a planter and an officer in the Confederacy
(Williamson 1986, p. 100). The notion of Tillman as a typical poor white
Populist leader who later became antiblack is false.

Reaction to Populism

The movement to disenfranchise blacks and to establish state-mandated
segregation was not part of the Populist revolt. In fact, this movement was
partly a reaction against Populism. This reaction was led not by white
workers or poor whites. It was led by the upper class in the South.

Kousser (1974) examined the social and party background of members
of the southern state legislatures and the electorate involved with the
disenfranchisement movement. He argued that most of the leaders of this

movement were wealthy planters from the black belt regions. Kousser (1974, p. 247) said,

> Not only did the vast majority of the leaders reside in the black belt, almost all of them were affluent and well-educated, and they often bore striking resemblances to antebellum "patricians." Indeed, almost every one was the son or grandson of a large planter, and several of the older chiefs had been slaveholders before the war.

In the majority of the states examined, Kousser (p. 248) found a positive correlation between wealth and the vote for disenfranchisement and a negative correlation between wealth and the vote against disenfranchisement. Votes against disenfranchisement came overwhelmingly from those areas outside the black belt inhabited primarily by yeoman farmers. Kousser's findings contradict the orthodox view that poor whites, white workers, and Herrenvolk democracy disenfranchised blacks.

This antidemocratic movement disenfranchised the very people likely to oppose planter hegemony: blacks and poor whites. Voter participation in the South declined by more than 90% among blacks. It declined measurably among whites as well (Bloom 1987). In Louisiana, between 1896 and 1900, the number of registered voters fell from about 127,000 to about 3,300 (Gossett 1971, p. 266). In Texas, voter participation among whites declined from a rate of 80% in 1900 to 27% by 1904 (Bloom, p. 49).

Bloom (1987) noted that most Jim Crow laws were enacted after the Populists were overthrown. For example, laws segregating places of employment—requiring black and white workers to use separate entrances, exits, toilets, drinking facilities, restrooms, and so on—were not enacted until after 1910. With the exception of South Carolina, states did not segregate hospitals until after 1901. With the exception of Arkansas, Georgia, and Mississippi, southern states segregated transportation facilities after 1900.

By 1910, southern state laws mandated the segregation of almost everything public: schools, recreation facilities, courtrooms, city halls, restaurants, hotels, theaters, cemeteries, funeral homes, drinking fountains, restrooms. These states prohibited most forms of interracial contact, including interracial marriage and fornication. New Orleans segregated bordellos; Atlanta, courtroom Bibles; Oklahoma, telephone booths. Florida and North Carolina forbade white and black students from exchanging textbooks. Alabama prohibited blacks and whites from playing checkers together (Sitkoff 1978).

Jim Crow laws were accompanied by increasing racial and social class disparities in the distribution of public resources. Focusing on public education expenditures, Bloom (1987) demonstrated that in the early 1900s, disparities in spending increased both between whites and blacks and between rich whites and poor whites. He noted that although educational expenditures in the South increased in the early 20th century, they increased marginally for blacks, a little more for poor whites, and substantially for rich whites. Illustrating the extent of these disparities, he cited figures for two counties in Mississippi in 1907: Itawamba, the poor one; and Washington, the well-to-do black belt one. Itawamba spent $5.65 per white pupil and $3.50 per black pupil. Washington county spent $80 per white pupil and $2.50 per black pupil (pp. 55-56). Bloom (p. 56) concluded,

> It is difficult to see where the great gains for lower-class whites are to be found in this situation. It seems, instead, apparent that the defeat of Populism and the subsequent disenfranchisement of blacks brought about a severe setback for these whites, as well. Many of them lost the right to vote. They were subject to the harsh terms of their employers, and they remained without labor unions to counter the power the wealthy retained.

In short, the Populist movement threatened planter hegemony. The planter-led Democrats responded to this threat by disenfranchising blacks and poor whites. Disenfranchisement removed the threat of Populism and ensured the political dominance of the planter class. After securing its hegemony, planters used the state to protect racially oppressive arrangements. Planters dominated southern politics and maintained these arrangements until the mid-1960s.

THE ROLE OF THE NATIONAL GOVERNMENT

The national government played a major role in sustaining and legitimizing this system of racial oppression. With few exceptions, the courts, presidents, and Congress supported racially oppressive arrangements in the South. This national support was not simply a policy of keeping hands off the southern problem. The national government played an active role in legitimizing these arrangements.

The U.S. Supreme Court

The U.S. Supreme Court played a critical role in narrowing the scope of the 14th Amendment, in eliminating state protection of the civil rights of African Americans, and in providing constitutional protection and legalistic justification for racial segregation. The 14th Amendment prohibits states from depriving any person of life, liberty, or property without due process and requires states to provide equal protection to all citizens. In the 1873 Slaughter House decision (*Butchers' Benevolent Association v. Crescent City Livestock*), the first case involving this amendment, the Court narrowed the purview of this amendment by claiming that it applied only to cases of gross discrimination against ex-slaves. In subsequent cases, the Court defined *gross discrimination* so narrowly that most forms of racial discrimination disappeared from the Court's sight. This myopia allowed the Court to ignore a wide range of civil rights violations. For example, in the 1876 *United States v. Reese* decision, the Court permitted local officials to deny the right to vote to blacks, so long as the denial was based on factors other than race. In this case, the Court legitimized the poll tax, which was used effectively to disenfranchise blacks. In subsequent cases, the Court allowed literacy and character tests. These devices disenfranchised almost every black in the Deep South. Of course, in the first three decades of the 20th century, the Court struck down local and state laws that expressly prohibited blacks from voting in primaries. It also invalidated the grandfather clause. However, the poll tax, literacy test, and character test—all legitimized by the Court—combined with violence and intimidation, kept most blacks from the polls in the Deep South until the mid-1960s.

In the *United States v. Cruikshank* (1876) decision, the Court struck down the section of the Enforcer Act of 1870 that made it a federal offense for the Ku Klux Klan to murder blacks. This case arose out of the 1873 Colfax massacre in Louisiana, in which a well-organized white military force massacred a large number of blacks. Nine whites were convicted in a federal district court. The U.S. Supreme Court overturned the conviction and nullified the provision of the Enforcer Act pertaining to Ku Klux Klan violence. The Court claimed that this case fell under state jurisdiction and that the federal government had exceeded its powers under the Constitution by encroaching on the rights of the states.

In the *Civil Rights Cases* of 1883, the Court invalidated provisions of the federal Civil Rights Act of 1875 that prohibited racial discrimination in public accommodations. Again, the Court maintained that the federal government had exceeded its powers and that the 14th Amendment prohibited state actions, not the actions of individuals.

The Court's attack on civil rights was based on shifting constitutional principles. That is, the Court's principles shifted to support its anti-civil rights position. Two cases in the 1870s illustrate this point. These cases involved the 10th Amendment, which says that those powers not expressly delegated to the national government are reserved for the states. This amendment restricts federal powers but enlarges state powers. In the 1877 Grange decision (Buck 1913, pp. 206-37), the Court cited this amendment as it underscored the power of states to regulate railroads. However, when the State of Louisiana passed laws to regulate railroads and to prohibit racial segregation on railroad cars, the Supreme Court lost sight of the states rights principle. In the 1878 *Hall v. DeCuir* decision, the Court argued that a Louisiana law barring racial segregation on all modes of public transportation placed an undue burden on those companies with trains or ships traveling across state lines. The Court insisted that these companies would be forced to segregate passengers in one state and to integrate them in another (Logan 1965). Thus the Court underscored state prerogatives to regulate railroads under the 10th Amendment in the Grange decision but contradicted this principle in the Louisiana case. The Court abandoned the 10th Amendment principle when this principle supported civil rights but adhered to this principle when it undermined civil rights.

In these cases, the Court not only bent the meaning of the Constitution to protect racially oppressive arrangements, it insisted that state-mandated segregation was rational; that the existing patterns of racial oppression were legitimate; and that state prohibition of segregation was irrational, intolerably burdensome, and unconstitutional. The Court reiterated this message in the 1896 *Plessy v. Ferguson* case. In this decision the Court reinterpreted the 14th Amendment to allow state-mandated segregation, so long as the separate facilities were equal. This separate but equal doctrine remained in effect until the 1954 *Brown v. Board of Education* decision.

The Court upheld state laws prohibiting miscegenation on grounds that these policies applied to both blacks and whites equally (*Pace v. Alabama* 1883). Laws prohibiting interracial marriages remained on the books until after the 1967 *Loving v. Virginia* decision. These cases illustrate this point: The Supreme Court functioned to justify and legitimize segregation and other racially oppressive laws (Logan 1965).

Presidents

With the exception of Harrison, who supported the 1892 Fair Election bill, presidents from Hayes to Hoover supported the southern system of racial oppression. This support ranged from tacit approval to active promotion. Hayes recognized all regimes in the South, including the ones that ascended through fraud and violence. He withdrew the last troops from the South and failed to provide any federal protection for blacks subjected to organized violence. Of course he vetoed bills designed to weaken civil rights protection and expressed concerns over the status of southern blacks. In 1892, Cleveland ran on a platform that vehemently denounced federal election laws designed to protect blacks' right to vote (Logan 1965, p. 89). McKinley praised the South for eliminating old sectional animosities at the time southerners were disenfranchising and lynching blacks in record-breaking numbers (Logan). Although Theodore Roosevelt expressed concern over lynchings and disenfranchisement, he did nothing to alleviate these problems (Dyer 1980). Woodrow Wilson segregated federal administrative offices in Washington, D.C. (Sitkoff 1978, p. 20). Warren Harding expanded the segregation efforts initiated by Wilson and actively campaigned against racial integration and social equality (Sitkoff, p. 27). Hoover opposed hiring blacks to work in federal offices. Despite insistence from the NAACP, Hoover's Commission on Law Enforcement refused to investigate lynching, peonage, disenfranchisement, or segregation. Both Hoover and Coolidge were adamantly opposed to any form of federal intervention to protect the civil rights of African Americans.

Congress

By 1877, the old antebellum southern regime was back in power in the South and back in Congress. By the turn of the century, having eliminated opposition and enjoying unopposed reelections, southern congressmen had secured an advantage on Capitol Hill, especially because seniority meant power in this institution. Because of this seniority system, southern congressmen were disproportionately represented as chairs of key congressional committees until the 1960s. This domination allowed southern representatives and senators to obstruct major civil rights legislation.

The entire political system—the courts, presidents, Congresses, and state governments—all operated to sustain racially oppressive arrangements. This state function arose out of oppressive economic arrangements that concentrated land ownership in the planter class. This economic structure did not determine the role of the state. It gave a substantial advantage to the planter class in a struggle between dominant and subordinate classes for control of the state. The planter-dominated Democratic party triumphed in this struggle, first over the Republican Reconstruction regime and then over the Populists. The planter class consolidated its power over the region, exercised considerable influence over state and national governments, and used the state to maintain racially oppressive arrangements in the South.

Once the planter class consolidated its power, it operated to legitimize the social and political order upon which its power was based. It mobilized its resources to convince other classes and the entire society that this order was natural, inevitable, and just. In this process, the planter class generated a dominant ideology and created a racially oppressive culture. This culture functioned to secure broad-based support for the racial social order.

CULTURE

Racially oppressive features of the culture of this period arose out of deliberate efforts of political and social leaders to justify the subordination of African Americans. Once created, this culture became a social force of its own, quite apart from its creators. This culture, which debased and dehumanized African Americans, was disseminated in just about every medium and institution in society: newspapers, magazines, books, theaters, cinema, and later in television and radio, as well as in Congress, courts, public schools, and universities.

Ideology and Cultural Formation

The discourse, worldviews, and ideology of the planter class played a major role in shaping the culture of this era. Although this period featured a diverse ideology, the ideas of the planter class emerged as the dominant perspective in the South. This perspective denigrated African Americans. It depicted the Reconstruction period, along with efforts to protect the rights of African Americans, as a nightmare of black domination. From this perspective, Reconstruction meant giving too much to blacks, giving too little to whites, and allowing inferior, uneducated blacks to rule over superior, more educated whites. It meant that illiterate and mindless blacks overtaxed and oppressed whites and grossly mismanaged, wasted, and stole state funds. This view maintained that ending Reconstruction and establishing white rule was the best arrangement for all races in the South and that granting voting rights to blacks would destroy the South and the nation. This perspective was not held by all southerners. There was a southern liberal perspective. However, this anti-Reconstruction and antiblack perspective was vigorously promoted, especially by members of the planter class. This view depicted oppressive arrangements as rational and alternative arrangements as irrational and destructive. It functioned to convince all others in society—blacks, whites, rich, poor—that existing racially oppressive arrangements were rational, legitimate, and good.

A number of southern politicians were major promoters of this southern planter perspective. Consider Wade Hampton for an example. Hampton, a Confederate general who was elected governor of South Carolina in 1876, argued for the disenfranchisement of blacks and for a rule of men of property, intelligence, and virtue. He said,

> In my opinion the voters who in any state represent the best elements, the capital, the intelligence, and the virtue, should govern, despite all fine-spun theories of fraternity and equality, the sacred brotherhood of mankind, and the divine right of universal suffrage. (quoted in Logan 1965, p. 78)

In an 1890 article titled, "The Race Problem," Hampton argued that granting blacks the right to vote during Reconstruction was "a crime against civilization, humanity, constitutional rights, and Christianity" (quoted in Fredrickson 1971, p. 264). He claimed that efforts to extend the vote to blacks arose from "the Anarchist, the Communist, the Nihilist, and all the other scum of European nations" (p. 265).

Another example is Ben Tillman, a Populist and advocate for poor white farmers who campaigned unabashedly and vigorously for the disenfranchisement of blacks. Tillman, who succeeded Hampton as governor of South Carolina in 1890, associated efforts to deny voting rights to blacks with democracy, white supremacy, and black inferiority. When South Carolina passed disenfranchising laws, Tillman hailed the move as "the triumph of democracy and white supremacy over mongrelism and anarchy" (quoted in Logan 1965, p. 83).

Also, James K. Vardaman, governor of Mississippi in the early 1900s, advocated terminating public education for blacks and claimed that the black man was a "lazy, lying, lustful animal which no conceivable amount of training can transform into a tolerable citizen" (quoted in Gossett 1971, p. 271).

Racist political discourse was not limited to southern politics. It occurred even in the U.S. Congress, particularly in reaction to congressional efforts to protect the civil rights of African Americans. A prime example of this type of reaction arose in response to the 1892 Fair Election Bill, introduced by Senator Henry Cabot Lodge. Although this bill simply allowed voters to petition the federal government to supervise a federal election if it was threatened by fraud or violence, southern opposition was vehement. Opposing this bill, John J. Hemphill of South Carolina argued that the law would put blacks in power and return the South to the horrors of Reconstruction (Logan 1965, p. 72). Tucker of Virginia suggested the bill would cost $12 million to implement (Logan, p. 73). Senator Pugh from Alabama argued that whites would not allow the enforcement of this bill and that it would give the vote to illiterate blacks, incapable of making intelligent decisions (Logan, p. 77).

This debasement and dehumanization of blacks continued long past the Lodge bill crisis, even though the bill was defeated. By the early 20th century, southern congressmen seemed quite comfortable in referring to blacks as savages, aliens, and vile and worthless brutes (Logan 1965, p. 99). In one example, David A. De Armond of Missouri described blacks as "almost too ignorant to eat, scarcely wise enough to breathe, mere existing human machines" (quoted in Logan, p. 99). John Sharp Williams of Mississippi said,

> You could ship-wreck 10,000 negroes, every one of whom was a graduate of Harvard University, and in less than three years, they would have retrograded governmentally, half of the men would have been killed, and the other half would have two wives apiece. (quoted in Logan, p. 99)

This debasement of blacks in public, in the U.S. Congress, by congressional leaders, legitimized and promoted racist discourse and worldviews that sustained racist culture.

Social Darwinism and Eugenics

The debasement of the African American was not limited to political discourse. Academic theories joined political ideas in a defense of racially oppressive arrangements and in a vitriolic verbal assault on black humanity. These academic theories included social Darwinism and eugenics.

Darwin, who published *The Origin of Species* in 1859, did not create social Darwinism. Herbert Spencer developed this new social doctrine (see Spencer 1891 and Duncan 1908). Like most social philosophers of the late 19th century, including Marx, Spencer adapted natural science models to his theory of social trends. Darwin's concepts of evolution and natural selection fit Spencer's grand theory of the social world.

Spencer's theory was based on a number of underlying assumptions. First, social Darwinists assumed that the social world, like the biological world, was in a process of evolving and that this process was leading to an improved society and to superior species of men. Second, social Darwinists saw this evolution as natural. Hence, they opposed any form of governmental interference. Spencer was a passionate proponent of laissez faire capitalism. He was a fierce opponent of public education, welfare, child labor laws, restrictions on convict labor, minimum wages, and limits on working hours. Most of his disciples believed that charity caused more harm than good precisely because it interfered with the natural evolutionary process. Third, they believed that conflicts among men were purifying processes that led to the creation of superior men. Spencer coined the term *survival of the fittest* to draw an analogy between human conflicts and the natural world. Proponents maintained that these conflicts would lead to the disappearance of inferior races and the triumph of superior races (Gossett 1971, pp. 144-50).

Social Darwinism is grounded in a racist view of the world. Spencer believed that "Rousseau's idea of the 'primitive equality of men' was 'absurd' " (quoted in Gossett 1971, p. 148). Spencer insisted that humanity was divided into superior and inferior races. He said that the "dominant races overrun the inferior races mainly in virtue of the greater quantity of energy in which this greater mental mass shows itself" (quoted in Gossett, p. 150). He classified nations as civilized or savage. He attributed the level of technological development of a nation to what he believed was the level of biological evolutionary development of its people. In other words, Spencer suggested that European nations were more civilized and technologically advanced than African nations because Europeans had evolved into a superior biological species compared to Africans. For Spencer, Africans were savages and an inferior species.

William Graham Sumner, professor of political science at Yale, was one of Spencer's most ardent disciples in the United States. Sumner argued that when Thomas Jefferson said that all men were equal, Jefferson had no intention of including blacks (Gossett 1971, p. 154). Sumner was a passionate opponent of any form of equality or social reform. He even opposed giving blacks the right to vote.

Joseph Le Conte, one of the South's most esteemed natural scientists, subscribed to social Darwinism. In 1892, he argued that the laws governing the evolution of species in the animal kingdom applied to the human world. He claimed that weaker races, notably blacks, were destined for "extinction . . . or else, relegation to a subordinate place in the economy of nature; the weaker is either destroyed or seeks safety by avoiding competition" (quoted in Fredrickson 1971, p. 247).

Another southern social Darwinist, Frederick L. Hoffman, maintained that slavery protected blacks from extinction but emancipation accelerated the process of eliminating them. As evidence of this process, Hoffman pointed to the high mortality rates among blacks. He attributed these high mortality rates to the inferior physical condition of blacks and to "an immense amount of immorality which is a race trait, and of which scrofala, syphilis, and even consumption are the inevitable consequences" (quoted in Fredrickson 1971, p. 251). Hoffman condemned any form of public or private assistance for blacks because he said that it would only prolong their agony (Fredrickson, p. 251).

The old polygenists of the days of slavery adjusted their views to the new social Darwinist school. Josiah C. Nott, who before the Civil War had believed that blacks were a separate species, argued at the turn of the century that blacks were so far below whites on the evolutionary scale that blacks were like a different species.

The eugenics movement emerged along with social Darwinism. This movement, initiated at the turn of the century, focused on proving that geniuses arose from superior races and that learning disabilities, poverty, promiscuity, and criminality were inherited traits found commonly in inferior races (Gossett 1971, p. 155). Proponents of this movement often used cognitive ability tests to prove these assumptions about inferior and superior races.

In the first decade of the 20th century, Alfred Binet, who opposed eugenics, developed a cognitive ability test designed to identify students with learning disabilities and special educational needs. Scores on the test were based on successful performance on a number of mental tasks. These scores corresponded to mental ages determined by the mean score for each age group. Cautious in interpreting test results, Binet established a number of caveats about this test. He maintained that its most important use was in identifying students with special educational needs. He insisted that intelligence was too complex to be captured with a single number. He feared that his test would be abused and used for oppressive ends: to label children, to set unwarranted limits on their mental development, and to exclude the undesirable; to tell some children that they inherited low intelligence and that they will never improve their intellectual performance beyond a fixed point. Binet did not think the test measured intelligence, nor did he believe that intelligence was either fixed or innate.

In 1916, Lewis Terman, a young professor at Stanford University, revised Binet's examination and created the Stanford-Binet test. Terman disregarded every one of Binet's caveats. Terman assumed that the revised test indeed measured intelligence and that intelligence was fixed and inborn. He used this test to provide scientific support for racial, ethnic, and class prejudices. He insisted that northern Europeans were superior to all other races; that the average intelligence of southern and eastern Europeans was well below the intelligence of northern Europeans; and that lower strata groups, African Americans, Mexicans, and Native Americans, were endowed with the lowest intelligence of all. He argued that the test scores proved his assertions. He indicated that the scores correlated with forms of moral behavior. He maintained that the higher IQs of northern Europeans enabled them to move into the upper class and predisposed them to higher ethical standards and that the lower IQs of African Americans prevented them from rising into the upper class and explained their high rates of crime, promiscuity, and other forms of degenerate moral behavior. In other words, he asserted that people were in the lower class because they were genetically endowed with a lower intelligence and their low intelligence prevented them from rising out of poverty. For the proponents of eugenics, social status and human behavior were determined by genes.

Social Darwinism and eugenics existed simultaneously. They differed in terms of public policy implications and ideological functions. Social Darwinists were ardently antigovernment. They demanded that government not tinker with society. They opposed public education, social welfare, and any form of government regulations. This ideology provided strong support for the racial hierarchy embedded in industrial capitalism, particularly prominent in the North in the last quarter of the 19th century and throughout much of the 20th century.

Proponents of eugenics often supported a strong role for government, especially in promoting the segregation and sterilization of inferior races. Moreover, some proponents wanted government to take an active role in excluding inferior races from higher status jobs. Whereas social Darwinism offered ideological support for the aversive racism of industrial capitalism in the North, eugenics provided ideological support for the dominative aversive racism of the rural South. Nevertheless, both of these ideologies operated to support a form of culture that dehumanized and oppressed African Americans.

Media and the Dissemination of Culture

This culture was transmitted by the media—newspapers, magazines, books, cinema, and so on. Rayford Logan conducted an analysis of newspapers, magazines, and books published between 1877 and 1918. He concluded that most of the articles related to African Americans glorified the plantation tradition, condemned Reconstruction, rationalized lynching, and reflected the general stereotypes of blacks of the times (Logan 1965, p. 371). Textbooks and scholarly journals also reflected these views.

Fictional stories and comic strips generally depicted blacks as animal-like, childlike, chicken-eating, or crap-shooting caricatures, who looked like monkeys, devoid of any humanity. These dehumanized images of blacks continued to flow across the print media throughout the first half of the 20th century. Even Walt Disney cartoons depicted Africans as half-naked cannibals. Childlike characters such as Stepin Fetchit became household names, images burned into the American psyche.

The movie, *The Birth of a Nation,* illustrates the process by which ideology affects the construction of culture. This movie contained the common stereotypes of blacks as either childlike or bestial. It expressed the planter's perspective of Reconstruction: that Reconstruction meant putting inferior, illiterate, and uncivilized blacks in power in the South and that emancipation unleashed black bestiality. In this film, black state legislators took off their shoes and put their feet on desks; ate fried chicken and threw the bones on the floor; talked in an unintelligent, almost incomprehensible dialect; seemed completely disorganized; and appeared incapable of making intelligent laws. The movie, based on the book *The Clansman,* focused on a large black man who raped a virtuous, innocent white woman. These conditions justified the rise of the Ku Klux Klan. The movie glorified this organization as the savior of the South from the horrors of black domination.

Thomas Dixon, the author of *The Clansman* and coproducer of the movie, was not an apolitical artist. He was born in 1864 of prominent parents in North Carolina. His parents had owned 32 slaves up until the end of the Civil War. His mother's family included wealthy planters. Her brother, LeRoy McAfee, became a colonel at age 25 in the Confederate army. McAfee, whom Dixon idolized, was one of the leaders of the Cleveland County, North Carolina, Ku Klux Klan (Williamson 1986). This movie not only embodied the planter perspective on Reconstruction. It impressed on the minds of Americans vivid images of black incompetence, inferiority, and bestiality. It contributed to the formation of a racist culture that contained images that dehumanized blacks and perspectives that legitimized oppression.

The Cultural Phenomenon of Rapes and Lynchings

An analysis of the lynching phenomenon illustrates some of the non-ideological forces and irrational drives undergirding racist culture. These forces and drives are best understood through psychoanalytical models. Until 1890, more whites were lynched than blacks. However, thereafter lynching emerged as a particular form of racial violence. In 1892, 69 whites and 162 blacks were lynched (Gossett 1971, p. 269). Although the number of lynchings declined in the early 1900s, 10 times as many blacks were lynched as whites. Between 1906 and 1916, about 620 blacks were lynched compared to about 61 whites (Gossett 1971, p. 270).

Lynching was an irrational and emotional assault on the black community. It functioned as an outlet for intensely hostile feelings. Illustrating this point, Williamson (1986, p. 124) cited an interview with a young Mississippian, who said, "You don't understand how we feel down here; when there is a row, we feel like killing a nigger whether he has done anything or not."

Lynchings have often been defended as a way of protecting white women from black rapists. For example, the governor of South Carolina, Ben Tillman, said, "There is only one crime that warrants lynching and Governor as I am, I would lead a mob to lynch the negro who ravishes a white woman" (quoted in Williamson 1986, p. 97). Also, the first woman to become a U.S. Senator, Rebecca Felton of Georgia said,

That week there were seven lynchings in Georgia from the fearful crime of rape. I told them that these crimes had grown and increased by reason of the corruption and debasement of the right of suffrage; that it would grow and increase with every election where white men equalized at the polls with an inferior race and controlled their votes by bribery and whiskey. A crime nearly unknown before and during the war had become an almost daily occurrence and mob law had also become omnipotent . . . if it takes lynching to protect woman's dearest possession from drunken, ravening human beast, then I say lynch a thousand a week if it becomes necessary. (quoted in Williamson 1986, p. 95)

Various psychoanalytical theories offer a number of perspectives on the association between rapes and lynchings, notably, repression/projection and displacement symbolism. The repression/projection theory assumes that sexual repression arises when the dominant culture defines sexuality as something evil, dirty, or debasing—a phenomenon common in the Bible Belt of the Deep South. Repressed sexuality is projected onto debased groups. Unable to accept their own sexuality, whites repress their sex drives and project them onto blacks. The sexual aggression they see in blacks is but the projection of their own sexuality (Adorno, Frenkel-Brunswik, Levinson, and Sanford, 1950; Fanon 1967).

The process of displacement symbolism offers a more powerful explanation for the connection between fear of rape and lynchings. This process was reflected in Rebecca Felton's speech, in which she suggested that rapes had "increased by reason of corruption and debasement of the right to suffrage" (quoted in Williamson 1986, p. 95). Felton associated her fear of rapes with the right of blacks to vote. Just as anxiety arising from childhood traumas is displaced and focused on objects (spiders, the dark, heights) and expressed in a phobia (arachnophobia, and so on), anxieties arising from social traumas were displaced and focused on a social object (blacks) and expressed in a phobia—negrophobia. The fear of black men raping white women embodied a profound sense of anxiety. This anxiety arose out of a deep fear of losing control over blacks and the possibility of blacks acquiring political power. Granting blacks the right to vote triggered these fears. This anxiety arose in a society that had created an image of free blacks as savage beasts, driven by an unrestrained sexuality. This image intensified anxieties and ignited a bonfire of negrophobia—a fear that this beast would ravish white society, symbolized by the white woman. The economic crisis in the South at the turn of the century, and the depression in the cotton market at the beginning of the 20th century, generated a great deal of anxiety.

Quite apart from these psychoanalytical theories, Gossett (1971) saw lynching as a form of social control that had little to do with rape. According to Gossett, out of a total of 3,911 blacks lynched between 1889 and 1941, only 641, or 17%, were associated with rape. Gossett (p. 270) added that blacks were more commonly lynched

[for] threatening to sue a white man, attempting to register to vote, enticing a white man's servant to leave his job, engaging in labor union activities, "being disrespectful to" or "disputing with" a white man, or sometimes for no discoverable reason at all.

Segregation and the Anal Character

Psychoanalytical theory also helps to explain segregation. By the early 20th century, almost every aspect of southern social life was segregated: restaurants, theaters, courtrooms, restrooms, trains, buses, drinking fountains, schools.

Segregation served a number of psychosocial functions. It functioned to subordinate blacks socially and to reinforce their inferior status psychologically. The "for whites only" and "no coloreds allowed" signs were constant reminders of blacks' status as an inferior, undesirable caste, much like the untouchables of India.

Segregation functioned as a quasi form of elimination. Williamson (1965, p. 276) argued that many southern whites had envisioned and hoped for the elimination of blacks after emancipation. They expected blacks to either die out as an unfit race or migrate back to Africa. However, given that blacks did not disappear and that their labor was needed, segregation achieved a quasi-social elimination of blacks without eliminating their labor. With segregation, whites could eliminate blacks from their social world, while continuing to exploit them in the economic realm.

Kovel (1984) associated segregation with the anal character type. Within the context of neo-Freudian psychology, this character type arises out of crises in the toilet training stage of childhood development. It is in this stage that the child is made to urinate and defecate in the toilet and to avoid soiling himself, his clothes, the floor, or anything around him. This stage focuses on body excrement, cleanliness, and order. The child learns that excrement is nasty, that its release from the body is to be controlled, that its presence is to be avoided, and that cleanliness is desirable. The anal character, fixated on this stage, tends to be orderly, punctual, obstinate, clean, and controlled (Erickson 1963; Fromm 1980). In the extreme case, this character divides the world between the pure and the dirty. He associates that which is a part of him as clean and that which is excreted from him as filthy. He sees people like him as clean and those farthest removed from him as filthy. It is this type of character that tends to classify poor whites as trash, poor blacks as scum, and the most undesirable people as feces. It is this type that tends to be preoccupied with the purity of blood.

Southern culture encouraged the development of this character type, which in turn operated to meticulously and rigidly enforce the system of segregation. Within the context of this culture and the anal character's mind, interracial marriages meant the contamination of pure white blood with filthy colored blood; integration of public schools meant exposing pure white children to dirty black children. White was pure, clean, and virtuous. Black was impure, dirty, and evil. This character was driven to maintain racial order and racial purity. It became part of the racist segregationist culture.

This culture operated to maintain racial oppression. It involved the ideology of the dominant class, which functioned to persuade the whole society of the legitimacy of racially oppressive arrangements. It also encompassed images of blacks as beasts, fantasies of unrestrained sexuality and dirt. It involved an anal-sadistic social character, driven to maintain the segregation and subordination of blacks.

DEBT PEONAGE AND DOMINATIVE AVERSIVE RACISM

Thus a new form of racism—*dominative aversive racism*—emerged after the death of slavery and lasted until the mid-1960s. This racism arose out of a new mode of production—sharecropping, a debt peonage system based on the exploitation of black labor. These economic arrangements sustained the old planter class.

This class maintained its power because of its concentrated ownership of land, because of its initial investment in southern industries, and because of its control of labor both on the land and in the industries. Its economic and political power was enhanced by the absence of an autonomous industrial class and a strong middle class. Ordinarily, these two classes function to counterbalance the power of the land-based aristocracy. Without these countervailing powers, the planter class—the land-based aristocracy—easily subverted democratic politics in the South, overthrew the Reconstruction regimes, derailed the Populist movement, and disenfranchised blacks and poor whites. The planters captured state governments in the South and exercised considerable influence over the national government.

Members of this class played a primary role in generating and per-petuating racist culture. Some of these members were involved in politics. They promoted a style of political discourse that dehumanized blacks, justified racial oppression, and advocated white supremacy. A few planters contributed to literary works that contained images of black bestiality, ideas of black incompetence and inferiority, and views justify-ing oppressive arrangements. Racist culture was disseminated in various media forms: newspapers, magazines, movies, plays, books, and others.

We call the racism of this period (1865 to 1965) of the South dominative aversive racism because it involved both the direct domination and repression of African Americans and their social segregation from European Americans. Direct domination entailed two sources. First, the planter directly controlled the black family working on the planter's land. The planter owned and controlled the land, the home in which the black family lived, the food they ate, and the clothes they wore. This class regulated the black family's life, setting the time to begin and to end work and directly supervising their labor. Thus the planter class directly subor-dinated and oppressed African Americans. Second, whites of all classes directly oppressed blacks through the enforcement of the norms of the racial caste system. This direct control was reminiscent of the earlier dominative racism.

Aversion characterized the social customs of segregation and the psychoculture of the anal character. Blacks were segregated in all forms of social life: at schools, theaters, buses, restaurants, restrooms, public drinking fountains, beaches, amusement parks. Many southern states forbade blacks and whites from meeting together in the same building. Most of these states prohibited interracial marriage. Behind this segrega-tion, and driving it, was an intensely anal social character that saw blacks as dirty, fecal, diseased. This character was obsessed with purity: the purity of races and the purity of blood. He was driven to dominate and to segregate; hence, he exuded dominative aversive racism.

6

Industrial Capitalism
and Aversive Racism

In the previous chapters, we demonstrated that white racism and white consciousness arose out of oppressive, exploitative, and dehumanizing economic arrangements, initially constructed and defended by the dominant class and later accepted by other subordinate classes. That is, the southern planter class, with its concentrated ownership of land, constructed a system of black subordination, first in the institution of slavery and later in the debt peonage arrangement. Racism persisted, as the dominant class used the state to defend oppressive arrangements and bombarded the whole society with its ideas, symbols, and images—ideas of the virtue of black subordination, symbols of black inferiority, and images of bestial black characters. Racism grew as members of all classes accepted these notions. Racism survived because the dominant class crushed social movements led by poor whites and poor blacks opposed to oppression.

In this chapter, we examine the perpetuation of racism under industrial capitalism, especially from about 1865 to 1965. Although racism changed form under this new mode of production, its persistence followed a pattern similar to the one in the slave and the debt peonage systems of the South. Racism, especially in the urban areas of the North, grew out of the exploitative, oppressive, and dehumanizing features of industrial capitalism. The dominant class, with its concentrated ownership of production facilities, controlled the process of organizing labor in production. (We reject the notion of a new class of managers with an interest separate from capital.) This class, the corporate elite—capitalists and their managers—created caste arrangements within the industrial labor force. This force contained an upper stratum of skilled workers who

118

joined the corporate elite in subordinating black workers. Moreover, caste arrangements in production generated racial conflicts, as workers with a sense of white consciousness and job entitlement fought to exclude blacks. In this system, race consciousness was more prevalent than class consciousness.

Industrialization and new transportation technology allowed for the reorganization of urban space and the production of class and racial segregation in residential areas. These new patterns of racial and class segregation in urban space augmented the caste system in industrial labor. Racial segregation in housing divided working-class communities, weakened the labor movement, strengthened race consciousness, and reinforced the racial order.

Under industrial capitalism, government played a paradoxical role, which resulted from the political struggle over government territory, pitting forces supporting the racial order against those opposing it. Corporate leaders, craft unionists, and planters stood on the side of the battle line supporting the existing racial order. Civil rights workers and radical industrial labor leaders stood on the other side, opposing this order.

In short, the exploitative and oppressive features of capitalism and the segregated structure of urban space provided the base out of which a culture and politics of racism emerged. In this chapter, we examine this base and the role of government policies and cultural formations in either modifying or sustaining patterns of racial oppression. We divide our examination into five parts. First, we underscore the exploitative features of industrial capitalism and illustrate the connection between these features and racism. We enlarge upon this connection with an overview of segmented labor theory and with an analysis of the race and labor literature.

Second, we discuss cases of race relations in specific industries and labor unions. We elaborate on the relationship between patterns of organization in production and patterns of race relations in particular industries and unions. We investigate the correlation between the power of radical industrial labor and the promotion of interracial labor solidarity. We outline the psychosocial processes out of which white consciousness arose.

Third, we outline the development of racial and class segregation in urban space. We associate industrial expansion and political decisions with the construction of segregated metropolitan areas. Fourth, we talk about the role of the state in sustaining and in altering this racial order. Finally, we show how these dimensions—exploitative features of capitalism, the role of labor and capital, urban space, the state, and psychoculture—interact to produce and maintain a particular form of racism—aversive racism.

EXPLOITATIVE FEATURES OF INDUSTRIAL CAPITALISM

Let us begin our discussion with the exploitative and oppressive features of industrial capitalism. These features include (a) the exploitation of labor; (b) class conflict, caste arrangements, and the reserve army of labor; (c) private property and inequality; (d) the centralization and concentration of capital, and (e) periodic crises.

Exploitation of Labor

Although labor under capitalism is free, it is exploited much as labor was under earlier modes of production. Like earlier forms of production, industrial production involves a dominant class that owns the means of production and a subordinate class that owns little. As Marx ([1867] 1975, p. 235) said,

> Wherever a part of society possesses the monopoly of the means of production, the laborer, free or not free, must add to the working-time necessary for his own maintenance an extra working-time in order to produce the means of subsistence for the owners of the means of production.

Consider the sharecropper and the planter in contrast to the industrial worker and the capitalist. The sharecropper owns nothing. The planter owns the land. Because he owns nothing, the sharecropper is forced by economic necessity to sell his labor power to the planter. This labor power creates value embodied in a crop. This crop is appropriated by the planter, who sells the crop and keeps the money. A part of this value is returned to the cropper in food and supplies to sustain his life—necessary value. The remaining value is used by the planter to purchase farm equipment, seeds, fences, and other items to maintain the plantation; he may also buy more land, save more money, maintain the mansion, invest in industry, or use the value for other sources of wealth.

Similarly, the worker owns nothing, and the capitalist owns production facilities. Although the worker under capitalism seems to be free, he is constrained by economic necessity to sell his labor power to the capitalist.

The capitalist purchases this labor power and therefore the right to use it to create value (derived from commodities sold for money). Marx divides the value created by this labor power into two types: necessary value and surplus value. Necessary value is required to provide for the worker's subsistence. Surplus value is used to generate wealth. It is the key to the process of accumulating wealth under capitalism (Marx 1975; Bottomore 1985; Gough 1985). Of course, Marx accounted for other aspects of the value of a commodity: the cost of purchasing raw material, maintaining the machinery of production, and so forth.

Class Conflict, Caste Arrangements, and the Reserve Army of Labor

This process of exploiting labor generates tensions between capitalists and laborers. Workers struggle for higher wages, better working conditions, and control over the workplace. They organize into unions to promote their objectives. Capitalists struggle to extract more surplus value from labor, a goal that is at odds with workers' objectives and generates conflict between the two classes.

Capitalists have the better position in this conflict for two reasons. First, they own capital. This ownership means they control the primary means through which workers earn money to sustain their lives. Engels ([1844] 1973, p. 115) made this point succinctly in *The Condition of the Working-Class in England*:

> The proletarian is helpless; left to himself, he cannot live a single day. The bourgeoisie has gained a monopoly of all means of existence in the broadest sense of the word. What the proletarian needs, he can obtain only from this bourgeoisie, which is protected in its monopoly by the power of the state. The proletarian is, therefore, in law and in fact, the slave of the bourgeois.

In other words, in a capitalist society, those individuals who do not own capital are constrained by the threat of starvation to work for those who do. The unskilled, unattached, and unemployed worker with no money or capital must either starve, steal, or work for an owner of a production facility, warehouse, retail establishment, or service company. Of course workers can and do organize and withhold their labor in exchange for some concessions. Nevertheless, this arrangement still favors the owners of capital and their executives.

Second, capitalists have the better position because they have a range of strategies available to them to weaken the power of organized labor and to depress wages. One strategy used by capitalists is to maintain a reserve army of labor, a large pool of unemployed or subemployed workers desperate for full-time work. The presence of this pool allows the capitalists to threaten workers with replacement and to pressure them into accepting lower wages or harsher working conditions. In another strategy, capitalists operate to exercise more direct control over workers and to accelerate the pace of production. Factory owners speed up the assembly line and invest in labor-saving technology or machines of production. Still another strategy involves capitalists' inciting conflicts and divisions among workers. Capitalists, especially in the early years of industrial capitalism, exploited racial and ethnic tensions to undermine labor solidarity. They created special privileged categories of labor, notably a stratum of skilled workers who operated to exclude other workers and to protect their privileges.

Stratification within specific industries generates secondary conflicts among workers, especially between high stratum craft workers and low stratum industrial workers. As upper stratum craft workers struggle for control over craft jobs, they create barriers to restrict entrance to the trade to only a few workers from the lower stratum. This exclusionary practice enhances the value of the trade, increases the price of skilled labor, and confers higher status and privileges on craft workers. As upper stratum workers struggle to maintain their privileged position, conflicts arise between them and lower status workers. These intraclass struggles overlap with racial conflicts, as white skilled workers operate to exclude black workers and restrict access to select white workers. This conflict among workers operates to maintain a labor and a racial caste system.

Private Property and Inequality

Under capitalism, the capitalist class owns the means of production as private property. This arrangement means two things. First, it means extreme inequality in wealth and income. This inequality arises from the fact that productive property is wealth and generates income. Concentrated ownership of this property in the hands of the capitalist class means concentrated wealth and concentrated income generated from this wealth (Edwards, Reich, and Weisskopt, 1978, p. 294).

Second, private ownership of production facilities means that production will be for profit and not for human need. This arrangement allows the capitalist class to subordinate the interests and welfare of the larger community to the interests of private profit.

Centralization and Concentration of Capital

There is a general tendency for competitive markets to transform into monopolistic or oligopolistic ones. This tendency arises out of the logic of competitive capitalism. In competitive markets, large numbers of firms compete with each other. Each firm operates to increase profits, to secure a greater share of its market, and to triumph over its competitors. Logically, one firm can increase profits and dominate its market by outperforming the other firms, forcing them out of business, or purchasing and absorbing competitors. This process—in which one or a few firms absorb or bankrupt competitors—creates monopolies or oligopolies.

When oligopolies are formed, control of the market becomes centralized in these few firms. When these firms are owned and controlled by a few individuals, we say that capital has become concentrated in the hands of a few. There is a general tendency for capital to become centralized and concentrated, as competitive capitalism transforms into monopoly capitalism. Signs of monopoly capitalism were evident in the United States at the end of the 19th century, particularly in the steel, oil, and railroad industries (Kolko 1963).

Periodic Crises

Capitalism is subject to periodic crises, characterized by high levels of unemployment. Economic theories have identified different types of crises and have offered different explanations for their causes— overproduction, underconsumption, and saturated markets (Sweezy 1970; Mandel 1973; Bottomore 1985). These crises contributed to shifts in political power and occasionally alterations in patterns of racial oppression.

CAPITALISM AND RACISM

These features of capitalism tend to precipitate and nourish racism: the exploitation of subordinate groups; the existence of extreme inequality; the private, monopolistic ownership of productive property; the conflict between capital and labor; the development of hierarchical labor structures; the presence of reserve armies of labor. Patterns of racial oppression emerge out of the interaction of race and these features of capitalism. That is, racism arises as blacks become concentrated in the reserve army of labor; as blacks remain among the most exploited groups; as lines of inequality overlap with lines of color; as capitalists use race to weaken the organization and the power of labor; as high skill and high status laborers exclude blacks in order to maintain the privileged position of whites. Racism persists under industrial capitalism precisely because human exploitation, extreme inequality, and oppression persist.

There are many forms and sources of racial oppression and racial conflict under capitalism. One source of racial conflict has been the use of blacks as strikebreakers, which generated intense racial conflicts in the late 19th and early 20th centuries (Cox 1970; Myrdal [1948] 1975; Bonacich 1976; Reich 1981; Fusfeld and Bates 1984). These conflicts deflected working-class hostility away from the capitalist class and toward black workers, constituting a redirected form of class conflict (Cox; Reich).

Another form of racial oppression under capitalism involved the concentration of blacks in the most dreadful jobs. This concentration of blacks in areas such as the blast furnaces of steel mills, with their high morbidity and mortality rates and low wages, constituted a form of superexploitation of black labor.

Another source of racial oppression has been the maintenance of a labor hierarchy. This hierarchy contained an upper stratum of skilled workers who operated with the corporate elite to exclude black workers from higher paying skilled jobs. This exclusion produced a racial caste system in the industrial labor force. Hence, black subordination involved more than just class conflict, as some claimed. It involved a racial caste system maintained by both capitalists and white workers.

This concentration of blacks in this stratum has crowded blacks into the least desirable, lowest paying, and most unstable jobs, contributing to their marginalization. That is, it explains why blacks suffer the highest rates of layoffs, unemployment, and poverty.

Although it arose with industrial capitalism in the early 20th century, the marginalization of black workers became most evident in the last quarter of that century. Of course, a number of scholars claim that the black unemployment rate was lower, relative to the white rate, prior to the civil rights era and that the higher black rates relative to whites resulted from the perverse effects of public policies of the 1960s (Wilson 1980; Sowell 1984). However, pre-1960 national unemployment rates for blacks mask black unemployment because a large proportion of blacks were employed as sharecroppers in the rural South. City data provide a more accurate picture of black unemployment under industrial capitalism. These data indicate that for the economic downturns of the early 1920s and the 1930s, black unemployment rates in selected cities and industries were two or three times the white rates (Sitkoff 1978; Foner 1981). For example, during the depression of 1921 in Detroit, black unemployment rates were five times the unemployment rates of native-born whites and twice the unemployment rates of foreign-born whites (Foner, p. 132). A 1931 U.S. Bureau of Census survey of unemployment among adult males in the industrial sector of 13 U.S. cities recorded a rate of 31.7% for native whites, 29.9% for foreign-born whites, and 52.0% for blacks (Foner, p. 190).

This concentration of blacks in the reserve army of labor served a number of social functions. It provided white workers with recession insurance. If blacks bore the brunt of unemployment during depressions or recessions, then fewer whites would have to suffer job losses. Moreover, this concentration of blacks in the ranks of the unemployed made higher levels of unemployment more socially tolerable and easier to justify. White society could be less sensitive to these high rates because the victims were disproportionately black. Moreover, racists could attribute high black unemployment rates to inferior black genes or decadent black culture.

This denigration of blacks has historically functioned to legitimize extreme oppression and inequality. As Kovel (1984) suggested, the existence of race and racism presupposes the existence of oppression. That is, the notion that the oppressed are of a different race than the majority of the population has long been used to desensitize society to the suffering of the oppressed and to make oppression appear natural and legitimate. Wallerstein (1991, p. 87) added that racism provides an "acceptable legitimation of the reality of large-scale collective inequalities."

The subordination and denigration of a group creates conditions conducive to the growth of racism and racial thinking. Steinberg (1989, p. 170) made this point as he demonstrated the structural economic basis of racism using examples of capitalist countries noted for the absence of people of African descent. In Switzerland, for example, Italians were migrant workers imported to do the most undesirable jobs. Intense prejudices, similar to race prejudice, emerged against these Italian workers. This situation illustrated what Steinberg called the revised iron law of ethnicity. This is, it is not difference per se that produces ethnic conflict. It is ethnic difference "in a hierarchy of power, wealth, and status" that produces the conflict (Steinberg, p. 170). Insofar as capitalism produces hierarchies of power, wealth, and status, it is bound to produce group, ethnic, and racial conflicts. However, although race and racism are social constructs arising out of hierarchical, exploitative, and oppressive economic arrangements, these constructs are real and have the potential for precipitating the most destructive of human actions.

Segmentation Theory

Segmentation theory provides another way of explaining the connection between capitalism and racism. Gordon et al. (1982), proponents of segmentation theory, associated stages of capital accumulation with phases of labor processes. They identified three stages of accumulation and labor processes under industrial capitalism:

Initial proletarianization of labor (1820-1890)

Homogenization of labor (1870-1940)

Segmentation of labor (1920-the present)

Our examination of industrial capitalism involves the latter two stages: homogenization and segmentation of labor.

The homogenization period involved the consolidation of capital and the homogenization of labor categories. In this period, wealth became more concentrated as the income share of the top 5% of the population increased from 25% to more than 33% (Gordon et al. 1982, p. 105). By the early 1900s, a number of corporations emerged to control well over 50% of their markets. By this time, the United States Steel Corporation, representing the consolidation of 165 companies, controlled about 60% of the U.S. steel market; International Harvester Company controlled 85% of the farm machine market (Gordon et al., p. 108). By 1899, Standard Oil refined 90% of the nation's oil; of course, after antitrust suits, its share fell to 45% by 1926 (Kolko 1963, p. 40). Nevertheless, Gordon et al. (p. 107) reported that 3,653 mergers occurred between 1898 and 1902 alone, a figure 25 times the number in the previous 3 years. Indeed, this was a period of tremendous consolidation.

This consolidation corresponded to the emergence of a homogenizing labor process. This new labor process resulted from capital's need to extract more surplus value from labor and to exert more control over workers. In other words, as large firms strove to dominate their respective markets, they used several techniques to secure greater control over their workers. First, they instituted more mass production techniques that relied less on difficult-to-control craft workers and more on unskilled and semiskilled workers.

A good example of this new labor process is found in the meat processing industry. This industry was once dominated by the butcher, a skilled craftsman who carved up the entire animal. During the 1870s and 1880s, meat processors established an assembly line method of processing meats. In this method, carcasses, hooked on a conveyor belt, moved to carvers who stood in one place and performed a single task. This new labor process reduced the industry's reliance on the skilled butcher and allowed for greater use of semiskilled or unskilled workers (Gordon et al. 1982). It spread rapidly to other industries, increasing labor efficiency and reducing labor costs.

Second, employers invested in large factories and labor saving machines. This trend led to further increases in production and decreases in labor costs. Third, they engaged in more direct supervision of workers and relied more on central personnel departments (Gordon et al. 1982). Finally, in this new labor phase, employers waged war on unions, especially militant industrial unions. It was during this period that employers used blacks to break strikes, divide workers, and weaken labor unions. White workers' hostility against blacks was most virulent during this era.

This labor arrangement was shattered during the Great Depression of the 1930s, a period characterized by falling prices, rising unemployment, high rates of business failure, and labor revolts. These revolts were severe; the number of strikes increased precipitously in this decade, increasing from an average of about 753 per year between 1927 and 1932, to an average of about 2,542 per year between 1933 and 1938 (Gordon et al. 1982, p. 177). The number of strikes peaked at 4,740 in 1937 (Gordon et al., p. 177). These strikes signal a serious crisis of the homogenization labor arrangement.

This crisis was resolved with the formation of a new labor process, which emerged after major macro- and microlevel changes in the economy. Macrolevel changes involved an enlarged government role in regulating the economy and labor relations and the emergence of multinational corporations after World War II. Microlevel changes entailed an expanded role of labor unions in the workplace and capital's concession of union rights to exist and to bargain for higher wages and better working conditions.

A segmented labor market emerged after these changes. This new market was characterized by a primary or core sector and a secondary or peripheral sector. Large multinational firms with a unionized workforce constituted the primary sector. Smaller businesses with high failure rates, limited capital, and low wage, nonunion workers constituted the secondary sector. Primary sector firms were able to reduce labor costs and the power of labor unions by contracting with or shifting operations to the secondary sector.

Gordon et al. (1982) attributed the economic subordination of blacks in the post-World War II period to their concentration in the secondary sector. They argued that black migration from the South to urban areas accelerated during World War II when industrial jobs in the primary sector were expanding. This process, which continued in the postwar years as industries declined, left blacks concentrated in the secondary sector. Of course, Gordon et al. underscored the role of racial discrimination in perpetuating this pattern of black concentration in the secondary sector.

The strength of segmentation theory is its focus on the big picture. Its weakness is that it overlooks other important but subtle relationships and processes involved in the subordination of blacks under capitalism. It overlooks the relationship between social relations in production and race relations in unions, the connection between skilled labor's alliance with capital and labor's exclusion of blacks, and the role of radical industrial labor leaders in promoting racial equality. Segmentation theory especially overlooks the psychological dynamics behind European immigrant workers' development of a sense of white consciousness. Race and labor studies focus on these issues.

ANALYSIS OF RACE AND LABOR MOVEMENT STUDIES

In our investigation of the race and labor literature, we pay close attention to the dynamics of race relations in labor unions. We underscore the association between particular social relations in production and particular patterns of racial conflict in labor organizations. We examine the relationship between racial conflicts in labor and the nature of leadership in labor unions and among the corporate elite (capital). We demonstrate that black exclusion in labor unions arose more readily in the more stratified industries where labor aristocracies were allied with capital. We also illustrate the process out of which white consciousness emerged in the mind of the European immigrant worker. We investigate race relations in selected labor movements and selected industries. We examine the United Mine Workers and the coal mining industry, the Knights of Labor, the International Workers of the World, the Railroad Brotherhoods and the railroad industry, the American Federation of Labor, and the steel and the automobile industries and their respective unions. We divide our discussion into two periods: the pre-New Deal and the post-New Deal (1930s to 1960) eras.

Coal Mining and the United Mine Workers of America

The case of the United Mine Workers of America (UMWA or UMW), is instructive for several reasons. This case illustrates the connection between organization in production and race relations in unions. It challenges the notion that racism originated with white workers.

During the first half of the 20th century, there was very little labor stratification in the coal mines. Most jobs were coal handlers; some were machine operators, and a few were maintenance. However, there was little range in wages or occupational status among these jobs.

In the early 20th Century and particularly in the southern Appalachian region, the number and proportion of blacks employed in the coal mines increased. The demand for black labor rose in this region because of the discovery of large supplies of high quality coal and the expansion of railroads after the 1890s. Moreover, the hazardous and arduous nature of mine labor repulsed workers who could find better jobs elsewhere. Immigrant labor, plentiful in the North, was scarce in the South. Hence, the demand for black labor in the southern mines remained high throughout the 1920s. Up until the Great Depression, blacks constituted more than 22% of the southern mining workforce (Northrup 1944, p. 157). Thus organizing mine workers in the South meant organizing both black and white miners.

Because there was little stratification in mine labor and because the work was confined to the mines, black and white workers labored together and shared the same dangers. From its inception in 1890, the UMW had integrated unions in the southern Appalachian region. Moreover, blacks were elected to leadership positions in both the local and the national organizations (Foner 1981). In the first decade of the 20th century, the

Alabama division, District 20 of the UMW, succeeded in forcing mine owners to eliminate racial wage differentials (Reich 1981, p. 240). This division also pressured the business community in Birmingham to allow the UMW to hold integrated meetings in halls owned by members of this community (Reich, p. 240). Antiblack hostility came primarily from owners, businessmen, and civic leaders who were opposed to the union. This point was illustrated in the violent strike of 1908, precipitated by the mine owners' refusal to renew the union contract. In this strike, a citizen committee informed the UMW that "the people of Alabama would never tolerate the organization and striking of Negroes along with white men" (quoted in Northrup 1944, p. 163). Subsequently, miners were burned out of the tent city where they had lived after being evicted from their company-owned homes. The governor of Alabama sided with the owners, saying he would not allow whites to live in tent cities under the UMW jurisdiction (Northrup, p. 163). The UMW was defeated; the Alabama division was destroyed. The state, the mine owners, the citizen committee, and the media's virulent opposition to both the union and to the integration of black and white workers within the union were largely responsible for this defeat. The hatred for black unionized miners was so intense in Alabama that the UMW leadership considered taking the black miners out of the state and making the strike a white miners' issue.

In 1928, the UMW again attempted to organize Alabama mine workers. This time the national union leaders succumbed to race baiting, as the mine owners used blacks as strikebreakers. Again the UMW failed.

Conditions changed in the 1930s. Although the union faced more desperate economic times, its right to organize was protected by the federal government, and the union did not compromise on the issue of racial equality. The union remained tenaciously committed to interracial solidarity (Northrup 1944, p. 165), fighting against antiblack organizations, including the Ku Klux Klan (Northrup, p. 165). It succeeded in reorganizing the Alabama mine workers and reconstructing the integrated unions.

The absence of a rigidly stratified mining labor force and the situation in the mines that forced blacks and whites to share dangers and experiences provided the social or structural context out of which integrated unions were formed. The formation of this integrated union was not necessarily hindered by the racism of the workers, although there was some evidence of this racism. It was hindered by mine owners and business and community leaders incensed over two things: (1) blacks who displayed dangerous signs of rebellion by joining the union; and (2) whites who threatened the racial order by creating an integrated organization. Racism and white supremacy initially arose, not from the white worker, but from the impulse to control blacks and to maintain the racial and social order. This impulse originated from the upper stratum.

The Noble Knights of Labor

The case of the Knights of Labor further illustrates this connection between anti-union violence and antiblack violence. It also underscores the role of both leadership and economic arrangements in determining the fate of unions and race relations.

Unlike the UMW, the Knights of Labor, established in 1869, was a federation of labor unions, including garment workers, longshoremen, and bricklayers. The Knights organized both industrial and craft workers. Although some locals excluded or segregated blacks, the national leadership was committed to interracial solidarity.

The 1886 convention in Richmond, Virginia, illustrated this commitment. At this convention, 60 white delegates from New York City refused to stay at a hotel that would not accept the one black delegate. These delegates stayed with black families and worshipped at black churches in protest against the racial segregation in the South. Knights' leaders demanded the integration of hotels and theaters in Richmond. This convention included an integrated parade and picnics. At the parade, white mounted marshals rode side by side with black mounted marshals representing the Knights. It was the largest integrated social affair in Richmond's history (Foner 1981, p. 55). Such integrated affairs were common at Knights' conventions.

In the late 1880s, the Knights attempted to organize black and white workers in the South. They were met with intimidation, arrests, murders, and lynchings. In 1887, A. W. Jackson of Milton, Florida, a prominent Knights leader and successful businessman, was gunned down in his own establishment after the Ku Klux Klan ordered him to leave the city (Foner 1981, p. 59). H. F. Hoover, a white organizer in South Carolina who recruited blacks into the Co-operative Workers of America, was assassinated in Warrenton, Georgia, on May 20, 1887 (Foner, p. 59). The murder occurred shortly after several leaders of the union were detained by local deputies and threatened with long imprisonment or death if they did not cease their organizing efforts (Foner).

In 1887, the Knights organized sugar workers and initiated a strike against sugar planters in Louisiana, near New Orleans. The governor sent the militia to suppress the strike. Union leaders, including two black officials, George and Henry Cox, were arrested. Later a white mob took the two black leaders from their cells and lynched them (Foner 1981, pp. 60-61). During the strike, a local militia unit attacked a black settlement of strikers who had been evicted from their homes on the sugar plantation. The militia massacred over 20 blacks. The strike was broken.

The Knights rose and fell rather quickly. Membership peaked in 1886 at over 700,000 members. It declined rapidly. By 1888, membership had fallen to only 221,618 (Foner 1981, p. 56) By 1895 there were only 20,000 members. The demise of the Knights is attributable to three major factors. First, the economic crisis of the 1890s idled many Knight organized workers. Second, the late 1880s and early 1890s were a period of relentless repression against labor unions. This repression escalated after the May 1886 Haymarket riot in Chicago. Employers and anti-union officials used this incident as an excuse for their assaults on unions. Following this incident, authorities in several cities arrested Knight leaders. In some cases, entire executive committees were arrested. In the Deep South, Knights organizers were gunned downed, jailed, and lynched (Foner 1981).

Finally, the leaders of the Knights failed to respond effectively in defense of their organization. They were reticent in denouncing the arrest of their officials and in condemning the murder of their organizers. Because of the violence, they retreated in their opposition to segregation. In their waning years, they became more tolerant of segregated unions.

Like the UMW instance, the Knights case illustrates that antiblack violence did not originate with the union. It originated with anti-union employers and business associations. However, union leadership played a role in determining how the union responded to this violence.

The Railroad Industry and the Railroad Brotherhoods

The experiences of the railroad industry and the railroad brotherhoods (unions) provide an instructive contrast to the cases of the UMW and the Knights of Labor. The example of the brotherhoods further illustrates the connection between stratification in an industry and racial exclusion in the union. It also underscores the structural context out of which racially exclusive labor unions arise.

Railroad jobs were heavily stratified. That is, they were divided into several categories, arranged from the highest to the lowest in status and in wages. These jobs included engineers, firemen, brakers, trainmen, switchmen, conductors, brakemen, porters, and others. Separate unions emerged to represent workers in these separate job categories. For example, the Brotherhood of Locomotive Engineers, founded in 1863, represented railroad engineers; the Brotherhood of Locomotive Firemen, founded in 1873, represented the firemen, and so forth. These unions excluded blacks and operated to maintain a racial caste system in the railroad industry, with blacks concentrated in the lower paying, least desirable porter jobs (Foner 1981).

Labor scholars differ over the origin of the racially exclusionary behavior of these unions. Northrup (1944) maintained that these unions did not always exclude blacks and that this practice arose in reaction to the manner in which owners used black workers against white workers. This view points to an economic motive for the exclusion. Indeed, in the late 19th century, railroad companies hired black workers at a cheaper rate than white workers to do the same jobs. Owners also used blacks as strikebreakers. Northrup argued that unions had two options in responding to these practices: to include blacks in the union on an equal basis or to exclude them altogether. They opted for the latter.

Foner (1981) insisted that railroad unions always excluded blacks. He noted that their original constitutions contained clauses barring blacks from membership. Moreover, the brotherhoods actively campaigned to eliminate blacks from skilled jobs. These unions used strikes, collective bargaining, and government to coerce employers to bar blacks from all but the least desirable railroad jobs.

For example, in 1890, the Brotherhood of Locomotive Trainmen initiated a strike against the Houston and Texas Central Railroad Company to force the company to fire black switchmen. At this time, blacks worked as engineers, firemen, brakemen, and switchmen, the same jobs as whites but often for less pay. The strike failed. Other strikes to eliminate blacks from the higher status railroad jobs erupted all over the country. They were more successful in the North, where unions were stronger (Foner 1981).

In 1909, the Brotherhood of Locomotive Firemen launched a more successful strike against the Georgia Railroad Company. The Brotherhood defined the strike as a struggle for white supremacy against a company that promoted black supremacy. E. A. Ball, vice president of the Brotherhood, pleading for public support for the strike, said,

It will be up to you to determine whether the white fireman now employed on the Georgia Railroad shall be accorded rights and privileges over the negro, or whether he shall be placed on the same equality with the negro. I stand for white superiority, and Mr. Scott [the manager of Georgia Railroad] stands for Negro superiority; let the South judge between us. (quoted in Foner 1981, p. 106)

The business community supported the strike, although this community was hostile to unions. The fact that this was a strike for white supremacy undoubtedly appealed to this community.

The strike, which lasted for 2 weeks, ended with an arbitration decision, allowing the company to continue to hire blacks but requiring it to pay them the same wages as whites for the same jobs. This decision eliminated the company's prime incentive for hiring blacks—lower labor costs. The company stopped hiring black firemen. Because engineers were recruited from the ranks of firemen, fewer blacks became engineers. Foner (1981) claimed that by 1915, there were no black railroad engineers in the country.

These white unions excluded blacks for reasons other than self-interest, as the experience of the Brotherhood of Engineers in Cuba demonstrates. In 1910, this Brotherhood had the opportunity to organize Cuban railroad engineers, a move that would have enhanced the size and power of the union. However, the Brotherhood declined this opportunity because it could not draw a color line. Explaining this decision in 1910, the assistant grand chief, F. A. Burgess said, "We did not organize any of the engineers in Cuba for what we considered the most excellent of reasons; that we were unable to distinguish the nigger from the white man" (quoted in Foner 1981, p. 107). These trade unions operated to exclude blacks and to maintain a rigid color line. This behavior cannot be explained simply in terms of economic self-interest. It arose out a peculiar sense of race consciousness. It also emerged out of the structural context of a highly stratified industry. The experience of the American Federation of Labor helps explains this peculiar behavior.

The American Federation of Labor

The experience of the American Federation of Labor (AFL) further illustrates the correlation between the stratified industry and the racially exclusionary union. This case also points to a connection between racial exclusion and a labor/capital alliance. Founded in 1881, the AFL was initially committed to racial equality. In its early years, it refused to either support or incorporate local unions that excluded blacks. For example, in 1892, it refused to charter the Brotherhood of Boiler Makers and the Iron Ship Builders of America because their constitutions excluded nonwhites (Foner 1981).

The first president of the AFL, Samuel Gompers, maintained that racial exclusionary policies harmed the labor movement because they would allow employers to divide and exploit workers and make one group of labor antagonistic to the other. Gompers urged the AFL to become involved in organizing black workers. However, he suggested that in areas where local unions barred blacks, the AFL should support the formation of separate black unions that gave black workers the same rights and privileges as white workers.

This endorsement of either integrated or separate but equal locals was shattered during the panic of 1893 and the ensuing depression, which lasted until 1898. Employers bent on destroying unions and undercutting wages hired blacks at wages well below the rates paid to whites, frequently used blacks to replace striking white workers, and vehemently attacked integrated unions.

These conditions threatened the survival of the AFL. In response to this crisis, the AFL embarked on three new policy directions:

1. It accommodated itself to capital.
2. It focused on craft unions.
3. It tolerated and supported racially exclusionary and segregated locals.

The AFL's new accommodationist position was exemplified when Gompers joined the National Civic Federation in 1900. Although Gompers served as vice president, this organization tended to be dominated by industrialists. It frowned on industrial unionism and fought vehemently against radical unions (Brooks 1971). Radical unionists were the most strongly committed to interracial solidarity (Foner 1981).

As the AFL worked to make itself more acceptable to capital, it shifted from a general strategy of organizing both craft and industrial unions to a focused strategy of organizing craft unions. In the process of doing so, it became more tolerant of racial segregation and exclusion. At first, it allowed a local union's informal policy of excluding blacks. By 1899, it began accepting locals with constitutions that explicitly barred blacks from union membership. After chartering the Order of Railroad Teleg-raphers and the Brotherhood of Railway Trackmen—two unions with "for whites only" clauses in their constitutions—Gompers encouraged the other racially exclusive railroad brotherhoods to join. He also advocated the maintenance of segregated unions and blamed blacks for the need for segregation (Foner 1981, p. 76).

Most of the craft unions incorporated into the AFL either ex-cluded blacks or segregated them in separate locals. Almost all of them tolerated some form of discrimination against blacks. This discrimination occurred even in those craft unions with antidiscrimination clauses in their constitutions. For example, although the Bricklayers and Masons' International Unions prohibited racial exclusion, this union tolerated racial discrimination. In a case cited by Foner (1981), which occurred in the early 1900s, black and white bricklayers from Chicago went to Cincinnati with special union traveling cards indicating they were all union members and entitled to work in this city. Cincinnati locals im-mediately honored the cards held by whites, allowing them to secure immediate employment as unionized workers, but did not honor the cards held by black workers, forcing them to find jobs in some other, generally lower-paying, unskilled work. Foner noted that this pattern occurred in other cities. He mentioned cases in which white bricklayers refused to work with black bricklayers, a practice that led to the dismissal of blacks. The union failed to protect blacks from these forms of discrimination, even though it had an expressed antidiscrimination clause in its constitu-tion (Foner 1981).

In some cases, trade unions affiliated with the AFL provoked racial hostilities in their fight against employers. One case in East Saint Louis contributed to a race riot in 1917. In April, the Aluminum Ore Company of St. Louis used blacks as scabs to defeat a strike. A month later, the Central Trade and Labor Union, an AFL affiliate, publicly announced that it would demand that local authorities take action against the "growing menace" of "undesirable Negroes" (Foner 1981, p. 137). Union officials met with the mayor and council members and told them that if local officials failed to act against blacks, violent measures would be employed to deal with the problem. Shortly after the meeting, small groups of whites attacked a few blacks. The race riot erupted a few weeks later (Foner, p. 137).

Craft unions affiliated with the AFL tended to either exclude blacks altogether or segregate them into separate all black locals and deny them rights granted to white union workers. Rights denied to blacks included representation in the national organization and access to preferred jobs. Racial exclusion and segregation in many of these skilled trades unions continued, more or less, throughout the entire 20th century.

The International Workers of the World

The case of the International Workers of the World (IWW) demonstrates that the more radical, class-conscious, industrial unions exhibited the strongest commitment to interracial solidarity. The IWW was founded in 1905 by radical and socialist labor leaders disenchanted with the AFL. These leaders focused on organizing industrial workers regardless of race, color, gender, religion, or nationality (Foner 1981, p. 107). They were convinced that the AFL was too committed to the craft unions to assist the industrial workers and too exclusionary to unite workers across racial, ethnic, and gender lines. IWW journals criticized the AFL for depicting blacks as natural scabs. They accused the AFL of forcing blacks to become strikebreakers by excluding skilled blacks from AFL locals. This exclusion gave skilled black workers the choice of either working in a lower paying, unskilled position or working as a scab. Not only did IWW leaders campaign to recruit blacks, they fought to eliminate race prejudice as well. They condemned segregation and lynching in the South as forms of antilabor savagery (Foner 1981, p. 110). They insisted that the recruitment of blacks as equals to whites was not simply a moral issue, but a practical and economic one as well; it circumvented capital's ability to use black labor to break strikes and to undersell white labor. This union endured police repression, race baiting, and violent assaults in its efforts to organize across racial lines. Foner (1981, p. 111) insists that the IWW is the only federation of unions in the history of the labor movement in the U.S. never to have chartered a single segregated local. Its union meetings were integrated even in southern states that prohibited blacks and whites from meeting in the same hall.

Like the Knights, the IWW rose and fell quickly. It fought many skirmishes with employers and local police. In the end, the combined efforts of federal, state, and local enforcement agencies destroyed this union. In 1917, under the wartime espionage acts, the federal government indicted 150 of its leaders, the entire national leadership. One of the founders of the IWW, the socialist leader Eugene V. Debs, was sentenced to 10 years in prison in 1918. Another founder, Big Bill Haywood, escaped after his conviction. He emigrated to the Soviet Union, where he died in 1928 (Brooks 1971, p. 123).

The Steel Industry and Its Unions

Organized labor and the steel industry provide another example of the complexity of race relations in labor unions. This industry has depended on a large supply of cheap labor. In the North, until World War I, European immigrants provided this labor supply. In the South, poor whites and poor blacks served this purpose.

Jobs in the steel industry were stratified into skilled, semiskilled, and unskilled positions. With one exception, blacks tended to be concentrated in the lower paying, least desirable, unskilled jobs. The exception was found in the South where blacks were employed in some skilled jobs in the foundries. This trend was attributable to the undesirability of skilled jobs in the coke ovens, where working conditions were intolerably hot and accident and mortality rates high. Because European immigrants settled in the North and because southern whites tended to avoid these jobs, southern employers hired blacks, especially in the Birmingham, Alabama, mills.

Efforts to organize steelworkers date back to the 1850s. The Sons of Vulcan, one of the earliest steel unions was formed in 1858. This union, like most of the unions of this era, organized skilled workers and excluded both black workers and industrial workers. Its constitution contained a "for whites only" clause.

The movement to organize industrial steelworkers arose in the 1870s, with the formation of the Amalgamated Association of Iron, Steel, and Tin Workers. This union combined craft steel workers with industrial steelworkers. Although this union did not have an explicit policy of black exclusion, many of its members were hostile to the notion of organizing blacks. Its locals tended either to exclude blacks or to organize them in segregated locals. Blacks reacted to this exclusion with hostility toward the union. Many became strikebreakers.

Just after World War I, the Amalgamated Association launched a massive effort to organize the steel industry. In 1919, more than 350,000 steelworkers went on strike to gain union recognition (Northrup 1944, p. 177; Reich 1981, p. 255). During this strike, steel employers in Chicago and Pittsburgh brought large numbers of black steelworkers from the South to use as strikebreakers. The union movement was crushed. It did not recover from this defeat until the 1930s, with the formation of the Steel Workers Organizing Committee of the Congress of Industrial Organization. This union was more committed to racial equality. It survived and later became the United Steelworkers Union of America.

THEORETICAL REFLECTIONS

These cases illustrate the complexity of race relations in the labor movement. They provide some support for a number of theories explaining racial exclusion and segregation in unions. These theories include the rational, the contextual, and psychocultural perspectives.

Rational Theory

Rational theory suggests that there are a number of rational reasons why white labor unions excluded black workers. Bonacich (1976), better known as a split-labor market theorist, suggested that black exclusion protected white labor from capital's efforts to use blacks to weaken or destroy unions, to reduce the price of white labor, and to replace the more expensive white workers with cheaper black workers. Others have claimed that black exclusion insulated white workers from the more devastating impacts of depressions and recessions (Baron and Sweezy 1968; Williams 1987; Shulman 1989). This exclusion guarded white craft workers from competition with black craft workers and reserved preferred jobs for privileged whites. It enhanced the financial position of white craft workers by reducing the overall supply of craft workers. Black exclusion also paid a psychological wage to white workers (Du Bois 1969a; Roediger 1991). That is, no matter how low the status or wage of the white worker, he had the advantage of being above the black worker in status and wages. Thus this perspective suggests that white labor's exclusion of blacks was a function of the self-interest and rational decisions of white workers, not of racism or a false consciousness (Williams 1987; Shulman 1989).

Contextual Theory

Contextual theory suggests that racially exclusionary decisions are best understood by examining the context in which they are made. These decisions are made, not in a vacuum, but under specific circumstances and within particular situations. Indeed, they are shaped by these circumstances and situations. We have identified three situations that strongly influenced the racially exclusionary behavior of labor unions.

The first situation entailed social relations within an industry. That is, the level of stratification and segregation in an industry corresponded to the level of racial exclusion or segregation in the union. Highly stratified industries were more likely to produce racially exclusionary unions. The highly stratified railroad industry was associated with the racially exclusionary railroad brotherhoods. Conversely, the less stratified industries correlated with unions committed to racial equality. The less stratified coal mining industry correlated with the racially integrated UMW. The second situation was the social status of the union and its relationship to capital. The higher status craft unions, with a close relationship to capital, were more likely to exclude blacks than the lower status industrial unions, with an antagonistic relationship to capital. For example, the IWW, hostile to capital, was most committed to racial equality. The higher status AFL, allied with capital, had affiliated unions with the most notorious reputations for excluding blacks.

Most of the higher status craft unions were racially exclusionary from their inception. This behavior arose partly from the tendency of these unions to restrict membership in order to raise the price of skilled labor and to protect white labor from competition with black labor—a rational theory perspective. It also emerged partly out of the union's quest for higher status and social privileges in the context of a stratified and racist society that conferred lower status on blacks and higher status on whites.

The third situation was one of pervasive violence against radical unions committed to racial equality. Both the AFL and the Knights of Labor became more tolerant of segregation in the social context of antiblack violence. These unions lost their commitment to racial equality in a milieu in which labor leaders faced violence in general and suffered relentless assaults for organizing blacks. Radical unions committed to racial equality, like the IWW, were crush by national, state, and local law enforcement agencies. Racially exclusionary behavior of unions like the AFL surfaced out of this context of violence against blacks and radical unions. One reason, among many, that racially exclusionary unions became so prevalent in the United States was that the dominant class and the state—whether intentionally or not—destroyed racially inclusionary unions and spared exclusionary unions that cowered to capital.

Psychocultural Explanation of White Labor Excluding Black Workers: The Case of the Irish Worker

Psychocultural theory suggests that black exclusion was not just a matter of white control of preferred jobs, white protection from black competition, or white union survival strategies. Black exclusion also involved the formation of white identity and white consciousness, the creation of a particular racial classification scheme, and the development of contempt for blackness.

The case of the railroad brotherhoods provides one illustration of the psychocultural aspect of black exclusion. Although expansion into Cuba would have increased the size and power of the Brotherhood of Engineers, this union would not organize in Cuba because it would not adjust to the Cuban racial classification scheme. The union was so fixated on the rigid black/white racial categorization scheme endemic to North American culture that it could not adjust to the more flexible Cuban scheme, which accepted blacks and whites in the same family. Because of presuppositions about race and beliefs in the unnaturalness and grotesque consequences of race mixing, attitudes deeply ingrained in North American culture, the North American mind could not imagine the possibility of blacks and whites belonging to the same family. This cultural context, which structured North American thinking and imagining about race, rather than rational decision making, best explains the brotherhoods' inability to organize in Cuba.

Roediger (1991) provided a more detailed analysis of the role of culture in explaining black exclusion. His study focused on Irish workers, the social construction of race, and the formation of white consciousness. Roediger noted that in the 1830s, Irish leaders in Ireland and the United States sympathized with African Americans. They condemned African slavery and oppression, as they saw themselves as oppressed by England. During this time, the Irish were not white, Roediger insisted. As an oppressed group, they were victimized by stereotypes similar to those used against blacks. The Irish were seen as overly promiscuous, prone to violence, and predisposed to drunkenness. They faced discrimination in the job market and contempt in social settings (Steinberg 1989; Roediger 1991).

The Irish in the United States changed during the 1840s and 1850s. In this period, the Irish population increased exponentially. The economic position of the Irish improved; the position of blacks declined (Roediger 1991). At the same time, the Irish became more acclimated to American culture. By the 1850s, Irish workers began to define themselves as white workers. White labor was defined in its contrast with black slavery. White labor was free, respectable, and acceptable. Black slavery was unacceptable, dreadful, and debasing. Irish Americans, who had equated their plight in Ireland with slavery, began to equate slavery with blackness. They called the most degrading, dangerous, or backbreaking work "nigger work."

In the early 1860s, the Irish displayed explicit signs of hostility toward blacks. Rational theory explains this hostility in terms of Irish workers' reaction to employers using blacks as strikebreakers. Indeed, a number of scholars explain the antiblack New York draft riots of 1863 in terms of the revolt of Irish workers against black strikebreakers. Fusfeld and Bates (1984, p. 17) contended that 3,000 Irish longshoremen in New York, who had lost a strike to black strikebreakers, led the antiblack draft riots. They feared that the Civil War would liberate more blacks, who would move north and take Irish jobs. This rational theory explains antiblack violence as arising out of black and white job competition (see Woodward 1951; Wilson 1980; Fredrickson 1982).

The problem with the rational choice model is that it accepts the antiblack sentiments as a rational, natural, and sensible reaction to a real threat. The problem with antiblack violence in the North was similar to the problem in the South: The black threat was exaggerated. Irish workers had already displaced blacks in various jobs. Hence, blacks posed little threat to Irish workers as competitors. Moreover, the Irish faced stronger opposition from native-born White Anglo-Saxon Protestant (WASP) workers, who complained that the Irish were underselling WASP labor, and from other European immigrants, especially from German, Italian, Polish, Russian, and Scandinavian immigrants, throughout the rest of the 19th century. Many of these immigrants were willing to work harder for less money and had few qualms about taking Irish jobs. In the last half of the 19th and first decade of 20th century, the black population in northern cities increased negligibly, whereas immigrant populations rose dramatically. Indeed, in many cities, the proportion of blacks in the total population declined between 1860 and 1910. For example, in Detroit, blacks constituted 3.1% of the total city population in 1860, 1.7% by 1890, and 1.2% by 1910 (Geschwender 1979, p. 59). Yet, although European immigrants posed a greater threat to them than black workers did, Irish workers focused their exclusionary efforts and violence at blacks.

Theodore W. Allen (1994), in *The Invention of the White Race,* provided a detailed historical analysis of the transformation of Irish Catholics from abolitionists in the 1840s to white Irish hostile to blacks and major participants in the antiblack draft riots of 1863. Allen suggested that three factors explain this metamorphosis: the Tammany Hall machine, the Catholic church, and the hegemony of white racist culture.

Allen maintained that the local Democratic party in the North was part of the slaveholders' Jacksonian party. Tammany Hall and other local machines supported slavery and white supremacy. This party, Allen argued, defined the Irish as white, bestowed special privileges on them as white workers, and promoted a racial order of white privilege and black subordination. This party played a major role in changing the Irish into whites. Allen argued that the Catholic church in the United States played a similar role. He suggested that although the pope condemned slavery, Irish Catholic leaders in New York City and other urban areas adjusted their position to accommodate the dominant culture. These leaders defined abolitionists as unpatriotic, anti-Catholic, Protestants, which abolitionists tended to be. They reinterpreted the pope's position as opposition to the slave trade rather than slavery per se. They compared support for slavery to patriotism.

Illustrating his arguments, Allen (1994) recounted a series of events beginning in 1861 and leading up to the 1863 riots. Between 1861 and 1862, the Democratic mayor of New York City, Fernando Wood, expressing sympathy for southern slaveholders, proposed that the city secede from the union; Archbishop Hughes of New York City claimed that any effort to abolish slavery would violate the Constitution; the Democratic party newspaper, *The Leader,* wrote that if a black was hired by the U.S. customs office, the entire white race would rise in rebellion against it; a series of newspaper articles appeared warning white workers that freed blacks were taking white jobs (Allen, pp. 189-91). These inflammatory statements did more to incite the draft riots than labor competition.

Allen (1994) argued that the threat of black labor competition was a bogus one. He noted that in 1855, the city labor market had four non-Irish, foreign-born workers to every one black worker and that between 1855 and 1863, the foreign-born population increased geometrically. Allen maintained that slavery posed a greater threat to white workers in New York than emancipation because blacks would be more likely to run north to escape oppression and more likely to stay in the South if they were free and no longer oppressed. He concluded that Irish hostility to blacks and opposition to abolishing slavery cannot be adequately explained by the labor competition view. This hostility can be better explained by focusing on the dominant white racist culture. This culture was promoted by various institutions, notably the local political party and the Catholic church.

The level and intensity of the violence against blacks during the draft riots cannot be explained in any rational context, such as labor competition. As Allen (1994, p. 197) said so eloquently, "No European immigrants were lynched, no 'white' orphanages were burned, for fear of 'competition' in the labor market."

Roediger (1991) offered two major reasons why the Irish targeted blacks. First, within the labor force, Irish workers defined themselves as white. They claimed entitlement to special privileges and jobs as white workers rather than as Irish workers. Roediger argued that if the Irish had staked a claim on skilled jobs in the name of Irish workers, they would have faced an immediate and fierce backlash from native-born craft workers who were already anti-immigrants. They acquired privileges as whites that they could not obtain as Irish.

Second, blacks were one of the most vulnerable groups in the United States. They were politically weak. When attacked, they were least likely to retaliate with any degree of effectiveness. More than any other group in North America, save the Native Americans, African Americans were denigrated and despised with impunity. Irish Americans found more security in identifying with the dominant white group and in directing their hostility to the weaker black group.

Other studies have underscored this process in which European immigrants—Irish, Italian, Polish, and others—acquired a white consciousness and identity (Steinberg 1989; Widick 1989). White identity and antiblack prejudices emerged as a common way in which European immigrants could deflect anti-immigrant hostility. Widick (p. 28) made this point cogently in his study of racial violence in Detroit: "Using the odious term 'niggers' gave the foreign-born worker (mainly Polish) a sense of identity with white society, and by throwing the spotlight of prejudice on the Negro, he turned it away from himself."

Of course, in some large cities, specific ethnic groups were able to capture and dominate a particular job category in the local government, thus facilitating some degree of ethnic identification and segregation in city jobs. Once one group established inroads into a particular job area, this group tended to recruit people more like themselves into the agency. Nevertheless, whereas European ethnic groups may have been segregated into specific job categories, blacks tended to be excluded from all but the least desirable jobs. See Pinderhughes (1987) and Rich (1982) for more details on the ethnic and racial dynamics of machine governments and the allocation of city jobs and resources.

Rather than defining themselves as an oppressed group and empathizing with blacks—the most vulnerable and oppressed group—immigrant groups defined themselves as white, identified with the dominant Anglo-Saxon group, and assisted in the subordination of blacks. This phenomenon of oppressed groups identifying with the dominant group and releasing their hostilities on the subordinate group is not an anomaly. It has been well documented in the psychoanalytical literature (Allport 1979). For example, psychologist Bruno Bettelheim (1967) documented cases in which Jews in Nazi concentration camps identified with the SS guards. In the concentration camps, anti-Semitic pressures were so brutal, so intense, and so relentless that they crushed the egos of these prisoners and forced them to abandon their sense of self and to identify with their oppressors. Also, psychoanalyst Erich Fromm (1965) illustrated the tendency of insecure groups or individuals to use sadomasochistic strategies to cope with feelings of unbearable anxiety and powerlessness arising out of an alien, intensely hostile, and frightening world. These strategies involve groups or individuals abandoning their freedom and identity and submitting to a dominant group. This absorption in and submission to the dominant group—masochism—allays their anxiety. They overcome their sense of powerlessness by controlling, humiliating, or hurting others who are outside the dominant group or members of subordinate groups. This sadism gives them a sense of power and efficacy in a world that makes them feel powerless and impotent (Fromm 1965). Allport (1979) provided a similar analysis of groups and prejudice, except that he used the terms *in groups* and *out groups* instead of dominant and subordinate.

Cultural agents such as the church, the local political party, local newspapers, and others played the most important role in the formation of white identity. However, to some degree, the transformation of initially nonwhite immigrants into whites, hostile to blacks, involved these sadomasochistic dynamics. That is, immigrants allayed their anxiety by submitting to the dominant white group (masochism). Sometimes they shed their ethnic identity. They obtained a sense of power and efficacy by defining themselves as white and by humiliating and assaulting blacks (sadism).

This psychocultural perspective contradicts traditional views of assimilation and black subordination. Assimilation theory explains black subordination under industrial capitalism as a function of blacks' late arrival to the city—the mid-20th century—long after European immigrants arrived, assimilated, and ascended to higher social positions (Sowell 1975). In this psychocultural perspective, European immigrants did not assimilate per se. They identified with the dominant WASP group. Sometimes they lost their ethnic identity and acquired a white identity.

This white identity and consciousness arose in a cultural context that incessantly shouted that whites were superior, civilized, pure, angelic, and intelligent; and that nonwhites were inferior, primitive, impure, evil, and moronic. In this cultural context, white identity enhanced the esteem, the status, and the efficacy of those who defined themselves as white. It endowed them with a sense of power and efficacy. It gave them special entitlements to better jobs. It functioned as a psychological defense mechanism, triggered by a society hostile to nonwhites and to immigrants. It emerged in an oppressive and exploitative capitalistic society, characterized by dominant and subordinate classes and prone to the types of economic crises that generate anxiety and insecurity. It operated to maintain a caste system in industrial labor that barred blacks from skilled jobs and concentrated them in the least desirable industrial jobs.

The False Consciousness Controversy

We will be remiss in our discussion of the formation of white consciousness if we neglect the false consciousness debate. A number of theorists have claimed that racism is a form of false consciousness because it disadvantages white workers by depressing wages and weakening labor unions (Reich 1981; Cherry 1989). Because white consciousness is seen as detrimental to the interest of labor and beneficial to capital, it is said to be a false working-class consciousness. Others disagree (Shulman 1989). They cite benefits that white workers obtain by excluding black workers: higher priced skilled labor and recession insurance as blacks crowd into lower status jobs and bare the brunt of layoffs. Because they see white consciousness and black exclusion as beneficial to white labor, these scholars see racial exclusion as a function of a valid consciousness and a self-interested choice. They reject the idea of a false consciousness.

Of course, Lukacs (1975) defined false consciousness as any form of consciousness other than revolutionary consciousness. For us, what is important is not whether the consciousness is false or true. What is important is understanding the dynamics of the formation of consciousness—white, revolutionary, or otherwise. The debate is limited because it operates in the rational choice paradigm and ignores the psychological dynamics behind the formation of white consciousness.

White consciousness and antiblack hostility can be explained as a psychocultural pathology. Moreover, this pathology arose out of the exploitative and oppressive features of industrial capitalism.

THE POST-NEW DEAL PERIOD: FROM THE 1930s TO THE 1960s

Things changed during the Great Depression of the 1930s. Industrial workers revolted. They organized, assaulted capital, pressured government for protection, and expressed commitment to racial equality. Capital retreated; it conceded to industrial unions a right to organize and bargain for higher wages and better working conditions. Government responded by creating the National Labor Relations Board (NLRB) to protect the rights of unions. During World War II, the position of black workers improved, particularly with the creation of the Fair Employment Practice Commission (FEPC) and the expressed commitment of industrial unions to interracial solidarity.

The Congress of Industrial Organizations

The role of the industrial union in promoting interracial solidarity is illustrated in the history of the Congress of Industrial Organization (CIO). In 1935, leaders within the AFL, frustrated over this union's bias in favor of craft unions and neglect of industrial workers, established the CIO (initially the Committee for Industrial Organization) as a committee within the AFL. This committee, expelled from the AFL in 1938, moved quickly to organize industrial workers in the areas of steel, auto, rubber, and textile production, shipbuilding, meat packing, and many others.

From its inception, the CIO expressed a commitment to interracial solidarity. This commitment arose from two sources: the crucial position of African Americans in industrial labor and the personal convictions of CIO leaders. First, the proportion of black industrial steelworkers was too large for the CIO to ignore. Blacks were concentrated in the most dangerous, least desirable steel jobs, the very area targeted by the CIO for unionization. Moreover, the proportion of black steelworkers increased substantially in the decades following World War I. By 1936, blacks constituted 20% of steel laborers and 6% of steel operators (Foner 1982, p. 218). Their numbers increased further during World War II.

Second, many of the founders of the CIO and the leaders charged with organizing steelworkers were from the UMW. Many organizers were radical labor organizers, some were socialists, some were members of the Communist party, and most were committed to racial equality. The list of CIO founders includes leaders such as John L. Lewis, former president of the UMW, and William Mitch, a UMW activist with a reputation for organizing mine workers in Alabama. Under Mitch's leadership, the number of Alabama UMW members increased from 225 in 1933 to 23,000 in 1935, the UMW locals remained integrated, black officers were elected to key positions, and the influence of the Ku Klux Klan was diminished (Foner 1982, p. 218).

In 1936, the CIO replaced the dying Amalgamated Association of Iron, Steel, and Tin (AAIST) with the Steel Workers Organizing Committee (SWOC). This organization moved with great speed to organize steelworkers and negotiate a contract with the industry. By the spring of 1937, the SWOC had about 325,000 members. By 1938, it represented about a half million steelworkers, including close to 85,000 black steelworkers (Foner 1982, p. 224). At the end of 1937, it had secured a contract with U.S. Steel, one of the world's largest steel producers. A year later, the SWOC became the United Steelworkers Union of America.

The Special Case of the United Auto Workers

One of the most instructive cases of race relations and the new industrial unions of the 1930s under the CIO is that of the United Auto Workers (UAW-CIO). This case illustrates a number of important points involving industrial labor and race relations in industrial unions. It shows the crucial position of black workers in the industrial workforce and the role of labor leaders in fostering interracial solidarity. It reveals problems with industrial unions gaining the trust of black workers. It underscores the persistent problem of racism among white workers. It demonstrates the role of the corporate elite in generating and perpetuating racial divisions in labor. It further emphasizes the relationship between organization in production and race relations in unions. It unveils the role of ideology in the formation of race relations in unions.

Prior to World War I, there were few blacks employed in the automobile industry. Because of the rapid expansion of this industry during and after the war, and because of the sharp decline in European immigration, this industry desperately needed workers. It had little choice but to recruit among southern blacks. Its direct recruitment efforts in the South contributed to a dramatic increase in the number of blacks employed in this industry. Nevertheless, blacks were hired in a racially discriminatory manner. With a few exceptions, they were excluded from skilled jobs, concentrated in the least desirable jobs, and segregated in particular areas.

In 1916, the Ford Motor Company employed a little more than 50 blacks (Meier and Rudwick 1981, p. 6). Black employment in this company increased exponentially throughout the war years to about 2,500 in 1920, according to Meier and Rudwick. Others provide even higher estimates (Geschwender 1979, p. 19; Widick 1989, p. 27). The number of blacks employed by Ford increased even more dramatically after Ford built its mammoth River Rouge plant, located just outside of Detroit. Most blacks hired by Ford were employed in this plant. By 1923, 5,000 blacks worked in this plant (Meier and Rudwick, p. 6; Geschwender figures are higher). This figure increased to 10,000 by 1926 (Meier and Rudwick, p. 6).

By the 1930s, blacks were employed by General Motors, Chrysler, and Packard, as well as Ford and a number of smaller firms. However, all of these firms recruited blacks in a manner that produced a segregated system in this industry. Blacks were rarely hired in plants outside the Michigan area, except in custodial jobs. Inside Michigan, blacks were highly concentrated in the most dangerous and least desirable jobs. Most blacks hired by Ford were employed at the River Rouge Complex. Chrysler hired blacks primarily in its Dodge Division, especially in the huge Dodge main facility located in Hamtramck, a small city inside the city of Detroit. General Motors hired blacks mainly in its Chevrolet Division in Pontiac and Saginaw; its Buick Division in Flint; and the Pontiac foundry in Pontiac (Geschwender 1979; Meier and Rudwick 1981). In these plants, blacks were concentrated in the burning foundries, the suffocating spray paint shops, the hot drying rooms, and the dangerous sanding and grinding areas. Meier and Rudwick (p. 7) said that up until 1930, "at Chrysler and Chevrolet, blacks were employed as paint-sprayers; at another firm 'certain dangerous emery steel grinding jobs were given only to Negroes.' "

In regards to automakers' treatment of blacks, the Ford Motor Company was both typical and unique. Ford was typical in the sense that it tended to segregate blacks in the River Rouge production facility, where they were concentrated in foundry jobs. Ford was unique in two ways. First, whereas other automakers were reluctant to employ blacks on the assembly line, Ford employed a few blacks in most areas at the River Rouge plant. Before World War II, Ford was the only automobile company to admit blacks into apprenticeship positions. Whereas most companies excluded blacks from the skilled trades, Ford hired River Rouge blacks as machine operators, tool and die makers, electricians, and mechanics. Ford employed more black foremen than all the other automakers combined. Whereas black foremen in other companies only supervised all-black crews, a few black foremen with Ford supervised mixed crews. In one case, a black foreman at the River Rouge plant supervised an all-Polish crew (Meier and Rudwick 1981, p. 9). Of course, although Ford was indeed the most progressive automaker in hiring and promoting blacks, black Ford workers were confined, throughout the 1940s and 1950s, almost exclusively to the River Rouge plant, concentrated in the foundry, and disproportionately underrepresented in skilled and supervisory positions.

The second unique feature of the Ford Company was its relationship to the black community in the Detroit area. Henry Ford gave generously to black churches, the NAACP, the Urban League, and other organizations committed to improving black life. Ford also recruited through black churches and black ministers. Ford endeared himself to the black community through his generous contributions, through the status and special privileges he conferred on black ministers, and through his well-publicized rapport with black scientists, such as George Washington Carver.

This relationship between Ford and the black community posed a serious obstacle to efforts to unionize black workers. Blacks were loyal to Ford and suspicious of white unions. At the same time, because of the crucial position of blacks in key areas of the automobile industry, unions could not afford to ignore black workers.

This situation required UAW leaders to exert special efforts to recruit black workers. The UAW's original constitution expressed a commitment to organizing all autoworkers regardless of race, color, creed, nationality, religion, or political affiliation. The first vice president of the UAW, Wyndham Mortimer, an ex-coal miner and a member of the Communist faction in the UAW, appealed directly to black workers and campaigned in black churches to win black support for the union. The UAW hired black organizers. It initiated educational programs to combat racism among white workers and to counteract the influence of the Ku Klux Klan, the Black Legion, and other antiblack organizations active in the Detroit area (Foner 1982, p. 223).

The UAW moved quickly to unionize autoworkers. It organized General Motors workers by early 1937. With the exception of the Flint Buick plant, where more blacks were employed, few blacks participated in the GM strikes for union recognition. In the same year, the UAW attempted to organize Ford workers. It failed. Because of the crucial position of blacks in the River Rouge complex, black participation was essential for any successful organizing drive against this automaker. In

1937, black autoworkers were still suspicious of the UAW, and black leaders were still loyal to Ford.

In the battle to unionize black Ford workers, a tremendous ideological struggle arose between the UAW and Ford, between those groups allied with workers and those allied with capital. Henry Ford and the black leaders he supported argued that unions were un-American, communistic, and antiblack. Black ministers insisted that Henry Ford was the black worker's best friend. For a while, Ford had the stronger position in this struggle for black support, especially because he had the allegiance of black ministers.

The UAW's position improved after an intensive recruitment drive with the support of pro-labor black organizations. A new, pro-labor black organization, the National Negro Congress, was established by more than 250 prominent black leaders, including A. Philip Randolph, president of the Brotherhood of Sleeping Car Porters; Ralph Bunche, Nobel Peace Prize recipient; poet Langston Hughes; James W. Ford of the Communist party; and others. The NAACP's national chapter, having become interested in the status of black workers, favored a closer relationship with organized labor. The national chapter directly pressured the conservative, pro-Ford, Detroit chapter to change its position on the Ford-UAW conflict to favor the UAW. These political maneuvers, combined with the efforts of many zealous black UAW organizers, proved decisive. In 1941, the UAW succeeded in organizing Ford workers.

For the most part, the CIO was successful in its movement to unionize along interracial lines. However, this success did not automatically eliminate the racial caste system in industry. Although notable advancement in the promotion of racial equality occurred in industries, especially during and after World War II, racial progress was limited by problems within labor; the role of capital; shifts in the role of government; segregation in urban space; and the culture of racism.

Problems Within Labor

Although CIO-affiliated unions were committed to interracial solidarity, their efforts to achieve racial equality within industries were hindered by racism among white workers, factional disputes, internal purges, and the reunion of the CIO with the AFL. Racism among industrial workers obstructed CIO efforts to achieve racial equality or to eliminate the racial caste system in industry. Any attempt to promote blacks beyond the most dreadful jobs provoked white hostility.

For example, in the late 1930s, black UAW leaders attempted to introduce resolutions at UAW conventions demanding that antidiscriminatory promotion and apprenticeship policies be placed in the collective bargaining contract. These resolutions died because of the UAW leadership's fear of a white backlash (Meier and Rudwick 1981). This backlash occurred during World War II, when the UAW, with the support of the FEPC, began to pressure automakers to promote blacks into some skilled jobs. These pressures arose out of the critical labor shortage precipitated by the expansion of war production and the loss of workers to the draft. Workers were desperately needed in all job areas. Black workers stepped forward to satisfy this need.

Numerous antiblack strikes occurred in the early 1940s, precipitated by the promotion of a small number of black workers into an all-white job area (Northrup 1944; Geschwender 1979; Meier and Rudwick 1981). Meier and Rudwick (p. 162) documented 12 antiblack strikes in the first 6 months of 1943. One of the more serious strikes occurred at a Packard plant and involved Local 190 of the UAW. In this strike, 25,000 white workers walked off their jobs in protest over the placement of three black workers into an all-white skilled area (Meier and Rudwick, pp. 162-70). This strike was particularly troublesome to the UAW leadership because Local 190 officials participated in it. Some shop stewards urged white workers to walk off the job. At mass UAW meetings, hundreds of white workers jeered UAW president R. J. Thomas, who called for interracial solidarity and spoke of the rights of black workers. The strike was settled after the War Labor Board, the Labor Department, and the Defense Department intervened and threatened to fire all the striking workers and bar them from working in any other defense-related industry. Nevertheless, this case illustrates the enormous problem the UAW had with racism and the extent to which racism obstructed UAW efforts to promote racial equality inside the industry. It also illustrates the tremendous potential of the state in eliminating the racial caste system.

Another factor that hindered industrial unions' ability to eliminate the industrial racial caste system was internal labor politics in the postwar period. These politics involved internal factions in labor and purges of leftist labor leaders. After World War II, the CIO and its affiliates eliminated their left wing. They purged themselves of radical labor leaders, the very leaders most committed to racial equality. This purge occurred as centrist labor leaders consolidated their power within the union and accommodated the union to capital and external political pressures, particularly to McCarthyism in the 1950s. This purge occurred because leftist union factions were hopelessly divided among Stalinists, Trotskyites, and socialists disenchanted with the Soviet Union. It occurred because unions were under attack by industrialists, anti-Communist forces, and the state. After World War II, Congress began to attack unions. At this time, the House Committee on Un-American Activities began to target labor unions. The Taft-Hartley Act, passed just after the war, contained a provision allowing the NLRB to decertify Communist-dominated unions. Either out of fear of being decertified or out of sheer opportunism—the use of this fear for political gain—centrist leaders expelled the left wing of their unions. This expulsion gave centrist leaders more power. At the same time, it meant the elimination of leaders most committed to racial equality (Foner 1982).

A final factor that weakened union commitment to racial equality was the reunion of the CIO with the AFL. The CIO had a demonstrated record of interracial solidarity, at least in the area of organizing black and white workers and at least in expressing a commitment to antidiscrimination policy. It had pressured its locals to organize workers regardless of race, color, creed, or gender. In contrast, the AFL and affiliates had a demonstrated record of racial exclusion and segregation. The AFL pressured its affiliates to purge themselves of Communists, as it threatened to decharter affiliates with Communist party members. At the same time, it continued to tolerate racially exclusionary affiliates. It had a heavy hand for Communists and a hands-off policy for the racists. In regard to racial equality, the merger of the CIO with the AFL was like mixing the hot black coffee of racial equality with the ice-cold milk of racial segregation; it yielded a cooler, more diluted by-product—a vague and weak commitment to racial equality (Foner 1982).

An exclusive focus on labor leaves the impression that white workers played the dominant role in excluding blacks from the better jobs and in maintaining the industrial caste system. Labor's record of racial exclusion was mixed. Most craft unions practiced exclusion or segregation. Industrial unions supported interracial solidarity. Nevertheless, it was the corporate elite that played the major role in constructing the racial caste system in specific industries in the first place.

The Corporate Elite

White labor, especially unorganized white labor, never had the power either to create or to maintain the racial caste system in labor. Although a considerable body of literature insists on placing the blame for the construction and maintenance of this system on the white worker (Lipset 1963; Wilson 1980), and although racism clearly infected these workers, several factors support the alternative thesis, which places much of the blame on the corporate elite. The Ford River Rouge complex offers strong evidence in support of the corporate elite thesis. Ford Motors hired blacks into skilled and supervisory positions with little opposition from white workers. White workers never had the power to stop Ford from promoting blacks. If a white worker complained he was fired. The power to organize labor in production—especially in ways to produce a racial caste system—clearly rested with the company, not with unorganized labor.

Henry Ford was one of the most progressive industrialists of this period. He did more for the black community in Detroit, more in hiring blacks in skilled and supervisory positions, and more in advancing the social status of blacks than any other industrialist of this era. Nevertheless, he was a product of his times. He viewed blacks as a subordinate group. Ford claimed that whites were superior to blacks and that only the Anglo-Saxon people were capable of sustaining democracy (Meier and Rudwick 1981, pp. 11-12). Like other automakers, he excluded blacks from most of his plants outside the state of Michigan. He advocated racial segregation. His racial perspective differed from other corporate elites in that Ford was paternalistic. Ford insisted that the superior races had an obligation to assist the inferior races (Meier and Rudwick, pp. 11-12). While he advocated social segregation, he believed blacks deserved decent lives. Specifically, Ford said, "Race lines are fixed. Nature punishes transgression. . . . Blacks should have decent neighborhoods, but residential segregation and social separation must prevail" (quoted in Meier and Rudwick, p. 12).

Ford saw blacks as a docile race, forever loyal to their employers. Apparently, he became bitter after blacks joined the UAW to unionize the River Rouge complex. After 1941, Ford changed his policy toward blacks and began excluding them. Meier and Rudwick (1981, p. 136) said that Ford's "hiring policies became the most discriminatory among Detroit's large corporations." Thus it was the corporate elite of Ford Motors that advanced blacks at the River Rouge plants. It was the corporate elite that instituted racially discriminatory hiring practices.

When white workers revolted against the advancement of black workers, employers tended to share their views and sympathize with them. In some cases, automakers encouraged antiblack strikes. An October 1941 antiblack strike at a Packard plant illustrates this point. This strike arose after the federal government ordered the union and company to transfer two blacks from an automobile plant to metal polishing jobs in a tank factory. In protest of the black workers' arrival, 250 white metal polishers sat down on the job. In a negotiating session between Packard's industrial relations manager, C. E. Weiss, and the FEPC caseworker, J. W. Duncan, the Packard manager insisted that metal polishing was a "white man's job" (Meier and Rudwick 1981, p. 129). This attitude was typical among leaders of the automobile producers. It encouraged subsequent hate strikes, as 25,000 Packard workers struck in 1943.

The point is that the corporate elite played the dominant role in placing black workers in a subordinate position in the automobile industry. Studies in other industries make the same point. For example, Greer's (1979) study of the steel industry underscored the role of corporate executives in subordinating the black worker. Before World War I, southern steel producers hired blacks, even in some skilled foundry jobs, primarily because of the difficulty of hiring whites. White labor was in low supply in the South, and few whites were attracted to the foundry jobs because of the high morbidity and mortality rates. Northern steel-producers initially excluded blacks but were pressured to hire them because of labor shortages brought on by the war. In the great steel strike of 1919, northern steel producers exported large numbers of black steel workers from the South to use as strike breakers (Reich 1981, pp. 255-56). However, throughout the 1920s and 1930s, northern steel producers deliberately restricted the proportion of blacks hired and excluded blacks from skilled jobs. Consequently, the proportion of black steelworkers employed in the skilled trades declined in this industry between 1920 and 1928 from 30% to 20% (Greer 1979, p. 39). Specifically, he said, "Negroes are nice, simple people. I don't approve of using them for skilled work—not that they couldn't do it, but we have enough competition within the skilled group. Let the Negroes scramble for the unskilled jobs" (quoted from Greer, p. 87).

Corporate leaders generally saw blacks as more suitable for the heavier, dirtier, hotter jobs. For example, Foner (1982, p. 133) cited the superintendent of a Kentucky plow factory who said in 1919, "Negroes do work white men won't do, such as common labor; heavy, hot, and dirty work; pouring crucibles; work in the grinding room; and so on." Foner (p. 133) quoted a foreman in a Pennsylvania steel mill who said, in the same year,

> They [blacks] are well fitted for this hot work, and we keep them because we appreciate this ability in them. . . . The door machines and the jam cutting are the most undesirable; it is hard to get white men to do this kind of work.

In some cases, industrialists deliberately excluded blacks from skilled jobs, even during World War II, when the need for black labor was the greatest. Some of these elites preferred to limit war production rather than hire blacks in skilled positions. This extreme form of racial exclusion was most evident in the aircraft factories and the shipbuilding industries. Foner (1982, p. 238), for example, quoted the president of the North American Aviation Company: "While we are in complete sympathy for the Negro; it is against company policy to employ them as aircraft workers or mechanics . . . regardless of their training. . . . There will be some jobs as janitors for Negroes." Foner noted that the shipyard companies in several southern cities—Houston, Galveston, Mobile, New Orleans, and Tampa—advertised in local newspapers for white youths and white women to train as welders and work in the shipyards. These companies were in desperate need of laborers. However, when the FEPC suggested that they hire already trained black welders, the company claimed that they did not need the workers. Foner (1982, p. 243) concluded that the companies were so adamant in their racially exclusionary policy that they kept production down just to avoid hiring blacks. This racially exclusionary behavior of corporate leaders produced the racially stratified labor force and subordinated black workers.

CLASS, RACE, SPACE, AND INDUSTRIAL CAPITALISM

Another factor reinforcing the racial caste system was space. Patterns of racial and class segregation in urban space augmented the caste system in industrial labor, weakened the labor movement, strengthened race consciousness, and reinforced the racial order. At the same time, these patterns were products of the expansion of industrial capitalism, as different spatial configurations corresponded to different stages of capitalist development. Segregation was nonexistent in the precapitalist city. Class segregation appeared in the 19th-century industrial city. Extreme racial and class segregation arose with the 20th-century industrial city.

Integrated Space and the Precapitalist City

The preindustrial commercial city was small in size and population as transportation technology was primitive and the predominant mode of production was agriculture. During this period (precolonial to 1860), farming was the dominant economic activity and about 90% of the population lived in rural areas. It was only after 1840 that the urban population exceeded 10% of the total national population (Judd 1979, p. 16). Judd described the commercial city as a walking city. Everything—workshops, stores, banks, bars, homes, and so on—was within walking distance from the center of town (p. 18).

In this city, the workplace was near to or inside the place of residence (Katznelson 1981). Shopkeepers, blacksmiths, merchants—all tended to live in or near their place of work. Small manufacturing production tended to be carried out by extended families or in small shops by a few workers who engaged in every stage of production from planning to finished product.

Although a class and racial caste system existed in this city, housing was integrated. This integration arose partially from the small size of the city and partially from the close proximity between place of residence and place of work. In the port city, black and white dockworkers lived in the same neighborhoods close to the dock. In the antebellum South, black servants, slave or free, often lived in the alleys or side streets near their employers (Kusmer 1976; Massey and Denton 1993). Southern whites intentionally dispersed urban slaves to prevent the formation of cohesive black organizations (Massey and Denton, p. 24). Although identifiable black sections existed in some cities, such as Chicago, Cincinnati, Cleveland, Detroit, Philadelphia, or New York, throughout the 19th century, these neighborhoods tended to be in several clusters throughout the city; most blacks lived in integrated neighborhoods (Kusmer 1976; Fusfeld and Bates 1984; Massey and Denton).

Segregation and the 19th-Century Industrial City

The revolution in industry and transportation profoundly changed the structure of urban space. The Industrial Revolution required and attracted a massive labor force located near production facilities, thus stimulating an exponential growth in the population of cities. The invention of the omnibus, the steam engine, the electric trolley, and later the internal combustion engine liberated people from the center of town and allowed them to move outward. This transportation revolution, combined with the population explosion, produced massive spatial growth. Indeed, these revolutions transformed a rural country into an urban one within 60 years, as the total population went from 20% urban in 1860 to more than 50% urban by 1920 (Judd 1979, p. 16).

These changes in the late 19th-century industrial city contributed to the formation of class segregation. In this city, factories were located in the core of the city near railroads and waterways. Densely populated working-class housing districts grew around the factories. Middle-class and upper-class residents moved to the outskirts of the city, pushed out by the congestion and unpleasant features of the inner ring and attracted by the pleasant surroundings of the outer rings (Gordon 1978, p. 43; Judd 1979; Jones 1983). Once outside the city, well-to-do neighbors excluded those from the classes below them, especially the working and lower classes. This exclusion created class segregation.

The ethnically identifiable neighborhood was another feature of the 19-century industrial city. This feature resulted primarily from the exclusionary practices of WASPs and from the role of local machines in steering newly arrived immigrants into ethnic enclaves. Of course, the desire of immigrants to locate in familiar communities also contributed to the formation of ethnic neighborhoods. More than 33.5 million European immigrants entered the United States in waves between 1820 and 1920. First came the British, Irish, and Germans, from 1820 to 1860, joined by the Scandinavians between 1860 and 1890; later came the Italians and then the Eastern Europeans from 1890 to 1920 (Judd 1979, p. 28).

The ethnic enclaves of the 19th century were different from the racial ghettos of the 20th century. Although new immigrants faced prejudice and harassment that kept them in their areas, ethnically identifiable neighborhoods were transitory. They functioned as way stations for the new immigrants on their journey to assimilation in American society. As immigrants became Americanized, they moved out of the ethnic enclaves. Moreover, ethnic ghettos were never homogeneous even though particular areas of the city were associated with a particular ethnic group. For example, in the area of Chicago called Little Italy, in 1890, there was not a single block in which every family was Italian. By 1930, the Irish section of Chicago contained only 3% of the city's Irish population; the Italian section contained 50% of the city's Italian population; and the Polish section contained 61% of the city's Polish population (Massey and Denton 1993). In contrast, the 20th-century racial ghetto was permanent, with impenetrable invisible walls. Moreover, in this century, most blacks lived in predominantly black neighborhoods. For example, by 1930 the black section of Chicago contained 93% of the city's black population (Clark 1965; Massey and Denton 1993).

Hyper-Segregation and the 20th-Century City

The 20th-century industrial city was one of hyper-class and hyper-racial segregation. Suburbanization enhanced class divisions in urban space. Violence, government action, and institutional practices produced racially homogeneous ghettos.

Suburbanization and Hyper-Class Segregation

Suburban cities began to proliferate just after corporations started to move their production facilities outside the city. These corporations were attracted to suburban areas because of the cheaper land. For example, in 1890, land in downtown Chicago cost about $3.5 million per acre compared to about $175 per acre in the suburbs (Greer 1979, pp. 54-56). Corporate elites also saw the construction of industrial suburbs as a way of reducing labor unrest (Ashton 1978; Gordon 1978; Greer). Examples of these suburbs include cities such as East St. Louis, Gary, River Rouge, and many others.

According to Greer (1979), engineers for U.S. Steel worked with city engineers to design Gary, Indiana. In this city, corporate engineers built housing for both its managerial staff and its skilled workers. The unskilled workers lived primarily in boardinghouses and apartment complexes. This housing pattern placed the skilled workers in a privileged position of home ownership, and it segregated them from the unskilled workers. It encouraged skilled workers to identify more with capital than with labor. This pattern of segregating skilled labor from unskilled labor in urban space and granting the privilege of homeownership to skilled workers was common in other metropolitan areas. It divided the working class. Moreover, it enhanced status and race consciousness among skilled workers as they identified more with higher status whites than with lower status workers, especially black workers.

The movement of industries to the suburbs accelerated the process of segregating metropolitan areas. Corporations joined other groups—upper-class residents, developers, the real estate industry—in demanding new state laws disallowing annexation and allowing the incorporation of suburban areas. This political movement led to the creation of suburban cities. Not only were industrial suburbs created, but affluent residential suburbs proliferated as well.

The incorporation of an affluent suburban city gave its residents greater control over land use and building codes. These affluent suburban towns enacted zoning and building policies designed to permit the construction of homes affordable only to the most affluent families (Danielson 1976). These policies included regulations prohibiting the creation of apartment complexes, building codes setting square footage limits on new houses so high that only the most expensive homes were built, and zoning laws creating lots so large that only the wealthy could afford to purchase land in the area (Danielson). These policies guaranteed that suburban towns would develop into affluent enclaves, separated from the working class both by distance and by government. We call this type of spatial division *hyper-class segregation.*

Hyper-Racial Segregation

Hyper-racial segregation emerged in the 20th century simultaneously with hyper-class segregation. This new, more intense form of racial segregation was imposed by violence and maintained by private institutional practices and government action.

A brief period of race liberalism existed between 1865 and 1885. Northern states such as Michigan, New York, and Ohio had civil rights laws that prohibited racial segregation and discrimination. Detroit had integrated schools. Black ghettos were practically nonexistent (Katzman 1975; also see Wilson 1980). Racial segregation in public accommodations emerged in the northern cities in the late 1880s, as the U.S. Supreme Court hacked away at federal civil rights laws and as northern state courts followed the federal example.

Racial segregation in residential areas emerged in the early 20th century, with the mass exodus of blacks from the South to the North. Blacks migrated from the South to northern cities in waves, beginning in 1900 and continuing throughout the century. Between 1900 and 1910 close to 200,000 blacks left the South for northern cities (Wilson 1980, p. 66; Massey and Denton 1993, p. 29). This number increased to about 525,000 between 1910 and 1920, and to about 875,000 during the 1920s (Wilson, p. 66; Massey and Denton, p. 29).

The black population in northern cities exploded in growth. Between 1910 and 1920, this population increased by 611.3% in Detroit, 307.8% in Cleveland, 148.2% in Chicago, and 1,283.6% in Gary (Fusfeld and Bates 1984, p. 26). In New York City, the black population increased by about 66%, from 91,709 in 1910 to 152,467 in 1920. This trend slowed in the 1930s but continued throughout the 1940s, 1950s, and 1960s. For example, Detroit's black population increased from 5,741 in 1910 to 40,838 in 1920; to 120,066 in 1930; to 149,119 in 1940; and to 300,506 in 1950.

Mechanism of Racial Segregation: Violence

Segregation was initially imposed on blacks by violence, as they began to pour into the city in the early part of the century. This violence arose for many reasons, some of which we already discussed—immigrants scorned by WASPs acquired a sense of white consciousness and black contempt; white-conscious workers developed a fear that blacks would take their jobs during strikes or undercut white wages; whites learned to use blacks as the lightning rod of whites' fears, frustrations, and anger; whites feared that blacks would encroach on white urban space, crowd white neighborhoods, and erode white status; whites feared that blacks would breed crime and vice. Regardless of the reasons for the violence, it functioned to force blacks into black neighborhoods. Blacks in all-white areas were often harassed or assaulted. Riots broke out in a number of cities between 1900 and 1920: New York City in 1900, Springfield, Illinois, in 1908; East St. Louis, Illinois, in 1917, Chicago in 1919. Blacks isolated in white neighborhoods were most vulnerable in these riots. Many blacks outside designated black areas saw their homes burned; they were beaten, shot, or lynched (Massey and Denton 1993).

Another form of violence more directly related to efforts to segregate blacks was bombing. This form of violence occurred frequently during and just after World War I. In Chicago between 1917 and 1921, 58 homes of black families were bombed because these families attempted to move into white neighborhoods (Tuttle 1982). Sometimes the homes of the real estate agents were bombed because agents sold a house to a black family in a white area. Bombings occurred in other cities, notably in Cleveland and Detroit.

Neighborhood improvement associations often were formed in white areas to organize efforts to exclude blacks. In many cases, the association would attempt to reason with black family members, to persuade them to move from the white area. Sometimes the association would raise money to purchase the home of the black family. When persuasion or money failed, these associations often turned to violence. In some cases, they paid agents to bomb the home. Often angry white mobs would gather in front of the black home in the white neighborhood. Sometimes these mobs would vandalize or burn down the house, forcing the black family to move.

Violence had some drawbacks. It sometimes led to arrests, lawsuits, or deaths. For example, in Chicago, in 1919, J. Yarbrough, a black property owner, sued—unsuccessfully, however—a neighborhood association when his apartment complex was bombed. Just before the bombing, leaders of the Chicago Hyde Park-Kenwood Association—some of whom were real estate agents who owned extensive property in the area and who insisted that black families depreciated property in the area—had threatened to bomb the homes of blacks living in the Hyde Park-Kenwood neighborhood. A suspect in the bombing of Yarbrough's apartment was an employee in the Dean and Meagher real estate firm. Dean, a leader of the association, paid the bail of the suspected bomber (Tuttle 1982, p. 178). It was this connection between the suspected bomber and the association that led Yarbrough to sue the association. Yarbrough lost.

In another case, a white male was shot and killed in Detroit in the fall of 1925 during a melee between a black family and a white mob as the black family attempted to move into an all-white area. A black doctor, Ossian Sweet, had armed himself, along with a few friends and relatives, because he expected that a white mob would attack his family and home. This expectation arose from his awareness of Ku Klux Klan rallies in Detroit the summer before the melee. At these rallies, the Klan had urged whites to form white neighborhood associations to fight to keep blacks out of white areas (Katzman 1975; Geschwender 1979, pp. 64-65).

Violence as a method of excluding blacks continued intermittently throughout the century, although it subsided as new, more subtle, but effective and systematic forms of racial discrimination emerged. These new forms involved both the public and the private sectors.

The Role of Government and Private Institutions in Sustaining Housing Segregation

Government became involved in racial segregation in the early part of the century. Between 1910 and 1916, several local governments passed racial segregation zoning laws. These laws established white zones and black zones. Blacks were mandated by law to live in the black-zoned section, and they were prohibited from moving into the white section. Of course, racial zoning laws were ruled unconstitutional in *Buchanan v. Warley* (1917).

Local governments participated in creating and maintaining segregation in other ways. Often local police departments refused to protect black families attempting to move into white areas or to adequately investigate cases of white violence calculated to expel blacks from white areas.

The private sector also operated to maintain racial segregation in housing. In her study of housing discrimination in Chicago, Rose Helper

(1969) identified 26 different methods employed by real estate agents to exclude blacks from white areas. These methods ranged from blatant refusal to show blacks homes in white neighborhoods, to denying (to blacks) that any homes were available in white areas. One common practice has been the use of double listing—one list for blacks for homes in black areas and another for whites for homes in white areas. The real estate agent would show black families only the listings in black areas. Another has been steering: showing blacks homes only in black or mixed areas in the process of becoming predominantly black. Steering and double listing have been common throughout the 20th century (Feagin and Feagin 1986; Tobin 1987; Massey and Denton 1993).

For the first half of the century, restrictive covenants were common. This device, often created by local real estate boards, was part of the deed. It obligated the homeowner to sell the home to a white family and forbade the owner from selling to a black or another nonwhite family. In the *Shelley v. Kraemer* (1948) decision, the U.S. Supreme Court ruled that state and federal governments were constitutionally bound not to honor or enforce restrictive covenants. This decision did not make the covenant illegal. It simply ordered the government not to enforce the covenant. These covenants did not disappear as private parties continued to honor them even without government enforcement.

Real estate agents have employed blockbusting as both a money-making scheme and a racially discriminatory device. In blockbusting, real estate agents tell whites in an area adjacent to a black neighborhood that whites should sell their homes quickly and cheaply because blacks are about to move in and take over. After frightening whites into selling cheaply, the agents increase the price of the homes and sell them to blacks. This process maintained segregation and yielded a huge profit for the industry (Feagin and Feagin 1986).

Real estate boards—local and national—were committed to maintaining racial segregation. This commitment has been expressed in the personal views of real estate agents and in the industry's published code of ethics. In her survey of the opinions of real estate agents, Helper (1969) found that 65% believe that the inclusion of a black family was detrimental to white neighborhoods. More than 90% sympathized with a philosophy of racial exclusion.

The code of ethics of this industry committed its members and agents to the preservation of separate white and black neighborhoods. Helper (1969, p. 201) cited the Code of Ethics of the National Association of Real Estate Brokers, which said, "A Realtor should never be instrumental in introducing into a neighborhood . . . members of any race or nationality . . . whose presence will clearly be detrimental to property values in that neighborhood." This code remained in effect until 1950 (Massey and Denton 1993).

The federal government became involved in the racial segregation business during the New Deal era, especially with the creation of the Federal Housing Administration (FHA). This agency, created in the mid-1930s, mirrored the racial code of ethics of the real estate industry. Throughout the 1930s and 1940s, the FHA explicitly promoted racial segregation in housing (Danielson 1976; Bullock and Lamb 1984; Feagin and Feagin 1986). This agency instructed its officials to investigate

> areas surrounding the location to determine whether or not incompatible racial and social groups are present, to the end that an intelligent prediction may be made regarding the possibility or probability of the location being invaded by such groups. If a neighborhood is to retain stability, it is necessary that properties shall continue to be occupied by the same social and racial classes. A change in social or racial occupancy generally leads to instability and a reduction in values. (quoted in Danielson 1976, p. 203)

These processes produced impenetrable walls of racial segregation in cities (Clark 1965). These walls were maintained by the real estate industry, federal agencies, white neighborhood associations, and individual white homeowners. Moreover, with the acceleration of the suburbanization movement after World War II, especially during the 1950s and 1960s, metropolitan areas became completely fragmented and segregated along class and racial lines.

Unskilled working class, white working class, black working class, skilled and professional, upper middle class, upper class, and other class and caste categories were segregated on the spatial plane. Within this plane, upper stratum white labor moved closer to white capital. White industrial workers living in a white area acquired special social status in their segregation from black workers. Moreover, white workers could maintain this status by keeping blacks out of white neighborhoods. This spatial arrangement augmented racial differences, widened the gulf between the black and the white worker, heightened race consciousness, and weakened class consciousness. This arrangement weakened the labor movement as a force for racial equality.

Despite this crippling effect of racial segregation in metropolitan areas, some progress was made in the political struggle for civil rights. Civil rights groups were able to get some support, however small, from the presidency and the Supreme Court. Congress remained committed to preserving the existing order, until the mid-1960s. Overall, the state played a paradoxical role in the area of civil rights.

THE PARADOXICAL ROLE OF THE STATE

For the most part, the struggle for racial equality in the workplace was carried on both within the industries and within the political arena. In this struggle, the national government was like a divided and contested battleground. Civil rights groups fought hard to hold on to small tracts of land in the valley while upper stratum labor, corporations, planters, and other more powerful groups held the high ground and considerable territory. The net outcome of this struggle was a government that played a shifting role in racial matters. In some areas and some periods, the government operated to legitimize and sustain racial caste arrangements. In other areas and other times, government challenged these arrangements and promoted racial equality. This role emerged out of a fragmented governmental structure, sensitive to interest-group pressure although biased in favor of upper stratum interests.

Progress in Civil Rights: Roosevelt and the Courts

On the positive side of the government score card, President Franklin D. Roosevelt and the courts began to take action against the racial caste system. Roosevelt was the first president in the 20th century who attempted to use the federal government to ameliorate racial oppression. No doubt the threat of a massive march on the nation's capital organized by A. Philip Randolph, the growth of black voting strength in northern cities, and the sensitivities of key advisors, such as Eleanor Roosevelt, to racial injustice, all influenced the direction of this administration.

President Roosevelt made a number of decisions and instituted several programs calculated to attack the race issue. He created a "Black Cabinet" to advise him on racial matters. He appointed Mary McLeod Bethune to this cabinet and to an advisory committee for the National Youth Administration.

In 1941, Roosevelt issued Executive Order 8802, which enjoined unions and employers to "provide for the equitable participation of all workers without discrimination because of race, creed, or color" (quoted in Hill 1985, p. 179). This order established the FEPC, charged with the responsibility of investigating complaints of violations against this order and of obtaining compliance through public exposure and persuasion. In extreme cases, the commission relied on the support of the War Productions Board and the War Labor Board to secure compliance. In 1943, with Executive Order 9346, Roosevelt expanded the purview of the FEPC to nondefense industries affecting the national interest.

Although the commission's powers were weak compared to those granted to other independent commissions—it did not have the power to issue cease and desist orders like the NLRB—it was relatively effective in securing the promotion of blacks into many skilled positions. Blacks made their greatest strides during the war years, with an expanding economy, the support of progressive industrial unions, and the aid of the FEPC.

Roosevelt had a profound effect on the makeup of the U.S. Supreme Court, as he appointed eight justices during his three terms. This Court radically changed government's role in protecting racially oppressive arrangements. Between 1938 and 1958, the Court issued a series of decisions that eroded the separate but equal doctrine of *Plessy v. Ferguson* (1896).

In *Missouri ex rel. Gaines v. Canada* (1938), the Court struck down a Missouri law that prohibited blacks from attending state-funded law schools, even though the state provided money for blacks to attend law schools in other states. The Court ruled that the state had violated the equal protection clause of the 14th Amendment by failing to provide a law school for blacks. In the 1950 *Sweatt v. Painter* case, the Court ruled that even a separate law school for blacks violated the equal protection clause. The Court argued that a separate black law school denied blacks intangible benefits such as contact with full-time law professors who were well connected in the legal community, access to the state's best law library, and association with the distinguished reputation of the all-white law school. In this decision, the court ruled—without overturning *Plessy*—that segregated law schools were inherently unequal. In the 1954-1955 *Brown v. Board of Education* decisions, the Court struck down the separate but equal doctrine established in *Plessy,* found state-mandated segregated schools in violation of the 14th Amendment, and ordered southern schools to desegregate with all deliberate speed.

This Court moved further to limit the power of states to protect the racial caste system in *Smith v. Allwright* (1944) and *Shelley v. Kraemer* (1948). In *Smith,* the Court decided that white primaries that excluded black voters violated the 15th Amendment. The *Shelley* case, discussed above, addressed the legality of restrictive covenants—homeowner deeds that prohibited the bearer from selling the home to blacks, Jews, or others. The Court prohibited states from enforcing these deeds; however, it did not outlaw them, and their use continued.

The presidency and the Courts made important advancements in the promotion of racial equality in the labor market, in education, and in the political arena. However, these advancements were limited and even contradicted by state action from other governmental agencies and institutions. No doubt the resurgence of capital, the influence of southern segregationists, and the weakening of labor influenced this regressive side of government.

Setbacks in Civil Rights:
Congress, Truman, and Federal Agencies

On the negative side of the government score card, several factors hamstrung state actions in support of racial equality: the short duration of the FEPC; the role of the NLRB in legitimizing racially exclusionary labor unions; the passage of the Taft-Hartley Act of 1946, which weakened the power of labor; the McCarthy movement, which tended to combine anti-civil rights with anti-Communist sentiments; the U.S. Congress, with a block of southern segregationists; and a Court constrained by public opinion.

The FEPC was abolished in 1946. It was killed by both the president and Congress. Problems arose before the end of World War II, particularly after the FEPC began investigating other federal agencies such as the U.S. Employment Services, the Veterans Employment Services, and the Office of Vocational Rehabilitation (Reed 1991, p. 322). The Roosevelt administration had already attempted to muzzle the FEPC because it found a number of federal, state, and local agencies guilty of discrimination. In 1945, a major dispute erupted between President Truman and the FEPC over its investigation of the Capital Transit Company in Washington, D.C. The FEPC found this company guilty of racial discrimination and was about to issue a public announcement of its findings. President Truman, who had used federal troops to operate the transit system after transit workers walked off their jobs over a wage dispute, ordered the FEPC not to make this announcement. Apparently, Truman did not want to be in the position of using federal troops to enforce an antidiscrimination recommendation from the FEPC. The chair of the FEPC resigned in protest of

Truman's order. Congress cut the funding for this agency at the end of 1945 and terminated the commission the following year. However, before it died, the FEPC issued a report on the resurgence of racial exclusion. It reported on hundreds of cases of blacks being laid off as industries scaled down for peacetime production. It listed numerous cases of firms sending requests to the U.S. Employment Service for whites only (Reed 1991, p. 330). The elimination of the FEPC was a substantial setback in government efforts to protect blacks from racial exclusion or discrimination in key job areas.

Other federal agencies and programs that legitimized or promoted racially discriminatory practices included the NLRB, the FHA, and various job training and social welfare programs. The NLRB, supported by organized labor, routinely certified craft unions with a long history of racially exclusionary practices. Civil rights groups challenged this NLRB policy on grounds that it functioned to promote and legalize a racial caste labor system that excluded blacks from higher level jobs. In response to this challenge, the NLRB invariably maintained that neither racial exclusion nor racial segregation violated fair labor laws. For example, Hill (1985, p. 119) cited a 1945 NLRB ruling stating that "neither exclusion from membership nor segregated membership per se represents evasion on the part of a labor organization of its statutory duty to afford equal representation." This NLRB position generated tensions between upper level labor, which benefited most from this policy, and civil rights groups. Hill noted that it was not until 1962 that the NLRB threatened to decertify a union for racial exclusion.

Other governmental agencies and programs involved in promoting racial discrimination included the FHA and the Public Housing Authority. These agencies were directly involved in promoting and maintaining racial segregation in housing, a point we investigate more carefully in the next section. Most federal programs in the South administered through state and county agencies engaged in some form of racial discrimination up until the passage of the 1964 Civil Rights Act. For example, county-administered Aid to Dependent Children (ADC) programs in the South routinely excluded blacks (Piven and Cloward 1972).

A bloc of southern Democrats committed to racial segregation was a serious weakness in the New Deal coalition and a major obstruction to the passage of any civil rights legislation. This coalition began to split at the seams with the slightest display of support for African Americans by the Roosevelt administration. For example, when Roosevelt chose a black minister to give the invocation and a black Congressman to deliver the opening address at the 1936 Democratic party National Convention, a number of southern congressmen protested. Senator Ellison Smith of Georgia stormed out of the convention. Smith said that he would never support "any political organization that looks upon the Negro and caters to him as a political and social equal" (quoted in Sitkoff 1978, p. 94). He added, "The doors of the white man's party have been thrown open to snare the Negro vote in the North. Political equality means social equality, and social equality means intermarriage, and that means mongrelizing of the American race" (p. 109). Supporting Smith, Senator Carter Glass of Virginia stated, "To any discerning person, it is perfectly obvious that the so-called Democratic party of the North is now the negro party, advocating actual social equality for the races" (quoted in Sitkoff, p. 109).

Southern congressional opposition to the New Deal became more vociferous as Roosevelt supported more substantive civil rights policies, such as anti-poll tax and antilynching laws. Although a Senate filibuster killed these bills, they provoked a stream of racist tirades from southern segregationists. For example, in 1938, following the defeat of the Wagner-Costigan antilynching act, Senator Bilbo lectured the Senate on the inferiority of blacks, the benefits of race consciousness, and the need to maintain race purity. Bilbo, an admirer of Hitler, introduced bills to deport all African Americans to Liberia (Sitkoff 1978, p. 117).

With few exceptions, southern congressmen denounced Roosevelt for alienating the South by supporting civil rights legislation linked to pro-labor and pro-black forces (Sitkoff 1978, p. 118). In the same year (1938) Congressman Martin Dies, chair of the House Committee on Un-American Activities, began to associate labor and civil rights leaders with Communists. Although this committee was established to investigate the possibility that agents from fascist European governments were operating in the United States or collaborating with American citizens, Dies used this committee to attack pro-labor, pro-civil rights, and pro-New Deal forces. Dies attacked the New Deal for spending too much, for going too far, and "for playing Santa Claus and wet nurse for every local community" (Sitkoff, p. 119). Conservative southern congressmen engaged in both race-baiting and red-baiting in their efforts to defeat the nascent civil rights, social welfare, and pro-labor proposals of the Roosevelt administration. Of course, the few liberal southern congressmen, such as Claude Pepper, vigorously and courageously criticized southerners for supporting segregation.

Because of the absence of party competition in the Deep South, Democratic candidates faced no opposition. Consequently, incumbent southern congressmen were ensured reelection (see Key 1984). Thus, southern Democrats stayed in office longer than the average congressmen. Because the chairships of key congressional committees tended to be awarded on the basis of seniority and because southerners tended to have higher seniority, they dominated the chairships of key committees. They used their positions to kill civil rights legislation.

INDUSTRIAL CAPITALISM AND AVERSIVE RACISM

The milieu of industrial capitalism produced a new form of racism, aversive racism, different from the dominative racism of the South. The dominative racism of the South involved the direct control and regulation of black life by white masters and landowners. It included white enforcement of a racial etiquette designed to subordinate and humiliate blacks daily in their contact with whites. It entailed whites acting directly to exploit blacks, to control their lives, and to deny them basic rights and freedoms such as the right to vote and the freedom to move freely from one area to another without permission.

Blacks enjoyed more freedom under industrial capitalism and aversive racism. They were free to vote, free to move to another city without permission from a white landlord, and free to enter into contracts honored and enforced by the state. Most of all, they were free to sell their labor for wages on an open market. Nevertheless, industrial capitalism contained exploitative and oppressive features that undergirded aversive racism. These features included the exploitation of labor, the concentration of wealth in the hands of a few, extreme inequality, class conflict, periodic crisis, the creation of stratified labor forces, and a system that thrived with a reserve army of labor. Aversive racism emerged out of these features of capitalism.

There have been many aspects of aversive racism. One aspect has entailed the overrepresentation of blacks in the reserve army of labor—the concentration of blacks in the least desirable jobs and the exclusion of blacks from preferred, high skilled jobs. The construction of these arrangements involved the structural features of industrial capitalism as well as the actions of leaders of corporations and of craft unions. These leaders created and maintained a stratified labor market that relegated blacks to the lowest strata and crowded them into the reserve army of labor.

Another aspect of aversive racism has been racial and class segregation in metropolitan areas. This segregation emerged with industrial capitalism as industrial expansion precipitated the growth of urban areas and as actors and agencies operated to segregate these areas. The entire real estate industry, developers, local governments, public officials, neighborhood associations, white residents, corporate leaders, and other agents collectively contributed to the construction and maintenance of class and racial segregation in residential areas. Racial segregation in urban areas became a prominent feature of aversive racism. This segregation further enhanced race consciousness, weakened working-class consciousness, and obstructed the formation of interracial working-class solidarity. Once established, this racial segregation persisted throughout the 20th century.

Another aspect of aversive racism entailed psychocultural processes that contributed to the formation of white identity and antiblack hostility. Various agents of this culture—the church, the local political party, the media, schools, public agencies, and others—operated to instill a sense of white identity and white superiority among European Americans. In some cases, this culture involved sadomasochistic processes that reinforced identification with the dominant white group and encouraged the abuse and humiliation of blacks.

The state played a paradoxical role in sustaining the racism of this period. On the negative side of the ledger, it did little to ameliorate even the most extreme forms of racial oppression, such as lynching in the South. The FHA promoted housing segregation. The NLRB certified labor unions with constitutions barring blacks. The Dixiecrats who dominated congressional committees operated to obstruct the passage of any civil rights or antilynching laws. In 1946, Harry Truman eliminated the FEPC. On the positive side, during World War II, the FEPC fought against racial discrimination in the defense industry. Between the late 1930s and the early 1970s, from *Missouri ex rel.* (1938), through *Smith v. Allwright* (1944) to *Brown v. Board of Education* (1954/1955) and beyond, the U.S. Supreme Court rendered a string of decisions that gradually expanded civil rights. These cases chipped away at racially oppressive arrangements. By the mid-1960s, the national government began to use the full weight of its power against some of the most egregious aspects of these oppressive arrangements.

7

Advanced Capitalism and Meta-Racism (1970 to the Present)

The two systems of racism—aversive and dominative aversive—existed side by side, in the same time period (1870 to 1965), although they were rooted in different modes of production. Aversive racism was grounded in industrial capitalism, prevalent in the North. Dominative aversive racism existed in the predominantly agricultural and nascent industrial economic system of the South. Nevertheless, by 1970 dominative aversive racism was dead and aversive racism was metamorphosing into a new form of racism—meta-racism.

Changes in agricultural production and the civil rights movement destroyed the southern system of racism. Mechanization in agriculture atrophied the economic base of dominative racism and provided the structural basis for a stronger, more successful civil rights movement. This movement killed the old dominative aversive racism of the South. It fiercely attacked aversive racism, alleviated racial oppression, and contributed to improved life chances for African Americans. However, this movement did not eliminate racism, root and branch.

For several reasons, aversive racism survived the civil rights movement. First, the movement was limited. It succeeded in some areas, partially succeeded in some, and failed in others. Second, racial segregation in metropolitan areas and racial discrimination in labor markets persisted in the post-civil rights era.

Third, the exploitative features of industrial capitalism did not disappear. They changed as the old industrial economy transformed into an advanced form of capitalism, as the Fordist period gave way to a post-Fordist era, as fixed capital yielded to a new milieu of flexible capital, as homogenous labor organization gave way to segmented labor markets, and as other new forms of exploiting labor replaced the old forms. These changes contributed to the erosion of working-class wages, the contraction of labor unions, the growth of extreme disparities between the rich and the poor, and the marginalization of industrial workers, especially black industrial workers. These economic changes, combined with the persistence of labor market discrimination and housing segregation, produced a new form of racial oppression, characterized by declining rates of labor force participation among black males, by disproportionately higher levels of black unemployment and black poverty, and by black poverty substantially concentrated in inner cities.

Fourth, the forces that benefited from aversive racism regrouped, reorganized, and counterattacked. These forces reformulated old racist theories and created a new racial ideology justifying the new racial order. Several politicians exploited and popularized the new racial ideology.

Finally, these political and economic changes produced a new culture of racism—meta-racism. Although meta-racism contained many elements of older forms of racism, it was a more advanced, rationalized, and bureaucratized form of racism.

In this chapter, we examine these issues in greater detail:

1. The change in southern agriculture and the structural basis of the civil rights movement
2. The limits of civil rights and the persistence of racial discrimination
3. Advanced capitalism and the persistence of racial oppression
4. The counterattack from the right and the reformulation of racial ideology
5. The culture of meta-racism

These factors explain the transformation of aversive racism into meta-racism and the persistence of racism throughout the last quarter of the 20th century.

THE CHANGE IN SOUTHERN AGRICULTURE AND THE STRUCTURAL BASIS OF THE CIVIL RIGHTS MOVEMENT

Planters' need for black labor, the economic basis of dominative aversive racism, had been declining throughout the 20th century, first with catastrophes in cotton production and later with mechanization in farming. In the first quarter of the 20th century, the boll weevil decimated cotton crops, and cotton prices fell sharply. Consequently, planters were compelled to reduce cotton production and shift to other cash crops requiring fewer farm workers. With this shift, hundreds and thousands of blacks left the plantations for the cities. In the first two decades of the century, about 844,000 nonwhites left 11 ex-Confederate southeastern states (Wilson 1980, p. 71). Most were bound for the urban areas of the North. This figure increased to 926,000 for the 1920s (Wilson, p. 71).

Mechanization in farm production pushed blacks off the land at a more accelerated rate, especially between 1940 and 1970. In the 1940s, about 1.5 million nonwhites left these same states, followed by another 1.4 million in the 1950s (Wilson 1980, p. 71). By 1970, tractors, chemical herbicides, and cotton-picking machines had replaced black farm workers, in a once labor-intensive and most oppressive mode of farm production. At the same time, blacks become urbanized. In 1900, close to 80% of the black population lived in rural areas; by 1970, more than 80% lived in urban areas (Wilson, p. 71). The economic base of the old southern system of racism was gone.

Black urbanization not only contributed to the demise of dominative racism, it created a stronger foundation for the civil rights movement. Urbanization meant that black families would no longer be isolated in rural areas directly under the control of planters. The concentration of blacks in the cities made mass organizing easier. The movement of blacks into industrial jobs in the cities also provided a link between the industrial labor movement and the civil rights movement. The increasing number of black workers put pressure on industrial unions to campaign against racism and for interracial labor solidarity (see Chapter 6 and Bloom 1987). In response to this campaign, civil rights groups supported industrial unions. In turn, industrial unions supported civil rights groups. Moreover, black union activists and labor leaders formed direct links between the two movements, as they participated in both.

A. Philip Randolph, the president of the Brotherhood of Sleeping Car Porters, epitomized this dual role of labor and civil rights leader. The president of the Montgomery, Alabama, local of the Brotherhood of Sleeping Car Porters was one of the leaders of the Montgomery bus boycotts in 1956 (Foner 1982, p. 316). Many of the founders of the Congress for Racial Equality, a civil rights organization formed in the 1940s, were initially union activists (Meier and Rudwick 1973, p. 6). This connection between labor and civil rights was critical during the height of the civil rights movement. For example, the United Packinghouse Workers contributed about $11,000 to the voters registration drive in the late 1950s (Foner, p. 316). The UAW contributed about $160,000 to the Southern Christian Leadership Conference (SCLC), just to assist with bail expenses during the 1963 Birmingham, Alabama, demonstrations (Flug 1987). The president of the UAW, Walter Reuther, and other labor leaders participated in the 1963 march on Washington.

Of course, black religious leaders and high school and college students played important roles in the success of this movement. Many civil rights leaders were religious leaders. Students invigorated the movement, especially as they engaged in sit-ins, freedom rides, marches, and demonstrations throughout the 1960s. Civil rights leaders such as Martin Luther King attempted to develop an alliance of religious, labor, and civil rights organizations. Of course, the labor-civil rights alliance had a weak link: race-conscious unions. As Chapter 6 illustrated, craft unions have a long history of racially exclusionary behavior, and they have long been opponents of civil rights policies. Throughout the late 1930s and the 1940s, the AFL had campaigned vigorously against efforts to give the National Labor Relations Board (NLRB) responsibility for prohibiting racial discrimination in employment (Foner 1982). Of course, in the merger agreement between the AFL and the CIO in the mid-1950s, the new AFL-CIO pledged its opposition to racial discrimination. Moreover, it established an AFL-CIO Committee on Civil Rights.

However, this pledge was vague and the Committee's actual commitment to racial equality was weak. Although the new AFL-CIO supported the enactment of civil rights laws in the late 1950s and early 1960s, it was reluctant to contribute direct support to civil rights organizations or to eliminate racial exclusion and segregation among its own affiliates. For example, the AFL-CIO supported the passage of the Civil Rights Act of 1957. In the same year, it admitted the Brotherhood of Locomotive Firemen and Enginemen and the Brotherhood of Railway Trainmen into the federation, both unions with constitutions that barred blacks from membership. Throughout the 1950s, the AFL-CIO expelled affiliates with corrupt or Communist leaders. At the same time, it refused to expel affiliates for practicing racial exclusion or segregation (Foner 1982, p. 322). The AFL-CIO supported the Civil Rights Act of 1964 and the Voting Rights Act of 1965. It did not support civil rights groups nor did it participate in the 1963 March on Washington.

Given craft unions' record of racial exclusion and the AFL-CIO's defense of these unions, conflicts between the AFL-CIO and civil rights groups were inevitable. Indeed, during the 1960s, civil rights groups, in their fight against racial exclusion in employment, often found themselves demonstrating against racially exclusionary craft unions. In 1961, the NAACP and the Negro American Labor Council (NALC) issued reports documenting antiblack practices of AFL-CIO-affiliated craft unions. These reports exacerbated tensions between the AFL-CIO and civil rights organizations, especially when George Meany, then president of the AFL-CIO, defended the affiliates and accused civil rights leaders of creating a gap between labor and civil rights (Foner 1982). This tenuous relationship between the AFL-CIO and civil rights groups created a fault line in the labor-civil rights coalition. This fault line explains the crack in the labor-civil rights coalition that appeared in the post-civil rights period.

THE LIMITS OF CIVIL RIGHTS AND THE PERSISTENCE OF DISCRIMINATION

Despite this weak link in the civil rights-labor coalition, the civil rights movement emerged as a powerful force for social and political change. It profoundly changed race thinking and race policies. It exorcised from the public mind the belief that blacks were biologically inferior to whites. It eliminated state-mandated segregation. It pulverized blatant forms of racial exclusion.

Moreover, this movement secured the passage of a range of new civil rights laws. Congress passed the Civil Rights Act of 1957, the first piece of civil rights legislation since the Reconstruction era. During the 1960s, Congress passed the Civil Rights Act of 1960, which allowed civil challenges to voting discrimination; the Civil Rights Act of 1964, which prohibited racial discrimination in public accommodations, employment, and programs receiving federal funds; the Voting Rights Act of 1965, which prohibited racial discrimination in voting and established a statistical guideline for finding counties guilty of this discrimination; and the Fair Housing Act of 1968, which prohibited housing discrimination.

A number of federal agencies were established with these laws: The Civil Rights Commission (1957); the Civil Rights Division of the Justice Department (1957); Office of Civil Rights (1964), located in the Department of Health, Education, and Welfare (now Health and Human Services); the Equal Employment Opportunity Commission (EEOC) (1964); the Office of Federal Contract Compliance Program (OFCCP), housed in the Department of Labor. These laws were complemented by a number of

Executive Orders. For example, Executive Order 11246, issued by President Johnson and implemented by the OFCCP, prohibited discrimination in agencies or businesses receiving federal contracts and required these contractors to take affirmative action in recruiting minority workers. In the mid-1970s, Congress required that 10% of the dollar value of federal contracts be set aside for minority contractors. Despite this impressive series of laws and majestic array of civil rights agencies, racial oppression persisted after the civil rights era.

There is nothing paradoxical about the persistence of racial oppression after the so-called civil rights revolution. The growth of concentrated black poverty after the passage of the most aggressive civil rights laws in American history is no mystery. It is not a matter of social class supplanting race as a major factor determining blacks' life chances nor is it the result of a mismatch between the level of education attained by inner-city blacks and the level of education required by the new jobs of the post-civil rights era, as a number of scholars such as Wilson (1980, 1987) and Kasarda (1985) have claimed. Concentrated black poverty arose in urban areas in the post-civil rights era for two primary reasons: Racial discrimination in housing and employment persisted, and exploitative and oppressive economic processes continued in this era.

Racial discrimination persisted in the post-civil rights era because civil rights policies were not successful in all areas. These policies succeeded in areas such as voting, public accommodations, and state-mandated segregation. They failed in the area of housing and achieved only modest success in employment. One reason for the mixed record of civil rights policies is that the movement succeeded in generating a cultural paradigm shift in some areas but failed to do so in others.

Paradigms and Effective Civil Rights Policies

One factor that has obstructed efforts to eliminate racial discrimination throughout the 20th century has been the dominance of a conservative discrimination paradigm. This paradigm focuses on explicit references to race. It uses a pure race test for discrimination. It looks for individual acts of discrimination, and it requires evidence of the deliberate intent to discriminate. Within the context of this paradigm, discrimination occurs when an identifiable prejudiced white individual intentionally excludes a black person, expressly on the basis of color. To demonstrate discrimination through this paradigm, one must identify this prejudiced individual, isolate the act of exclusion, find the victim, and prove that the exclusionary act was committed with the deliberate intent to exclude. In this paradigm, discrimination does not occur if race-neutral practices exclude blacks or if racial exclusion is mixed with class exclusion. That is, this paradigm could not imagine a literacy test violating the Constitution because it disenfranchised well over 95% of the black voting-age population if this test excluded low income whites as well and appeared to be race-neutral on the surface.

This paradigm's focus on explicit references to race allowed it to see the more blatant forms of discrimination but blinded it to a wide range of subtle but effective forms of discrimination. Freeman (1978) maintained that this conservative paradigm functioned to legitimize racial discrimination. For example, before 1965 in the area of voting rights policy, the U.S. Supreme Court, operating under the conservative paradigm, invalidated white primaries because they excluded blacks explicitly on the basis of race; but at the same time, it allowed literacy tests, poll taxes, character tests, and other devices that effectively disenfranchised blacks. The Court legitimized racial discrimination by opposing the most blatant acts of discrimination while validating the more subtle yet effective ones.

Within the liberal paradigm, racial discrimination is equated with persistent statistical patterns and institutional practices of discrimination, especially in an overall atmosphere of racial tension. This model maintains that racial discrimination can occur in the absence of an identifiable prejudiced individual or the intent to discriminate. It offers affirmative action as a remedy for persistent and pervasive patterns of discrimination. In extreme cases, it allows for the use of statistical goals or quotas as remedies. Consider the case of voting rights as an example of the implications of these two paradigms.

The Voting Rights Act of 1965

Prior to 1965, the federal government operated under the conservative paradigm in the voting rights area. Under this paradigm, the Court allowed literacy tests, poll taxes, and character tests, even though these devices kept as much as 95% of the black voting-age population from the polls. When sued, southern officials maintained that these devices were race-neutral, that they did not violate the Constitution, that the Constitution gave states the prerogative to establish requirements for voting, and that no one intended to discriminate against blacks. The conservative paradigm required plaintiffs in civil rights cases to identify the individual responsible for violating blacks' voting rights and to prove that this individual intended to violate these rights. This standard of proof was nearly impossible. Despite the numerous cases of violence against blacks attempting to register to vote; despite the discriminatory manner in which poll taxes, literacy tests, and character tests have been used; and despite the fact that these devices effectively disenfranchised more than 90% of the black population in several counties in the Deep South, the federal courts did not see any violations of the 15th Amendment. This conservative paradigm left the courts blind and blacks defenseless. It prevailed until the passage of the 1965 Voting Rights Act.

The civil rights movement effected a paradigm shift. This movement popularized the liberal paradigm and influenced the passage of the 1965 Voting Rights Act. This Act established a 50% threshold for determining voting discrimination; that is, it targeted southern counties and mandated a federal response if less than 50% of eligible black voters were actually registered in the county.

This Act had a profound impact on black voter registration rates. For example, as of March 1965, the percentage of the voting-age black population actually registered was 7% for Mississippi, 19% for Alabama, and 27% for Georgia. By 1968, less than 3 years after the passage of the Voting Rights Act, the black registration rate for the Deep South was 62%. At the same time, the rate for every southern county exceeded 50% (Bullock and Lamb 1984, p. 42).

The success of the 1965 Voting Rights Act radically changed the face of politics in the United States. Since its passage, more blacks have been elected to political offices at all levels of government—federal, state, and local—than ever before in U.S. history. In 1951, there were only 82 black elected officials in the nation, at all levels of government; most of them were state and local representatives in northern states (Jaynes and Williams 1989, p. 240). There were only two blacks in Congress and no black mayors. By 1985, there were about 6,016 black elected officials, about 286 black mayors, and 20 black representatives in Congress (Jaynes and Williams, p. 240). In 1996, there were 39 voting black members of Congress, 38 in the House and 1 in the Senate. (These figures do not include the two non-voting members representing the District of Columbia and the Virgin Islands.) If ever a civil rights revolution occurred, it was in the voting rights area. Of course, the Supreme Court has recently invalidated a number of congressional districts because the lines were drawn in such a peculiar way that they could be explained only by deliberate efforts to enhance black representation. Nevertheless, blacks remain disproportionately underrepresented in Congress. That is, they constitute more than 12% of the population but only 7% of the members of Congress.

Clearly, the federal government made the most progress in eliminating discrimination when it operated under the liberal discrimination paradigm. It made the least progress when it operated under the conservative discrimination paradigm. It succeeded in the areas of voting rights and public accommodations, and somewhat in the area of public education in the South. It failed in the housing area and had modest success in employment.

Discrimination in housing and employment persisted long after the passage of the civil rights policies of the 1960s. Public policies were weak to moderate in these areas. Moreover, the persistence of discrimination in these areas contributed directly to the growth of concentrated black poverty. To understand these problems, we must analyze these areas in more detail. Let us begin our analysis with housing policies.

Fair Housing and Housing Segregation

Racial discrimination in the housing market continued from the passage of the 1968 Fair Housing Act to the present. This discrimination reinforced the hyper-segregation that arose under industrial capitalism and contributed to the growth of concentrated black poverty in central cities.

However, a number of scholars have a different perspective. They assume that the black middle class has been moving out of the central cities into integrated suburban areas; that the persistence of segregation is a function of past history, choice, and social class, not race; and that deliberate racial segregation in housing is a thing of the past. Nevertheless, studies of housing segregation refute these assumptions. These studies demonstrate that fair housing laws were weak and relatively ineffective; and that local governments, federal agencies, real estate industries, and other private parties contributed to the maintenance of housing segregation; and that racial segregation was a function of race, not a by-product of class.

The Fair Housing Act of 1968 prohibited discrimination on the basis of race, color, religion, gender, or national origin in the sale or rental of housing. The law, consistent with the conservative paradigm, forbade the blatant forms of racial exclusion, especially the for-whites-only signs. It ignored the subtle but systematic forms of discrimination such as steering, blockbusting, double listing, and others. Of course, federal district courts outlawed steering if this practice was couched in explicit racial language

(*Zuch v. Hussey* 1975) and forms of blockbusting, particularly those that explicitly exploited racial fears (*United States v. Mitchell* 1971). Nevertheless, unlike the Voting Rights Act, the Fair Housing law failed to provide either a standard way of measuring progress toward implementation or a statistical threshold to measure prima facie discrimination. It offered few guidelines on how to promote fair housing. As with most civil rights laws arising from the conservative paradigm, this one provided little protection against subtle forms of racial discrimination.

The Role of Federal Agencies in Sustaining Housing Segregation

Congress charged all federal agencies with the responsibility of implementing the Fair Housing Act. Some of these agencies were guilty of supporting or tolerating housing discrimination. Few gave the policy a high priority. For example, the Federal Housing Administration (FHA) had a long history of promoting housing segregation (see Chapter 6). Even after the passage of the Fair Housing Act, studies of housing segregation implicated the FHA. Summarizing a number of these studies of the early 1970s, Danielson (1976, p. 204) concluded that the FHA indirectly promoted segregation by failing to deal forcefully with real estate firms engaged in discriminating against blacks, by refusing to take affirmative measures to undo the segregation it had created in earlier years, and by relying on private builders and financial institutions in stimulating suburban expansion. Studies in the early 1970s found clear patterns of racial discrimination in the awarding of home loans by banks and federal agencies (Danielson 1976; Bullock and Lamb 1984). Of course, the Federal Home Loan Bank Board (FHLBB) issued a series of regulations throughout the mid- to late-1970s reaffirming the law's prohibition of racial discrimination in the awarding of loan applications.

The Department of Housing and Urban Development (HUD) has had a mixed record. In its early years, HUD was found guilty of supporting racially discriminatory behavior. For example, in 1971, the Supreme Court found the Chicago Housing Authority guilty of deliberately segregating public housing and HUD guilty of authorizing the use of federal funds in a program that engaged in racial discrimination. In a follow-up Chicago case, the Supreme Court found HUD guilty of not enforcing a court order mandating nondiscrimination in public housing. As a remedy, the Court ordered the scattering of subsidized housing through the city and suburbs (*Hills v. Gautreaux* 1976).

A 1979 Civil Rights Commission report on HUD's fair housing record listed a number of problem in HUD's enforcement pattern. The report claimed that HUD was reluctant to terminate grant recipients who violated civil rights policies, that HUD's fair housing guidelines were vague, and that HUD did little to monitor compliance with fair housing laws (Amaker 1988, p. 88). Nevertheless, HUD has taken some steps to implement the Fair Housing Act. It created the Office of Fair Housing and Equal Opportunity. This agency has played a major role in investigating housing discrimination and in referring cases to the Justice Department for prosecution. HUD revised its fair housing regulations by 1980. However, the Reagan and Bush administrations emphasized devolving federal responsibilities to state and local governments. During the 1980s, HUD expected state and local agencies to assume more of the responsibility for preventing housing discrimination. This practice worked well in those local areas already committed to fair housing. It meant no civil rights protection in other areas.

The Clinton administration has experimented with targeting a few selected suburban areas for scattered site housing—a strategy for dispersing low- to moderate-income housing throughout the metropolitan area. This policy revised plans derived from the *Hills v. Gautreaux* decision. However, few resources have been committed to this policy, and the few affected communities have successfully opposed efforts to build these homes.

Congress has demonstrated an interest in fair housing, as it passed the Home Mortgage Disclosure Act of 1975 and the Fair Housing Amendment Act of 1974 and 1988. These laws, along with a series of FHLBB and Federal Reserve Board regulations, played an important role in reducing cases of racial discrimination in the home loan business. These policies have reduced, although not eliminated, redlining—the banking practice of drawing a red line around a predominantly black area and denying loans to applicants in that area. Of course, studies assessing the extent of redlining and mortgage discrimination are mixed. The Fair Housing Amendment of 1988 strengthened the enforcement provisions of the 1968 Act. However, despite these gains, a number of institutional practices— public and private—continue to sustain racial segregation in housing, most notably, the exclusionary zoning and building code policies of local governments, the discriminatory practices of the real estate industry, and the low tolerance for integrated housing among white homeowners. Collectively these practices contributed to a pattern of both class and racial segregation. This racial segregation cut across class lines; that is, the segregation was based on race, not class.

Exclusionary Zoning Policies of Local Government

Suburban governments have been successful in maintaining class and racial segregation through the passage of exclusionary zoning ordinances. These laws involve establishing minimum lot sizes and minimum square footage for the construction of new homes. They often prohibit the construction of low- to moderate-income homes and forbid the building of apartment complexes. They set minimum limits for lot sizes and building square footage for new homes so high that only more expensive homes will be constructed. Affluent suburban cities use these laws effectively to exclude all but the most well-to-do families. These laws guarantee class segregation (Danielson 1976). They enjoy substantial support from the judicial system. Although they operate mainly to sustain class segregation, they have been used deliberately to exclude blacks, particularly low-income blacks. Exclusionary zoning laws function to segregate low-income blacks in central cities.

The Black Jack, Missouri, case best illustrates this point. In 1970, two churches proposed to construct about 210 federally subsidized, moderately priced town houses near an unincorporated subdivision of St. Louis County named Black Jack. The proposal was designed to facilitate integrated housing in a suburban area. Once they learned of this proposal, residents of Black Jack reacted against it. They collected petitions condemning it and lobbied federal officials in Washington, D.C., to oppose it. The most common concern that residents expressed to newspaper reporters was that the project would attract low-income blacks (Judd 1979, p. 189). They were afraid that a black housing project would be created in their all-white enclave. Thus the residents incorporated and introduced zoning ordinances prohibiting the construction of low- to moderate-income subsidized housing.

The construction company hired by the churches to build the houses filed suit against the city. The U.S. District Court sympathized with the residents of Black Jack. It ruled in favor of the city on grounds that no one was harmed by the zoning ordinance and that the city based its decision on "valid reasons." These reasons included the impact that the housing project would have on road congestion, the quality of city schools, and the value of property. The Eighth Circuit Court of Appeals reversed the lower court's decision. The Appeals Court maintained that the district court had not sufficiently considered the historical context in which the ordinance was enacted nor the ultimate impact of the exclusionary policy. The city appealed to the U.S. Supreme Court. Of course, before the case reached the Supreme Court, the construction company was out of business. The homes were never built.

Black Jack is not an isolated case. Similar cases have arisen in other suburbs. In Birmingham, Michigan, in 1978, residents revolted when their liberal mayor, Ruth McNarmee, supported a proposal for low- to moderate-income housing. The mayor described the reaction to the proposal as hostile and racist (Darden, Hill, Thomas, and Thomas, 1987, p. 144), and residents initiated a recall drive against her.

The case of Warren, Michigan, provides another illustration of the racial component of suburban exclusion. In 1970, HUD threatened to withhold federal funds from Warren unless the city established a human relations commission to address its problem of racial exclusion. The city was over 99% white, although 30% of the workers in its auto plants were black. HUD believed the problem of exclusion was one of race, not class, because the black autoworkers could afford to purchase homes in Warren. However, Warren residents called for the resignation of the HUD secretary, George Romney (Darden et al. 1987, pp. 142-43). Romney backed down and said that HUD would not attempt to force integration of the suburbs.

During the early 1970s, suburban residents throughout the nation resisted attempts to locate subsidized housing in their area. One state, California, amended its constitution to require local voter approval for any subsidized housing proposal. The Supreme Court sympathized with suburban residents. In the *James v. Valtierra* decision (1971), civil rights groups challenged this state constitutional amendment on grounds that it violated the equal protection clause of the 14th Amendment, especially for poor blacks. In this case, the Court sided with the state and upheld the constitutional provision. Justice Black, in the majority opinion, said there was no evidence that the provision was directed at any racial minority. Justice Marshall, in a dissenting opinion said,

> It is far too late in the day to contend that the Fourteenth Amendment prohibits only racial discrimination; and to me, singling out the poor to bear a burden not placed on any other class of citizens tramples the values that the 14th Amendment was designed to protect. (*James v. Valtierra* 1971).

The issue of whether a local government has the right to exclude subsided housing or any form of low- to moderate-income housing was settled in the *Village of Arlington Heights v. Metropolitan Housing*

Development Corporation (1977). In this case, civil rights groups challenged the village's zoning policy on grounds that it had a racially discriminatory effect. The Court acknowledged the policy's discriminatory effect but required proof of a discriminatory intent. The effect of this decision was to eviscerate any challenge of exclusionary zoning policies in the courts.

Local zoning and building code laws continued to operate throughout the 1980s and 1990s to maintain class segregation in metropolitan areas. These laws acted as impenetrable walls excluding low- to moderate-income homes from the well-to-do suburbs. This exclusion trapped low- to moderate-income families in the central city and forced the central city to bear the major responsibility of housing these families. These policies contributed directly to the growth of concentrated poverty in the central cities.

Discriminatory Practices of the Real Estate Industry

While exclusionary zoning policies perpetuated class segregation, a range of real estate practices operated to maintain racial segregation. These practices were subtle but effective. They included various forms of differential treatment and persisted throughout the 1980s and 1990s, producing the kind of racial segregation that cut across class lines.

A great deal of the data demonstrating the persistence of racial discrimination in housing markets comes from housing audits conducted by local or federal fair housing agencies. A typical housing audit study involves the matching of a black couple with a white couple in income, education, occupation, age, and other factors. Couples are trained to present similar outward appearances. Almost everything about the two couples is the same, except their race. In this way, differential treatment can be attributed to race, not class. Invariably these audits found a persistent pattern of racial discrimination.

Yinger (1987) provided a summary of several of these studies conducted in the 1970s and 1980s. He indicated that discrimination took many forms. The most common form involved (a) differential rates of showing homes, (b) differences in providing credit information, (c) steering, and (d) different overall treatment. In a 1981 Boston study by Feins, Bratt, and Hollister, blacks were shown fewer homes or apartments than whites in more than 60% of the cases. In studies of Boston in the early 1980s, whites received far more credit information than blacks (Tobin 1987, p. 55). In a 1982 Denver study, researchers found no discrimination in the availability of housing but substantial discrimination on credit information (Yinger, p. 56). Overall, Tobin found that blacks were more likely to be shown fewer homes and not to be given credit information. Moreover, steering was quite prevalent. In one study of the Detroit area, almost all the black couples were steered to neighborhoods that were either predominantly black or increasing in black composition (Yinger, p. 56).

Massey and Denton (1993) also provided a summary of housing discrimination studies. Although they pointed to different studies, they reached similar conclusions. In one study of the Cleveland area in the late 1970s, they noted that about 70% of the real estate firms engaged in some form of steering. White couples were rarely shown homes in integrated areas, unless they specifically requested it. Blacks were almost routinely shown homes in racially mixed areas or areas adjacent to predominantly black areas (Massey and Denton, p. 100). Noting Yinger's analysis of the 1988 HUD audit study, Massey and Denton (p. 103) noted that the HUD data indicated blacks had a 53% chance of experiencing discrimination in the housing rental or sales markets. This probability increased to 60% when steering is factored in. The cumulative effect of discrimination increased to 90% when blacks visited at least three realtors (Massey and Denton, p. 103). Jaynes and Williams's (1989, p. 142) assessment of the 1977 HUD study concluded that 90% of the black and white couples were steered.

There are a number of indicators that discrimination in housing is a function of race rather than class. Although it is common to assume that blacks do not purchase homes in affluent white areas because they cannot afford these homes, a large body of research refutes this assumption. This research can be divided into three major areas: segregation indexes, trends in black suburbanization, and public opinion data.

Housing segregation studies rely on an figure called the black-white dissimilarity index. This index measures the percentage of all blacks who must move in order for each census tract in the metropolitan area to become racial integrated (Massey and Denton 1993, p. 63). That is, if blacks constitute 12% of the metropolitan population, the index is the percentage of blacks who must move in order for each census tract to become 12% black. Massey and Denton summarized this index for the 30 Standard Metropolitan Statistical Areas (SMSAs) with the largest black populations. These areas contain more than 50% of the nation's black population. Their data indicated two things. First, the level of segregation has changed little in the post-civil rights era. In northern areas, this index averaged more than 80%, and it declined by only 4 points between 1970 and 1980 (Massey and Denton, p. 63). Segregation decreased in areas such as Columbus, Ohio, Los Angeles, and San Francisco, but increased in areas like New York City and Newark (Massey and Denton, p. 63). Second, the segregation index was relatively stable across class lines, although it tended to be slightly higher among low-income blacks, compared to middle- or upper-middle-income blacks. However, this index was higher among the upper-middle-income blacks compared to middle-income blacks. That is, according to 1980 data, for blacks with an income below $2,500, the index was 86, compared to an index of 81 for blacks with an income between $25,000 and $27,500 and an index of 83 for blacks with an income above $50,000 (Massey and Denton 1993, p. 86). For Chicago, this index was 91 for low-income, 85.8 for middle-income, and 86.3 for upper middle-income blacks. Most empirical studies have demonstrated that affluent blacks and whites live in separate neighborhoods and so do poor blacks and whites (Darden 1987, p. 17).

A number of alternative hypotheses have been offered to explain the high level of segregation among upper-income blacks, who could easily afford to purchase homes in the middle-income suburbs. One hypothesis maintains that blacks lack market information on the availability of homes in these areas. Another hypothesis insists that blacks choose to live in predominantly black areas. In both hypotheses, racial discrimination is dismissed as an irrelevant factor. However, public opinion data reject these two hypotheses. For example, in a survey of blacks' awareness of the Detroit housing market, Farley, Bianchi, and Colasanti (1979) found that blacks were quite knowledgeable about housing costs, locations, and other aspects of the housing market. Lack of information could not explain the racial segregation.

Surveys of black and white attitudes toward housing integration refute the free choice hypothesis: that blacks choose to locate in segregated neighborhoods. These studies indicated that blacks are more likely to favor integration than whites, that whites are more likely than blacks to move out of or to avoid integrated neighborhoods. In a classic study of the Detroit area, Farley presented five different configurations of integrated neighborhoods to black and white respondents. More than 95% of the black respondents were willing to move into one form of integrated neighborhood or another, so long as they were not the only black family. Their major reason for not wanting to be the only black family was fear of racial harassment or violence against their family. Nevertheless, 38% of the black respondents claimed that they would move into an all-white area even if they were the only black family. These surveys demonstrate that the persistent segregation of middle- and upper middle-income black families is a function of race factors, not choice or poor information. It is certainly not a function of social class.

Low Tolerance for Integrated Housing Among White Homeowners

Survey data indicate that whites are much more accepting of integration today than they were 20 or 30 years ago. At the same time, the data indicate that white homeowners have a much lower tolerance for integration than expected. When Farley (1976) presented respondents with a picture of a neighborhood with one black family out of 15 families, 24% of the white respondents claimed they would feel uncomfortable and 27% said they were unwilling to move into such a neighborhood. When the number of black families increased to 3 out of 15, 50% of the white respondents claimed that they would not move into the area and 24% said they would move out. When the number of black families reached 5 out of 15, 73% of the white respondents said they would not move into such an area and 41% said they would move out.

Clearly, integration has a different meaning for whites than it does for blacks. For blacks it means a neighborhood with two or more black families. Moreover, blacks feel comfortable in neighborhoods that are 55% white, 45% black. However, most whites are reluctant to move into a neighborhood that is more than 20% black (Farley 1976; Jaynes and Williams 1989).

Most whites still harbor stereotypes of blacks, according to a survey conducted by Farley et al. and published in 1979. This Detroit area survey found that 59% of white respondents believed that blacks were prone to violence, 70% felt that blacks did not take care of their property, and almost half believed that blacks were less moral than whites.

White attitudes alone offer a strong explanation for the perpetuation of racial segregation in metropolitan areas. If the surveys are correct, then neighborhoods with one black family would be relatively stable, but neighborhoods become unstable when the black population equals 20%. About 24% of whites would move out of such a neighborhood, and most whites would refuse to move in. As whites move out, blacks would be more likely than whites to move in. This process would transform an unstable, integrated area into a segregated neighborhood. These changes often occur in suburban neighborhoods adjacent to central cities. In fact, studies of black suburbanization have indicated that as the members of the black middle class leave the central cities, they move into unstable integrated suburban areas that soon become segregated black middle-class neighborhoods (Darden et al. 1987; Farley 1987).

Thus the whole assumption that the black middle class is leaving the segregated central city for the integrated suburb is exaggerated on two counts. First, black suburbanization does not mean integration. It appears that blacks are leaving the central city for select adjacent areas that tend to be in transition. That is, blacks appear to be moving into areas with a reputation for tolerance and avoiding areas with a reputation for strong antiblack sentiments. Moreover, as they move into all-white areas, it appears that these areas change from stable integrated, to unstable integrated, and finally into newly segregated suburban areas (Darden et al. 1987; Farley 1987; Tobin 1987). Summarizing the literature on black suburbanization, Farley (p. 111) concluded that "the forces perpetuating segregation are as much at work in the suburbs as in the city."

Second, the magnitude of black suburbanization tends to be exaggerated. For example, the proportion of blacks in the Detroit SMSA living in the suburbs increased from 13% to 15% from 1970 to 1980, hardly a level of increase one could consider massive (Carter Wilson 1992).

The Failure of Fair Housing Policies

Racial and class segregation persists in the post-civil rights era because policies designed to prevent housing discrimination have been ineffective. This segregation is not simply an artifact of the past. It is the result of processes operating in the present. Although federal and state housing policies have eliminated the more blatant forms of discrimination, a number of processes continue to function to perpetuate patterns of segregation. These processes include local zoning and building code regulations, a range of real estate practices, the behavior of white homeowners, and the reputation of suburban areas for antiblack sentiments. These processes create invisible walls around black neighborhoods. They leave blacks trapped in segregated areas. They partially explain the growth of concentrated black poverty in central cities.

Anti-Employment Discrimination Policy

The effectiveness of anti-employment discrimination policy was somewhere between voting rights and fair housing. That is, it was not as effective as the Voting Rights Act but more effective than fair housing policies. Throughout this period (1964-present), the state vacillated between the liberal and the conservative discrimination paradigms. It began the period in the conservative paradigm and shifted in and out of this framework throughout the 1970s and 1980s. With all of the strident criticism against affirmative action policies, at no time did the state ever tolerate more expansive approaches to remedying employment discrimination. On balance, the Court has maintained a moderate to slightly conservative position, although by the early 1990s it had a solid conservative majority. Congress continued to fight to preserve civil rights protections, at least until 1994, when the Republicans captured a majority in both houses. Presidents Reagan and Bush fought bitterly to pull this policy completely back into the conservative framework. Little progress has occurred under the Clinton administration.

The Equal Employment Opportunity Commission

The legislative basis of anti-employment discrimination policy is found in Title 7 of the 1964 Civil Rights Act. This Act prohibits discrimination on the basis of race, color, gender, religion, or national origin in the hiring or classification of workers. This Act also created the Equal Employment Opportunity Commission (EEOC), charged with the responsibility of implementing this law.

During its first few years of operation, the EEOC was ineffective primarily because it operated under the conservative paradigm and because it had limited resources and authority. In its first 7 years of existence, it received well over 100,000 complaints, of which it investigated about 41,000; 6% were successfully resolved (Bullock and Lamb 1984, p. 96). Estimates of the proportion of the total complaints that were valid range from 50% to 80% (Wolkinson 1973, p. 145; Bullock and Lamb, p. 96). A number of problems contributed to this dismal record. The EEOC had pursued antidiscrimination policy on a case by case basis. Apparently, it saw discrimination as an individual rather than an industry-wide or systematic problem. Its five commissioners and limited staff were ill equipped to handle the large caseloads. Its powers were limited; it even lacked the authority to initiate lawsuits against recalcitrant firms or labor unions and was required to turn cases over to the Justice Department for litigation.

In the early 1970s, several changes occurred that enhanced the effectiveness of anti-employment discrimination policies. Most notably, the Courts and the EEOC moved away from the narrow paradigm toward the expansive one. This move was evident in a number of Supreme Court decisions, notably *Griggs v. Duke Power Company* (1971).

This case emerged after a group of black Duke Power Company workers sued the company for discriminating against them. Prior to the passage of the 1964 Civil Rights Act, the company segregated blacks into the lowest paying, least desirable laborer jobs as a matter of company policy. After the passage of the Act, the company established two criteria for hirings, promotions, or transfers: a satisfactory score on two aptitude tests and the possession of a high school diploma. At that time, only 34% of white males and 12% of black males in the state of Louisiana had completed high school (*Griggs v. Duke Power Company,* 1971). Blacks sued because the new tests barred them from other higher paying menial jobs such as coal handler, maintenance, and operator. The company maintained that there was no evidence it had intentionally engaged in racial discrimination in violation of Title 7, although it had discriminated in the past.

Having moved away from the conservative paradigm, the Court recognized institutional forms of discrimination. In this unanimous decision, Chief Justice Burger maintained that hiring and promotion practices can be "fair in form but discriminatory in operation" (*Griggs v. Duke Power Company,* 1971). That is, they can be subterfuges for systematic discrimination. Whereas a number of scholars claim that in this case the Court attacked merit and reduced standards (see Glazer 1978), the Court underscored the need to maintain standards and to support merit systems. At the same time, it required that standards be fair and nonarbitrary. The Court required that standards be demonstrably related to job performance. That is, if a standard is unrelated to the job and discriminates against minorities, then it is deemed in violation of Title 7. However, if a standard is demonstrably related to the job and discriminates against minorities, then it is not in violation of Title 7. The Court ruled against the power company because the standards were unrelated to job performance and because they discriminated against blacks. While operating in this more liberal paradigm, the Courts and the EEOC made substantial progress in ameliorating the problem of discrimination in employment.

Other changes in anti-employment discrimination policy that occurred in the early 1970s included the EEOC's shift from a case by case approach to an industry-wide approach, attacking institutional discrimination; an increased use of affirmative action plans as remedies for discrimination; and the expansion of EEOC powers to include the authority to initiate lawsuits. Of course, the EEOC remained limited in that it never acquired the power to issue cease and desist orders as other more powerful regulatory agencies could do.

Throughout the late 1970s and 1980s, the Court oscillated between the two paradigms. It has upheld affirmative action remedies, although by slim majorities. In *Regents of the University of California v. Bakke* (1978), the Court rejected the notion of societal discrimination, although this paradigm found some support in the dissenting opinions of Justices Brennan and Marshall. Justice Brennan argued that blacks had been harmed by "a cultural tradition of race prejudice," cultivated both by a past history of slavery and segregation and a present climate of resistance to desegregation and aversion to blacks. He maintained that blacks applying to the University of California at Davis's Medical School were clearly victims of racial discrimination. Justice Powell, writing the prevailing but fragmented decision, rejected this notion of societal discrimination on grounds that it was too "amorphous as a concept of injury" and too "ageless in its reach into the past."

Of course, a few years before *Bakke,* the Court had failed to find a remedy to one of the most serious, concrete, and immediate factors disadvantaging low income, minority, grade school students: inequality in the distribution of educational resources. The *San Antonio Independent School District v. Rodriguez* (1973) decision involved two school districts: one poor and predominantly minority, Edgewood; the other, rich and predominantly white, Alamo Heights. Edgewood, with one of the highest tax rates in the area, was only able to raise $37 per pupil, $231 with state support. With a lower tax rate, Alamo raised $412 per pupil, $543 with state support. The parents of Edgewood charged that these disparities in school funding violated the equal protection clause of the 14th Amendment and directly harmed the children of Edgewood. Justice Powell argued that the 14th Amendment did not require an equal distribution of government funds, only that no one be denied an opportunity for some state funding; and that race was not a factor in this case. Edgewood was 4% white, 90% Mexican, and 6% black. Alamo was 18% Mexican and about 1% black. Marshall, in his dissenting opinion, argued that the 14th Amendment may not require an equal distribution of funds, but it certainly required the state to give the children of Edgewood, and other low income, predominantly minority school districts, a fairer, more equitable chance than it was currently giving them. The presence of the conservative paradigm made it difficult for the Court to see these disparities as a form of invidious discrimination.

More than 20 years after this decision, these disparities have worsened. Kozol (1991, p. 223) noted that in Texas, public school expenditures range from $2,000 per pupil for the poorest districts to about $19,000 for the richest. Kozol also provided several case studies indicating wide disparities in the allocation of resources for public education in other states. These disparities fall along racial and class lines, with poor central city school districts and poor industrial suburban districts—districts with large, low-income black and low-income white student populations—getting fewer resources, and predominantly rich and white suburban districts getting more resources. These disparities restrict the opportunities of both poor whites and poor blacks, much as the patterns in the South did at the beginning of the century.

Nevertheless, the *Bakke* decision rejected the notion of societal discrimination because the concept appeared too elusive and indirect. The *Rodriguez* decision blocked efforts to remedy a significant source of societal discrimination: fewer educational resources for low income, predominantly minority school districts. *Bakke* and *Rodriguez* represent a retreat from the more expansive liberal discrimination paradigm and a movement back toward the conservative one. At no time has the Court moved beyond a modest liberal paradigm toward a societal paradigm. The whole notion that the Court was too liberal in the area of civil rights is not supported by a careful review of these cases.

The Affirmative Action Issue

Although the *Bakke* decision did not prohibit affirmative action, it established a number of limits on and guidelines for this policy. It required affirmative action programs to impose the least harm on nonminorities. It rejected special admissions programs. It disallowed affirmative action as a remedy for past or societal discrimination. It left open the question of whether quotas were permissible or not.

Despite all the public clamor about affirmative action and assertions that this policy is a form of reverse discrimination, that it harms white males, and that it advances less qualified minority candidates over more qualified white males, the case law on this policy portrays a different picture from the one presented by opponents. Almost every major affirmative action case involved at least prima facie evidence of discrimination. Every remedy was limited in the sense of imposing the least harm on nonminorities; yet, every decision entailed the charge that affirmative action harmed white males. Consider these cases: *Weber, Johnson, Sheet Metal Workers,* and *Paradise.*

In *United Steelworkers of America v. Weber* (1979), Brian Weber, a white male, claimed he was harmed by an affirmative action skilled training program that had rejected him. He claimed that he was excluded because he was white and because 50% of the trainees were black. Both the Kaiser Aluminum Company and the United Steelworkers had agreed to establish the special training program because, by 1974, only 5 out of 272 craft workers at Kaiser were black and because of an unspoken acknowledgment that both the union and company had excluded blacks from the skilled trades in the past. The affirmative action program was small and remedial. It consisted of only 13 trainees, 7 black and 6 white. Justice Brennan, setting forth the majority opinion, argued that Brian Weber was not harmed by this program because he did not lose his job and the program created new opportunities for both black and white workers that would not have existed otherwise. Brennan added,

> It would be ironic indeed if a law [Title VII] triggered by a Nation's concern over centuries of racial injustice and intended to improve the lot of those who had "been excluded from the American dream for so long" . . . , constituted the first legislative prohibition of all voluntary, private, race-conscious efforts to abolish traditional patterns of racial segregation and hierarchy.

In the *Johnson v. Transportation Agency* (1987) decision, a white male, Paul Johnson, claimed that he was denied a promotion because an affirmative action program promoted a less qualified minority—a white female—over him. This case entailed substantial statistical evidence of discrimination in the Santa Clara County (California) Transportation Agency. In this agency, women constituted 76% of the clerical workers but only 7.1% of the agency officials and administrators and 0% of the 238 skilled craft workers. In 1974, a woman, Diane Joyce, applied for a dispatcher position but was turned down because the job required road maintenance experience and women were excluded from road maintenance jobs, a clear violation of Title 7. In 1975, Joyce became the first woman to join the road maintenance department, where she remained for the next 4 years, occasionally working out of class as a dispatcher. She then applied for a dispatcher job, becoming one of seven candidates deemed well qualified for the position. However, believing one of the interviewers to be biased because he made a comment about her wearing a skirt, she contacted the director of the county's affirmative action office, who contacted the agency director. The director of the transportation agency offered Joyce the job.

Johnson's complaint was based on the fact that he had an interview score of 75, compared to Joyce's 73. The agency director maintained that the interview scores were assigned subjectively and were meaningless. With her seniority and experience working out of class as a dispatcher, Joyce believed she was the better qualified candidate. In a split (6-3) decision, the Court ruled in favor of Joyce. Nevertheless, Bradford Reynolds, the director of the Civil Rights Division of the Justice Department under President Reagan, claimed that this was a typical case of affirmative action giving a job to a less qualified minority and discriminating against a more qualified white male. Clearly, Reynolds's claim was exaggerated.

In the *Sheet Metal Workers v. Equal Employment Opportunity Commission* (1986) decision, the Supreme Court upheld a 29% minority hiring quota imposed on Local 28 of the Sheet Metal Workers' International Association located in New York. In this split (5-4) decision, Justice Brennan argued that the union's long history of racial exclusion, blatant disregard for the law, and raw contempt for the justice system gave the lower courts little recourse except to impose this quota. This union was found guilty of racial exclusion from 1964 to the time the case reached the U.S. Supreme Court in 1986. In 1964, the State of New York, under its civil rights laws, ordered this union to stop discriminating. Although the union agreed to stop excluding blacks, it continued to do so under a wide range of subterfuges throughout the 1970s and the 1980s. At one time, it recruited apprentices exclusively on recommendations from its members—a practice that lead to nepotism and racial exclusion. When this practice was prohibited, the union found other ways of excluding blacks. It used union funds to "subsidize special training sessions for friends and relatives of union members taking the apprenticeship examination" (*Sheet Metal Workers v. EEOC,* 1986). It reduced the size of its apprenticeship classes deliberately to reduce the number of nonwhite applicants. It accepted transfers from all unions except those with a large minority membership. It organized nonunion sheet metal shops and allowed only whites to transfer to its local. It accepted only white applicants transferring from other locals. The union deliberately and contemptuously circumvented efforts to end its practice of racial exclusion. Thus the 29% quota, which reflected the proportion of qualified minorities available in the workforce, was not imposed to correct for a past history of slavery or segregation—as opponents of affirmative action often charge. It was imposed because the union stubbornly refused to stop excluding blacks in the present. This quota emerged as a desperate effort to prevent the perpetuation of racial discrimination.

This was not the only decision upholding quotas. The Court upheld a 10% set-aside program in *Fullilove v. Klutznick* (1980) and a 50% promotion quota, contingent on the availability of qualified minorities, in *United States v. Paradise* (1987). A substantial and incessant pattern of discrimination in the allocation of federal contracts justified the establishment of the 10% set-aside. The Court imposed quota of one black promoted for every white promoted only after the state refused to promote qualified black officers.

Evidence of racial discrimination appeared even in the cases where affirmative action lost. For example, *Firefighters Local Union No. 1784 v. Stotts* (1984), which decided that seniority systems take priority over affirmative action, began as a racial discrimination suit initiated by a black member of the Memphis Fire Department. Blacks were disproportionately underrepresented, and the hiring process was suspect. The suit resulted in an affirmative action consent decree in which the city hired a significant number of black firefighters. This hiring was a remedy for alleged discriminatory hiring practices. However, budget deficits forced the city to cut back. The city responded to these financial pressures by laying off the new hires. Civil rights groups challenged the dismissals, claiming they violated the consent decree. Although the Supreme Court sided with the city in this case, affirmative action emerged as a remedy for stubborn patterns of discrimination. The *Wygant v. Jackson Board of Education* (1986) decision is similar to the *Stotts* case insofar as it began as an affirmative action consent degree to remedy an alleged pattern of discrimination. In another case, *City of Richmond v. J. A. Croson Co.* (1989), the Court struck down a 30% set-aside program for minority contractors in Richmond, Virginia. The city established this program after it discovered that less than one half of 1% of prime city contracts were awarded to minority contractors, although blacks constituted over 50% of the city's population.

Of course, the Court did not find set-aside programs ipso facto unconstitutional. Instead, the Court established more rigorous tests for justifying them. These tests involved demonstrating racial disparities in awarding government contracts by comparing the percentage of actual minority business enterprises within specific areas—construction, public relations, electrician, and so on—with the proportion of government contracts actually awarded to minorities in each category. Set-aside programs must be justified with relevant statistical data demonstrating a pattern of discrimination. They are to be temporary remedies, narrowly tailored to the nature of the discrimination problem. Thus although the Court has moved away from the liberal discrimination paradigm and has eroded civil rights protections, it has not moved completely back into the old conservative paradigm. It has not eliminated affirmative action.

Shifts in Antidiscrimination Policies: A Return to the Conservative Paradigm

In the 1980s, the Reagan and Bush administrations struggled to reestablish the conservative paradigm in the area of civil rights. Reagan and his top administrators actively campaigned against affirmative action. Although they pledged their opposition to racial discrimination of any sort, they argued for race-neutral policies, demanded evidence of intent to discriminate, and lobbied for the case by case approach—all characteristics of the conservative paradigm.

The EEOC and the Justice Department under Reagan moved much closer to the conservative paradigm than the Supreme Court. In the first 2 years of Reagan's administration, the EEOC began to resume the case by case approach. For example, in the year before Reagan took office, there were about 62 industry-wide pattern of practice cases (Amaker 1988, p. 110). In 1982, there were no industry-wide cases. In early 1986, the head of the EEOC, Clarence Thomas—now a Supreme Court Justice in place of Justice Marshall—announced that his agency would abandon affirmative action as a remedy for discrimination. About the same time, the Justice Department sent letters to more than 51 cities, counties, school districts, and state agencies telling them to stop using numerical goals in hiring African Americans, women, Mexican Americans, or other minorities (Center for Popular Economics 1986, p. 53). Ed Meese, Bradford Reynolds, and Clarence Thomas claimed that race-conscious remedies violated the Constitution. Thomas suggested that they stigmatized blacks. Of course, after the *Sheet Metal* decision later in the year, Thomas (quoted in Amaker 1988, p. 114) said, "The Court has ruled. . . . That's the law of the land, whether I like it or not." Begrudgingly, this administration was pressured into tolerating at least limited forms of affirmative action.

President George Bush continued the assault on affirmative action in his opposition to the 1990 Civil Rights Act. In his veto message, Bush said that racial discrimination was an evil that tore at the fabric of our society, one that we all must oppose. However, he vetoed the civil rights bill because he felt it would require quotas. He argued that the bill contained

> an unduly narrow definition of "business necessity" that is significantly more restrictive than that established by the Supreme Court in [*Griggs v. Duke Power*] and in two decades of subsequent decisions. Thus, unable to defend legitimate practices in court, employers will be driven to adopt quotas . . . to avoid liability. (October 22, 1990)

This act attempted to respond to a number of Supreme Court decisions that clearly reflected the conservative paradigm: *Martin v. Wilks* (1989), *Patterson v. McLean Credit Union* (1988), *Lorance v. AT&T Technologies, Inc., Independent Federation of Flight Attendants v. Zipes,* and *Wards Cove Packing Co., Inc. v. Atonio* (1989). The *Martin* decision allowed collateral lawsuits against consent decrees. In *Patterson v. McLean,* the Court maintained that civil rights law, especially the Civil Rights Act of 1866, forbade racial discrimination in contracts but did not prohibit racial harassment in the implementation of the contract or on the job. The Court claimed, in *Zipes,* that attorney fees cannot be dumped on the losing party in Title VII suits. In the *AT&T Technologies* case, female employees claimed that when the company switched from a plant-wide to a department-wide seniority system, it discriminated against women who were recently promoted and transferred to new departments. Because the women employees initiated the suit when the company began to enforce a reduction in workforce plan, the district court dismissed the case on grounds that the 180-day statute of limitations had run out. The women appealed on the grounds that the time should have begun the moment the harm occurred—at the time the company began implementing the reduction in force plan—not when the new seniority system was established. The Supreme Court sided with the company.

The main conflict over the 1990 Civil Rights Act centered on the *Wards Cove* (1989) decision. This case arose when minority workers filed suit against the Wards Cove Packing Company in Alaska. In this company, Filipino and Native American workers were concentrated in lower level jobs and segregated in lunchrooms and dormitory facilities. These workers argued that a range of practices—notably, subjective hiring standards, separate hiring channels, a practice of not promoting from within, and nepotism—created a racially stratified workforce with minorities on the bottom. The Court ruled in favor of the company. Writing the majority (5-4) decision, Justice White explained that the plaintiffs, the nonwhite cannery workers, had used the wrong statistics. He said they "relied solely on . . . statistics showing a high percentage of nonwhite workers in the cannery jobs and a low percentage of such workers in the noncannery positions" (*Wards Cove,* 1989). These were irrelevant statistics, noted White. The relevant statistics would be data comparing the percentage of minorities in the relevant labor force with those hired in noncannery jobs, White contended. He added,

> Moreover, isolating the cannery workers as the potential "labor force" for unskilled noncannery positions is at once both too broad and too narrow in its focus. It is too broad because the vast majority of these cannery workers did not seek jobs in unskilled noncannery positions; there is no showing that many of them would have done so even if none of the arguably "deterring practices" existed.

Also, White required plaintiffs to identify and isolate specific employment practices and demonstrate how these practices are "allegedly responsible for any observed statistical disparities." Rather than overturning *Griggs,* White reinterpreted it to require far more stringent standards for proving discrimination. This reinterpretation of *Griggs* shifted the burden of proof in discrimination cases from the defendant to the plaintiff. White suggested that a less stringent standard might induce employers to use quotas. Apparently, White and President Bush had similar interpretations of *Griggs.* Nevertheless, in his dissenting opinion, Blackmun noted that the cannery industry had a reputation for discrimination, that the employment patterns in this case formed a caste system similar to the old southern plantations, and that the Court had placed too great a burden of proof on plaintiffs in discrimination cases.

Congress attempted to overturn the *Atonio* decision by adding the *Griggs* decision and EEOC regulations pursuant to *Griggs* to the 1990 Civil Rights Act. Although he claimed to agree with *Griggs,* Bush vetoed the bill. In a compromise version of the bill written the following year, Congress deleted the *Griggs* regulations while keeping those aspects of the decision agreeable to Bush. In the 1991 Civil Rights Act, Congress left the interpretation of *Griggs* principles up to the Court.

Recently, the Court has become more conservative than it was at the time of *Atonio.* Since 1990, moderate Ginsburg replaced conservative White (1993), a shift in the liberal direction. However, moderate Breyer replaced liberal Blackmun (1994), moderate Souter replaced liberal Brennan (1990), and ultraconservative Thomas replaced liberal

Marshall (1991), a net conservative shift. There are no more liberals on the Court; there is a solid conservative block with Kennedy, O'Connor, Rehnquist, and Stevens; and there is an ultraconservative block with Thomas and Scalia. Breyer, Ginsburg, and Souter form a moderate minority, with Souter shifting back and forth to the conservative block and Stevens occasionally joining the moderates. These changes in Supreme Court justices point to a likely shift further toward the conservative paradigm.

Measuring the Persistence of Labor Market Discrimination and the Effectiveness of Antidiscrimination Policies

Anti-employment discrimination policies have been moderately successful, although they have not eliminated discrimination. Because racial discrimination cuts across class lines, these policies, especially affirmative action, benefited all classes of African Americans. Just as affirmative action advanced middle-class blacks in professional positions, affirmative action apprenticeship programs advanced blue-collar black workers into skilled positions. Of course, a few studies argue that affirmative action benefited only African Americans with higher levels of education (Wilson 1987). Nevertheless, affirmative action programs were limited. As case law demonstrates, these programs tended to be small, narrowly tailored, and vulnerable to attack. Whereas some progress occurred, racial discrimination persisted.

The Statistical Approach

There are several approaches to measuring discrimination and the effectiveness of antidiscrimination policies. One approach is the use of black/white income disparity data. These data indicate both progress and persistent problems. In 1939, the black per capita income as a percentage of white per capita income was only 42.4% (see Table 7.1). This figure increased to 56.7% by 1969 and 58.7% by 1989. Although the increase indicates progress, black per capita income still lags substantially behind the white rate. Moreover, most of the black gains between 1939 and 1959 are attributable to black migration from the poverty belt of the rural South to urban areas.

Other income data suggest persisting problems. For example, Swinton (1993) presented income data by race and gender from 1967 to 1991. According to his data, drawn from census reports, in 1967 the median income of black males was only 57.2% of the median income of white

Table 7.1   Black/White Disparities in Per Capita Income, 1939-1989

Black per capita income as a percentage of white per capita income:	*1939*	*1949*	*1959*	*Year* *1969*	*1979*	*1989*
	42.4	45.3	49.6	56.7	57.3	58.7[a]

SOURCE: Jaynes and Williams 1989, p. 295; and (a) Swinton 1993, p. 149.

males. At the same time, black female median income was 78.7% of white female median income. By 1976, black male median income was 60.2% of white male median income and black female median income was 94.2% of white female median income. By 1990, the median income of black males had crept up to 60.6% of white male income and black female income had fallen to 80.7% of white female income (Swinton, p. 153).

Of course, the use of income disparity data as indicators of persisting discrimination has met with loud criticism from a number of economists. They claim that these disparities are explained by race-neutral demographic variables such as age, level of education, and skills (Sowell 1975, 1981). Nevertheless, some degree of disparity remains even after accounting for these variables. For example, Reynolds Farley concluded that in 1959, 19% to 35% of the black/white income disparity could not be explained by skill, education, experience, and other production-related characteristics. By 1979, this unexplained proportion had declined to 12% to 24% (Farley 1984). This unexplained proportion may be attributable to discrimination. Farley's study suggested that although the magnitude of discrimination has declined, some degree of discrimination persists.

Occupational data offer another indicator of both progress and persistent discrimination. In Table 7.2, we present changes in three occupational categories from 1970 to 1990. The data indicate that a great deal of progress occurred between 1970 and 1990. In 1970, the proportion of whites in the managerial and professional category was more than twice the proportion of blacks. Between 1970 and 1990, the black proportion in this category had more than doubled. Today the proportion of black workers who are managers or professionals is much closer to the white proportion, a clear indication of progress. However, blacks still lag behind whites in this area, an indication of persistent problems.

In 1970, blacks were concentrated in the operators, fabricators, and laborers category, as they were crowded in the least desirable and most laborious jobs in the manufacturing sector. Today, there is less black

Table 7.2 Race and Three Occupational Categories, 1970-1990

Occupational Category	1970		1980		1990	
	Whites	Blacks	Whites	Blacks	Whites	Blacks
Managerial and professional	20.0	9.1	23.9	14.1	28.5	18.5
Clerical, sales, and administrative support	30.4	18.2	31.1	25.2	32.6	29.4
Operators, fabricators, and laborers	20.2	31.0	17.1	26.7	13.4	20.8

SOURCE: U.S. Bureau of the Census, Department of Commerce, United States Summary, Social and Economic Characteristics, 1980 and 1990.

NOTE: The figures for whites represent the number of whites in each occupational category divided by the total number of white workers. The figure for blacks represents the number of blacks in the occupational category divided by the total number of black workers.

concentration in this area. Of course, many of these jobs have disappeared, an issue we will explore in more detail later.

These data offer some support for our discussion of civil rights and market discrimination. That is, African Americans have made significant progress over the years, but some problems remain. Although the data indicate the persistence of discrimination, the use of such data to make this point is still controversial. The most convincing evidence of the persistence of labor market discrimination has come from survey data.

John Kasarda, a proponent of the economic restructuring and job/skills mismatch thesis, presented data that point to labor market discrimination. Kasarda examined black and white unemployment rates with controls for levels of education to demonstrate the obvious correlation between education and employment. He presented both national and regional data for 1969, 1977, and 1982. Table 7.3 provides a summary of his 1982 data, which demonstrate that black males suffer higher levels of unemployment than white males even after controlling for education. Moreover, in every region except the West, blacks with 1 or more years of college experienced higher levels of unemployment than whites who had completed high school only.

Worse, in some regions, blacks with 1 or more years of college had higher unemployment rates than white high school dropouts. For example, in the Northeast, the unemployment rate for blacks with 1 or more years of college was 18.6%, compared to a rate of 17.2% for whites who had not completed high school. In the South, blacks with 1 or more years

Table 7.3 Unemployment Rates of Central City Males Ages 16-64 by Race and Years of Schooling, 1982 Only

Region and Schooling	White	Black
All regions		
Did not complete high school	17.7	29.7
Completed high school only	11.0	23.5
Attended college 1 year or more	4.4	16.1
All education levels	9.5	23.4
Northeast		
Did not complete high school	17.2	26.2
Completed high school only	10.3	21.9
Attended college 1 year or more	4.8	18.6
All education levels	10.2	22.6
North central		
Did not complete high school	24.3	34.8
Completed high school only	14.5	35.8
Attended college 1 year or more	3.8	22.2
All education levels	12.2	32.0
South		
Did not complete high school	13.2	28.2
Completed high school only	6.8	16.6
Attended college 1 year or more	2.9	13.6
All education levels	6.4	19.9
West		
Did not complete high school	17.3	32.9
Completed high school only	13.4	15.9
Attended college 1 year or more	6.0	9.0
All education levels	10.1	16.5

SOURCE: John Kasarda, "Urban Change And Minority Opportunities," in *The New Urban Reality*, edited by Paul Peterson, 1985, p. 57. Copyright © Brookings Institution. Used with permission.

of college had an unemployment rate of 13.6% compared to 13.2% for whites who had not completed high school.

Audits and Surveys

Survey data provide the most direct evidence of racial discrimination in metropolitan labor markets. Just as federal and local fair housing agencies have audited the housing market to determine the extent of housing discrimination, researchers have begun to audit metropolitan labor markets to determine the extent of labor market discrimination. In

1990, the Urban Institute conducted a total of 476 hiring audits in the Washington, D.C., and Chicago areas. They matched 10 pairs of young men, ages 19 to 24, recruited from area universities. Each pair contained one white male and one black male. Each pair was matched in size, dress, education, elocution, background, and other factors that might affect hiring decisions. They all attended special training sessions to teach them to behave similarly during interviews (Turner, Fix, and Struyk 1991). The Urban Institute drew a random sample of jobs from the classified ads of local newspapers, sent the pairs of young men, testers, to respond to the ads, and recorded the results. The institute concluded that in 20% of the cases, the white applicant was able to advance further than the black applicant in the hiring process. Specifically, the report said, "the study's finding indicated that unfavorable treatment of black job seekers is widespread, and that discrimination contributes to black male unemployment and nonparticipation in the labor force" (Turner et al. 1991, p. 2). The report contended that the data contradict the notion that affirmative action and reverse discrimination are commonplace. It found levels of discrimination in the suburbs to be similar to central city levels, disconfirming the belief that space rather than race explains black unemployment. It discovered that discrimination levels were higher for the Washington, D.C., area than for Chicago, even though Washington's economy was expanding and Chicago's was stagnating.

One weakness of the institute's study is that it focused on jobs advertised in the newspaper. This focus tells us much about direct discrimination in the selection of candidates for well-publicized jobs. It tells us little about institutional discrimination such as techniques of hiring that avoid advertising jobs in the newspaper and that rely on informal communication networks that exclude blacks. The *Sheet Metal Workers* case illustrates some of these techniques. A neglect of these forms of discrimination underestimates the extent of black exclusion from metropolitan job markets.

Kirschenman and Neckerman (1991) complemented the Urban Institute's study with a survey of employer attitudes toward hiring blacks. They interviewed, with both open and closed surveys, 185 employers in the Chicago and Cook County area. Most of the employers' perceptions of inner-city blacks reflected common notions about the so-called urban underclass: that inner-city blacks are uneducated, illiterate, unmotivated, unstable, likely to be associated with gangs and drug users, and lacking in a work ethic and family values. Some employers refused to hire blacks at all. One manager of a large, all-white manufacturing facility expressed a perspective common in housing surveys. He said that he felt comfortable hiring one black, but he would feel uncomfortable hiring more than one because doing so would cause conflicts among his white workers (p. 211). Another employer of an all-white restaurant claimed he would not hire blacks because his customers are predominantly white. Specifically, he said, "My clientele is 95% white. I simply wouldn't last very long if I had some black waitresses out there" (p. 220). One restaurant owner reported that some customers complained when he hired black waitresses. The manager of a drugstore refused to hire black males because he believed them all to be dishonest and lazy.

In addition to finding direct forms of discrimination, Kirschenman and Neckerman (1991) found signs of institutional discrimination. For example, employers were recruiting less through newspaper ads and walk-in applications and more through employee referrals. This recruitment strategy was evident both in the survey data and in a report by the Chicago Association of Commerce and Industry. Employers targeted their job searches on specific neighborhoods and specific ethnic groups. One company advertised for skilled job openings only in Polish- and German-language newspapers. These recruitment strategies tended to exclude blacks.

Kirschenman and Neckerman (1991, p. 229) concluded that racial stereotypes influence hiring decisions, but more so when there are fewer standards for choosing the best candidate. That is, for jobs requiring little to no training or skills, stereotypes are more likely to influence the hiring decision.

NEW EXPLOITATIVE AND OPPRESSIVE ARRANGEMENTS: ADVANCED CAPITALISM AND CONTEMPORARY RACIAL OPPRESSION

Racial oppression in the post-civil rights era involves the persistence of racial discrimination in both the job and the housing markets. This discrimination, in conjunction with substantial economic changes, contributed to the formation of the most visible feature of racial oppression today: concentrated black poverty in central cities. This feature is not the perverse or paradoxical effect of civil rights policies, as some scholars claim. It is the result of stubborn racism deeply embedded in this society and of civil rights policies weakened by a shift back to the old conservative paradigm.

Racial oppression in this era, as in previous periods, is grounded in exploitative and oppressive economic arrangements designed to accumulate wealth for the dominant classes. Herein lies the economic basis of contemporary racism: corporate changes that undergird a shift from the Fordist to the post-Fordist era. These changes arose out of the accumulation and legitimation crisis of the late 1960s and early 1970s. Although scholars offer various explanations for and descriptions of these changes, studies converge on this single issue: The changes had a devastating impact on labor and catastrophic effects on black labor. They produced wide disparities in the distribution of income, reduced the power and size of labor unions, and eroded the status of middle-class workers. They contributed to an erosion of the economic position of the middle class. These economic changes especially contributed to two factors related to racial oppression and racism. First, in conjunction with the persistence of housing and labor market discrimination, these changes generated the growth of concentrated black poverty in central cities. Second, these changes generated a deep and pervasive sense of anxiety that fueled the resurgence of racism in the 1990s.

From Fordism to Post-Fordism

After the crisis of the late 1960s and early 1970s, capitalists began to move at the speed of light to reorganize production in ways designed to reduce the costs of labor and the power of unions. This crisis was characterized by declining corporate profits and rising private and public debt. Corporate profits as a percentage of gross national product (GNP) fell from 22% in 1950 to 10% in 1970 (Castells 1980, p. 102). Corporate debt as a percentage of GNP reached 36% in 1973 and climbed to 44% by 1987 (Harvey 1993, p. 167). This accumulation crisis was accompanied by a legitimation crisis as the number of labor strikes increased during the 1968 to 1972 period (Gordon et al. 1982; Harvey, p. 142).

Harvey (1993) explained capital's responses to this crisis in terms of a shift from a Fordist, Keynesian, fixed-capital milieu to a new post-Fordist, flexible-capital era. In the former era, industrialists paid production workers a middle-class wage, embraced labor unions, and accepted an expanded role of the state in its accumulation and legitimation roles. In the Fordist milieu, production facilities were fixed to a specific area: fixed by their dependency on railroad lines and waterways and fixed by the enormous sum of money invested in mammoth factories. In the new era, industrialists struggled to reduced labor costs, destroy unions, roll back corporate tax burdens, shrink the social welfare functions of the state, and enhance corporate influence over government. With revolutions in transportation, communications, and production, capital became more flexible. That is, production became less dependent on railroad transportation. It relied more on trucking. Moreover, new production facilities were smaller, more compact, and easier to relocate to another region or country.

Although Harvey suggested that Fordist regimes began to shift after the 1968 to 1972 crisis, other scholars, such as Bonacich (1976) and Gordon et al. (1982) claimed that the movement to reduce labor costs and weaken labor unions began in the 1940s. Still others argued that this impulse to reduce labor costs and bust unions is an inherent feature of capitalism; it is a requirement for capital accumulation (Baron and Sweezy 1968; Edwards et al. 1978; Gordon 1978).

Whichever conceptual framework was used, the conclusions were the same. The following corporate trends severely affected workers:

1. Greater mobility of capital and restructuring of production
2. Direct assault on labor
3. Consolidation—merger mania

Capital Mobility and Restructuring

Several technological changes transformed fixed capital into hyper-mobile capital. The trucking industry emerged, especially after World War II, and liberated capital from its dependency on railroads and waterways. The revolution in telecommunications made it possible for executives in Chicago or New York to engage in high-quality, instant audio and visual communications with managers anywhere in the world. Advancements in air travel allowed executives to fly to any city in the world in a matter of hours. Changes in production technology—the creation of smaller and more automated factories—enhanced the possibilities for rapid deployment of factories anywhere in the world. These revolutions and advancements super-condensed time and space and allowed for the rapid movement of capital anywhere in the world.

With the hyper-mobility of capital, many corporations, especially those involved in textiles, apparel, electronics, footwear, and others, reorganized much of their operations into a global division of labor. That is, many of these firms moved the labor-intensive aspects of their operations to areas where wages are low and unions either nonexistent or under repressive government control. These firms have tended to keep the research, development, design, engineering, testing, and coordinating aspects of their operations in the United States. Of course, some firms are now exporting even these aspects (Reich 1992).

Almost every major U.S. electronics firm has transferred production and assembly operations to plants located in a foreign country. As early as 1971, 54% of black-and-white televisions, 91% of radios, and 18% of color televisions were manufactured in a foreign country (Blumberg 1981, p. 155). In 1977, Zenith joined RCA, General Electric (GE), Sylvania, and Admiral in using assembly plants overseas. In fact, Zenith eliminated 25% of its domestic jobs as it transferred a substantial proportion of its assembly operations abroad.

The case of RCA illustrates the use of mobile capital to reduce labor costs and union power. In the late 1960s, RCA built a new production facility in Memphis, Tennessee. When Memphis workers organized a union, RCA closed the facility and opened a new one in Taiwan (Bluestone and Harrison 1982, pp. 170-71). In another case, GE closed a production facility in Providence, Rhode Island, and opened a new facility in Mexico. General Electric was candid about the relocation. A representative for the corporation admitted that the company relocated the plant in Mexico because of the cheaper labor (Bluestone and Harrison, p. 172).

Today, no American-brand black-and-white television or radio is manufactured in the United States (Blumberg 1981, p. 155). About 90% of the value of the parts of American-made color televisions are assembled abroad (Harrison and Bluestone 1990, p. 30). Most U.S. personal computer firms have relocated assembly operations abroad because assembly tends to be labor-intensive, routine, and requiring few skills. Most important, labor is cheap. The IBM computer is designed in the United States but assembled abroad (Harrison and Bluestone 1990, p. 31). Other electronics firms, such as Texas Instruments, Hewlett Packard, and National Semi-Conductor, have joined the movement to locate assembly operations abroad.

Automobile plants have joined the movement to locate assembly operations where labor is cheap and unions weak. Ford, General Motors, and Chrysler have located a number of plants in Mexico. Chrysler has more than 23 plants south of the U.S. border (Harrison and Bluestone 1990, p. 30).

A number of firms have begun to shift service jobs overseas. For example, American Airlines has moved its data entry services to Barbados. This data service operation is connected to the airline's accounting division in Tulsa, Oklahoma, by way of satellite telecommunications (Harrison and Bluestone 1990, p. 31).

Cheap labor attracts firms like a magnet. Labor costs in some Third World countries are a small fraction of labor costs in the United States. For example, in 1982 the average hourly wage for a production worker was $11.79 in the United States, $1.97 in Mexico, $1.77 in Singapore, $1.57 in Taiwan, and $1.22 in South Korea (Harrison and Bluestone 1990). Taiwan and South Korea have become favorite spots for U.S. apparel factories. Mexico has become a haven for runaway U.S. firms.

Direct Assault on Labor

Although the relocation of assembly operations abroad hurt American workers, it accounted for only about a third of the loss of unionized jobs in this country (Harrison and Bluestone 1990). Other factors affected unions. Corporate leaders assaulted unionized labor directly. They employed a number of tactics including outsourcing, use of temporary workers and part-timers, union squeezing, and union busting.

In outsourcing, a major corporation closes down or cuts back a particular division and subcontracts with a smaller nonunion firm to do the division's work. This subcontracting occurs in a range of areas including advertising, design, finance, marketing, and parts production (Harrison and Bluestone 1990; Harvey 1993). Harrison and Bluestone provided an example of outsourcing in the case of pipe fitters who worked for the U.S. Steel Corporation under a union contract, earning $13 an hour with benefits. Workers were laid off but found new jobs working for a non-unionized firm, making $5 an hour, creating parts to sell to U.S. Steel. Automobile companies do a great deal of subcontracting with small firms to produce auto parts.

Outsourcing occurs on an international scale as U.S.-based companies subcontract for both manufacturing parts and services. For example, Saztec International, a data processing firm with headquarters in Kansas City, subcontracts data services with firms located in the United States and in the Philippines (Reich 1992, p. 211).

Also, to reduce vulnerability to strikes, automobile producers have engaged in parallel production and outsourcing. That is, auto parts are made not only by private companies in the United States but by a foreign division, a subsidiary, or another unrelated parts producer overseas. For example, parts for the Ford Escort are made in divisions, subsidiaries, or by parts producers found in 16 different countries on three continents (Bluestone and Harrison 1982, p. 176). If there is a strike in one company in one country, other parts producers in other countries can speed up production to compensate for the impact of the strike.

The proportion of the total U.S. workforce employed by these smaller subcontractors has been growing. Increased employment in this area contributes to a contraction of the core labor force—blue- and white-collar unionized workers paid a middle-class wage with benefits—and an increase in the peripheral sector—nonunion blue-collar and white-collar workers paid low wages with few benefits.

Another but more subtle way of assaulting labor entails an increased use of part-time and temporary workers. Harrison and Bluestone (1990) reported that the number of involuntary part-time, temporary, sub-contracted, and home workers grew from 8 million in 1980 to 18 million in 1985, almost 17% of the workforce. Further illustrating the extent of the rise of part-timers, they noted that in the Minneapolis-St. Paul area, the proportion of registered nurses employed part-time increased from about 30% in 1977 to about 70% in 1984.

Bankruptcy, buyouts, and reorganization emerged in the 1980s as a common way of eliminating unions and cutting labor costs. When a company declares bankruptcy or succumbs to a takeover or buyout, it shuts down operations, lays off its unionized labor force, reorganizes, and hires a new, nonunion workforce. A good example of this union-busting strategy is the 1982 case of Texas Air Corporation's buyout of Continental Airlines. After the buyout, Texas Air declared bankruptcy, repudiated union contracts, laid off two thirds of its workforce, and cut wages in half (Reich 1988, p. 139).

For companies with strong unions and no chance of declaring bankruptcy, negotiated concessions became an effective way of reducing labor costs. Most newly negotiated union contracts in the 1970s had cost of living clauses (COLA—which automatically increased wages when the cost of living increased); by 1980, only 40% of new contracts had such clauses. A year later, this figure had declined to 33%, and by 1986, it was down to only 15% (Harrison and Bluestone 1990, p. 40). Wage freezes or cuts were practically unheard of in the 1970s; in the 1981-1982 period, 44% of the unionized workforce accepted either a wage freeze or a wage cut. In 1986, the United Steel Workers at LTV Steel conceded to a $3.15 an hour wage cut (Harrison and Bluestone, p. 40).

A number of unions, such as the UAW, given a choice between wage cuts or layoffs, took the layoff. When the company sought more concessions, many of these unions conceded to cuts in entry-level salaries. Although these cuts did not affect the employed union workers, over time average wages eroded as older workers retired and new workers were hired under substantially reduced entry-level salaries.

Merger Mania

Another trend that severely affected the U.S. workforce is the tremendous upsurge in mergers and the rise of conglomerates on both the national and international levels. We call this trend a merger frenzy because the number of mergers and the amount of money involved were staggering and unprecedented. Between 1983 and 1986, over 12,000 firms, almost $500 billion, and close to one fifth of the value of all the stocks traded in 1986 were involved in mergers or acquisitions (Harrison and Bluestone 1990, p. 59). While this merger frenzy was driven more by the passion to accumulate wealth than a desire to hurt labor, it redirected capital in ways that contributed to further erosion of the industrial base and substantial losses of manufacturing jobs. That is, a number of industries, instead of reinvesting in obsolete industrial facilities, bought other firms in other areas. They called this investment pattern *acquisitions and diversification*. The steel industry is a prime example of this trend. As a former president of U.S. Steel once remarked, this industry is in business to make money, not steel. During the late 1970s and throughout the 1980s, the industry disinvested in steel, closing down several major plants and idling tens of thousands of workers. In 1979, U.S. Steel shut down about 16 plants and eliminated about 13,000 steel worker jobs, 8% of the U.S. Steel workforce (Blumberg 1981, p. 118). In the mid-1980s, U.S. Steel, now USX, spent $6 billion to buy Marathon Oil and $3.6 billion to purchase Texas Oil and Gas (Reich 1988, p. 127).

Merger mania involved both domestic and international markets. For example, by 1986, Chrysler owned about 25% of Mitsubishi's stock, and Ford owned 25% of Mazda's stock. U.S. firms are able to close down U.S. facilities and import parts made by foreign subsidiaries and related firms (Reich 1988, p. 82). Merger mania also involves U.S. firms purchasing other U.S. firms, closing them down, and contracting with foreign firms. Consider the GE case. In the early 1980s, GE bought RCA and NBC for $6.56 billion. GE then closed down RCA's production facilities in the United States, relocating some facilities abroad and subcontracting with other foreign firms. In 1985, GE spent $1.4 billion to buy and bring to the United States electrical appliances manufactured abroad. Of course, these appliances bore the GE label. More and more goods made under a U.S. label are not made in the United States or by U.S. workers.

Impacts

Private ownership of capital means that investments and corporate policies will be driven by the desire to make profits and to accumulate wealth, not to satisfy human needs or to build communities. These corporate investment patterns and corporate practices increased profits. At the same time, they contributed to the destruction of communities and the erosion of living standards. They devastated unions, increased inequality, and marginalized workers. Their most devastating impacts were felt on black workers.

Unions

These trends decimated the ranks of union workers. The proportion of nonagricultural American workers belonging to a union declined from 35% in 1960 to 25% in 1970, and 17% in 1989—13.4% if we exclude government employees (Reich 1992, p. 212). During the 1980s, the UAW lost over 500,000 members, one third of its membership.

Labor Markets

The labor market changes that took place in this period are inconsistent with the jobs/skills mismatch thesis. There is little evidence that a substantial number of knowledge-intensive jobs have been replacing the jobs lost in the industrial sector. Fainstein (1986-1987) demonstrated that the data presented by Kasarda (1985), which supported the jobs/skills thesis, were substantially biased. Kasarda divided jobs into two categories based on the mean level of education of jobholders: entry-level jobs have a mean of less than 12 years of education, and knowledge-intensive jobs have a mean of over 14 years of education. Fainstein pointed out that these two groups capture only a proportion of the jobs in the metropolitan labor market. They exclude jobs that fall in the 12 to 14 years of education range. More than half the jobs fall in this area. Fainstein concluded that when the universe of metropolitan jobs is examined, it becomes clear that low wage, service-sector jobs grew at a substantially faster rate than higher wage, knowledge-intensive jobs.

In a study of changes in Detroit's labor market from 1970 to 1980 (Carter Wilson 1992), we found substantial increases in service-sector jobs, but not the kind of jobs expected by the jobs/skills mismatch theory. We found that Wayne County, anchored by Detroit, experienced a 10% growth in such jobs; Oakland and Macomb counties, both adjacent to Wayne, experienced a 172% increase and 128% increase respectively. For Oakland County, with the highest growth rate in service-sector jobs, 55% were in two areas: business service and health service, with large proportions of these jobs in temporary help-supply services, building, mailing, and stenographic services. Only a small proportion of the jobs fell in the knowledge category.

Other studies supported the trend found in the Detroit area. Sassen-Koob (1984, pp. 154-55), for example, demonstrated the low wage business sector to be the fastest-growing labor sector for New York City. Harrison and Bluestone (1990), using national data, found that most of the growth in service-sector jobs was among the ranks of waiters, waitresses, doormen, store clerks, janitors, fast-food workers, hotel clerks, and other low wage positions.

Clearly, there is little job growth in the high wage, knowledge-intensive area but substantial growth in the low wage, service sector. These changes support the notion that the core sector is declining—jobs in large corporations paying a middle-class wage with benefits are dwindling—and the periphery is expanding (Fainstein 1986-1987; Harvey 1993, p. 151). These changes are contributing to an erosion of income and an increase in inequality.

Consistent with this declining core theory, Harrison and Bluestone presented evidence of an increase in the proportion of low income workers. They defined low income as annual income below $11,000 (in 1986 dollars). They examined the proportion of those workers (who are employed) earning $11,000 or less in various years. In 1970, 12% were low income. By 1980, this figure had increased to 15%; by 1986, it was 17.2% (Harrison and Bluestone 1990, pp. 122-23). They attributed this increase to the upsurge in low income service jobs.

Harrison and Bluestone (1990, pp. 132-35) also maintained that the proportion of families falling into the middle class—those with incomes between $20,000 and $50,000—has declined from 53% in 1973 to 47.9% in 1984. Although a small proportion of these families rose into the upper-middle class, the majority of them fell into the lower-middle and lower classes.

By most measures, inequality increased in the decades of the 1970s and 1980s. One way of measuring this inequality is by comparing the share of total family income earned by the poorest family with the share earned by the richest family. In 1969, the poorest fifth of all U.S. families earned 5.6% of the total of all family incomes in the United States, and the richest fifth earned 40.6% of this total. Throughout the 1970s and 1980s, the share earned by the poorest fifth declined, while the top fifth increased. By 1992, the poorest fifth earned 4.4% compared to 44.6% earned by the richest fifth (Hudson 1995, p. 235). A congressional study reported that between 1977 and 1990, the income of the richest fifth increased by 15% while the income of the poorest fifth declined by 7% (Hudson 1995, p. 234).

Another way of examining income changes of the 1980s is to focus on the status of displaced workers. In the late 1980s, the Department of Labor conducted a 5-year survey of displaced workers: those who had worked for a firm for 3 years or more and had lost their jobs because of employment cutbacks or plant closings between 1979 and 1984. The department identified about 5.1 million displaced workers. By January 1986, 30% of them had found jobs paying as much or more than their previous job. However, 30% found jobs paying less, and 40% were either unemployed or had dropped out of the labor force entirely (Levy 1988, p. 93).

Race, Marginalization, and Concentrated Poverty

These changes contributed to the marginalization of workers: those who have dropped out of the labor force, the long-term unemployed who are still looking for a job, the part-time or temporary workers who would prefer to work full-time, and the working poor. These marginalized workers make up what Marx called the reserve army of labor. The increase in their numbers tends to depress wages and weaken the power of organized wages.

The marginalization of the industrial worker has had its most devastating impact on black workers, who suffered the highest rate of job losses from the contraction of the industrial sector and have the greatest difficulty moving back into the shrinking core sector's jobs.

The city of Detroit graphically illustrates the impact of these changes on African Americans. Between 1977 and 1982, Detroit lost 21% of its industrial operations (Rich 1989, p. 129). The number of manufacturing establishments with 20 or more employees declined by about 42% between 1972 and 1982, from 821 to 477 (Carter Wilson 1992). This translated into the loss of more than 69,000 manufacturing jobs. These losses affected both black and white workers, but black Detroiters suffered more, because a higher proportions of them worked in the industrial sector in Detroit, as in the nation, and because a higher proportion of black Detroiters, compared to white Detroiters, worked in factories inside the city (Carter Wilson 1992). The long-term impact of this industrial decline was a decrease in black labor force participation, an increase in black unemployment, and an increase in black poverty.

Black poverty became more concentrated in Detroit, especially between 1970 and 1980. Although Detroit's population declined during this period, the number of poor increased by 14% (Carter Wilson 1992). At the same time, the proportion of the total population and the proportion of the poor population living in concentrated poverty areas—census tracts with poverty rates above 20%—increased. In 1970, 20% of the total population and 45% of the poor lived in concentrated poverty tracts. By 1980, over half of Detroit's population and 75% of the poor lived in concentrated areas (Carter Wilson 1992).

The changes in Detroit were part of a national trend. According to Richard Nathan's (1987) study of the nation's 50 largest cities, between 1970 and 1980, the population declined by 5.1%, the number of poor increased by 11.7%, and concentrated poverty populations increased by 30.5%. Other studies found concentrated poverty increasing in larger cities. Jargowsky and Bane (1991, p. 255) found that five cities—New York, Chicago, Detroit, Philadelphia, and Newark—accounted for two thirds of the total increase in concentrated poverty. Poverty declined substantially in rural areas and small towns but increased in the larger central cities. Jencks (1991) maintained that poverty did not increase but became more concentrated in central cities, especially between the mid-1970s and the late 1980s.

Nevertheless, blacks suffered substantially higher poverty and unemployment rates relative to whites in these metropolitan areas. For example, according to 1990 Census data, the poverty rate for black families was 29.8% in Detroit's Prime Metropolitan Statistical Area (PMSA), 26.5% in the Chicago PMSA, 21.6% in New York's PMSA, and 21.1% for Philadelphia's Central Metropolitan Statistical Area (CMSA). These figures compare to white poverty rates of 5.4% in Detroit's PMSA, 3.8% in Chicago's PMSA, 7.8% in New York's PMSA, and 3.6% in Philadelphia's CMSA. These figures indicate that black poverty rates are more that five times the white rates in Detroit, Chicago, and Philadelphia, and more than three times the white rate in New York (U.S. Department of Commerce 1990a, 1990b, 1990c, 1990d).

Unemployment rates were substantially higher for blacks compared to whites. Census data for 1990 indicate that black unemployment rates were 20.6% for Detroit's PMSA, 17.6% for Chicago's PMSA, 12.2% for New York City, and 12.6% for Philadelphia's CMSA. These figures compare to white unemployment rates of 6.1% for Detroit's PMSA, 4.3% for Chicago's PMSA, 4.0% for Philadelphia's CMSA, and 5.3% for New York City. That is, black unemployment rates are more than twice the white rates for these metropolitan areas (U.S. Department of Commerce 1990a, 1990b, 1990c, 1990d).

The New Race Politics

Persistent and concentrated black poverty characterizes the racial oppression of the post-Fordist milieu. This oppression is legitimized by a new race politics led by the resurgence of upper-stratum interests and strengthened by a decline in subordinate groups. As upper-stratum groups emerged to dominate the political arena, the prevailing political rhetoric increasingly shifted blame for deteriorating economic conditions from the corporate sector to blacks and to the lower classes. Post-Fordist politics has become politics for the rich and against the poor.

The reemergence of upper-stratum dominance in American politics is evident in studies of voting behavior and of interest groups. Voter turnout in the United States, especially in presidential elections, has declined. In the 1950s and 1960s, it hovered around 60% (Janda, Berry, and Goldman, 1995, p. 239); in 1960, it was 63% (Lineberry 1986, p. 278). By the 1980s, it had declined to just above 50%. Reagan was elected in 1980 with little more than 26% of the eligible voters voting for him, as voter turnout was 52%, and only 51% of those voting voted for Reagan (Chomsky 1985; Carter Wilson 1992, p. 193). Voter turnout correlates with socioeconomic status. It declines as income, education, and occupational status decline. The decline in voter turnout has been more substantial in the lower classes. Thus elections have acquired a profound bias in favor of the upper classes.

The interest-group lobbying system in the United States has always had a bias in favor of upper level groups (Schattschneider 1975). However, by the 1980s and 1990s, this bias became a matter of substantial corporate sector dominance of the political arena. A 1986 study of over 7,000 lobbying organizations in Washington, D.C., found a clear business-class bias. Of the total, 70% represented corporations, trade associations, and general business organizations (Hudson 1995, p. 191). Groups representing labor constituted only 1.7%; citizen groups made up 4.1% (Hudson, p. 191).

The sheer number of corporate Political Action Committees (PACs) increased exponentially from the mid-1970s to the mid-1980s, while labor union PACs declined. In 1975, there were barely 100 corporate PACS. This figure increased to about 1,500 in 1980, and by the end of the 1980s, there were close to 2,000 corporate PACs. Labor union PACs increased from about 250 in 1975 to almost 500 in 1982, but by 1988, there were only 200 (James Q. Wilson 1992, p. 188).

What these changes suggest is that the rise of the new race politics of the late 20th century corresponds to the decline of industrial labor unions, the weakening of the civil rights coalition, and the emergence of a politicized corporate sector. The assault on civil rights, affirmative action, and antipoverty programs is not the result of a revolt of working-class Democrats shifting to the Republican party. It is the result of a political arena substantially biased against lower level groups and in favor of upper level voters and corporate political action committees. Of course, the conservative coalition is far from unified, as other factions such as the National Rifle Association, the Christian Coalition, and anti-abortion groups, who make up this coalition, are often at odds with corporate leaders.

Nonetheless, subtle, antiblack sentiments undergird the political rhetoric of this conservative movement. This rhetoric characterizes liberal policies as irrational—having gone too far to the left. It depicts affirmative action as a program that takes jobs and educational opportunities from well-qualified whites and gives them to less qualified blacks. It insists that welfare does more harm than good, as it promotes dependency and drains federal resources. Conservative rhetoric demands harsher penalties for criminals as the best way to protect society from lawless elements. It portrays policies protecting the rights of criminals as dangerous and detached from the reality of today's violent world.

Although these proposals seem reasonable on the surface, they shift public attention away from changes benefiting the corporate sector. For example, in 1950 corporate income taxes were 26.5% of federal tax receipts. By 1985, the corporate share had declined to 9.0% (Center for Popular Economics 1986). Moreover, after the tax cuts of the early 1980s (1982-1984), many corporations paid little or no taxes, and the rich received the largest tax breaks. For example, General Electric "earned $9.5 billion in profits over the 1981-1984 period, paid no taxes, and got

$98 million in tax rebates" (Center for Popular Economics, p. 149). Moreover, when the effects of inflation and social security tax increases were factored in after the 1982-1984 cuts, taxpayers earning over $200,000 enjoyed a 15% tax cut, whereas those making between $30,000 and $50,000 got a break of only 1% (Center for Popular Economics, p. 146). Taxpayers making less than $30,000 paid more in taxes (Center for Popular Economics, p. 146).

The new conservative rhetoric shifts public attention away from corporate practices and federal policies that benefit the corporate sector at the expense of subordinate classes and redirects that attention to issues related to race: affirmative action, family values, capital punishment, the urban underclass, and welfare. Whether intended or not, this rhetoric both exploits and generates negrophobia. That is, behind the anti-affirmative action campaign lurks the fear that blacks are taking white jobs, white seats in colleges, and white apprenticeship positions. Behind the anticrime crusade hides the fear of black street criminals and dangerous black males. Behind the call for family values is the fear of black underclass values—the antithesis of middle-class values: two-parent families, education, hard work, respect for private property, and puritanical ethics.

To some extent, this phobia arises out of the pervasive anxiety generated by post-Fordist economic arrangements (a point that will be demonstrated in our forthcoming discussion of meta-racism). Fear of blacks provides an objective outlet for this anxiety. Although this negrophobia remains hidden behind this discourse, occasionally racial stereotypes and images appear in the conservative rhetoric. For example, Ronald Reagan often used the stereotype of the black welfare queen in his attack on welfare. Another example is the use of Willie Horton's image by Bush's campaign staff during the 1988 presidential election. Willie Horton was a black convict who committed rape and assault after he was set free by an early release program in Massachusetts under Governor Michael Dukakis, Bush's Democratic opponent. The intimation of Bush's campaign advertisement was that Dukakis represents the type of liberal who will release from prison violent black men who assault and rape innocent middle-class people. Still another example is Jesse Helms's 1992 campaign advertisement, featuring white hands being replaced by black hands.

The point is that conservative rhetoric embodies antiblack sentiments. These sentiments are expressed by politicians, radio talk hosts, popular magazines, and newspapers. These public expressions contribute to the formation and maintenance of meta-racism.

THE NEW RACISM: META-RACISM

Of course, politics alone did not produce meta-racism. Meta-racism emerged under specific historical circumstances and material conditions. That is, it arose after the disintegration of dominative racism, after the civil rights movement, and with the post-Fordist milieu. It is well-grounded in new exploitative and oppressive economic arrangements, characterized by a decline in the status and well-being of middle-class workers and the growth of concentrated urban poverty. These conditions and circumstances have contributed to three major trends supporting the ascension of meta-racism:

The new economic arrangements have diminished economic opportunities and have generated a pervasive sense of anxiety that has heightened racial fears.

It is precisely this decline in opportunities, especially for the sons and daughters of middle-class workers, that has generated the rise of the fear, anxiety, and anger that undergird the new racism.

These new economic arrangements, combined with persistent discrimination in housing and employment, have produced black poverty concentrated in central cities.

This concentrated black poverty characterizes racial oppression of the post-civil rights era. Black poverty, especially under conditions of pervasive anxiety and fear, contributes to racist imagery and racist ideology. Concentrated poverty, anxiety, fear, and extreme inequality have provided the atmosphere of insecurity and anxiety that makes the public more receptive to the resurgence of older forms of racism such as those represented in Richard Herrnstein and Charles Murray's book *The Bell Curve*.

These conditions contributed to the formation of a more bureaucratized racism.

With the death of dominative racism and the modest success of the civil rights movement, blatant racial exclusion is no longer acceptable in contemporary culture. At the same time, the presence of racist images and discourse heightens the impulse to exclude blacks. This culture encourages the formation of bureaucratized and rationalized forms of racial discrimination.

 Upper level interests—upper-income voters, corporate PACs, and so on— dominate the political arena, and they have become bolder about exploiting racial fears to divert political hostility from the corporate sector.

This use of this fear has contributed to the rhetoric of the new race politics.

What has emerged under advanced capitalism is not one racism, but meta-racism. Meta-racism is a conglomeration of many forms of racism with dynamics similar to older forms of racism: scapegoat racism, ideological racism, institutional racism, aversive racism, racist imagery, and symbolic racism. It is also a more bureaucratized form of racism.

Institutional and Bureaucratic Racism

Institutional racism became more evident after the passage of the 1964 Civil Rights Act. It involves large organizations using practices, rules, or standard operating procedures that are unjust or arbitrary and that discriminate against blacks. The *Griggs* case provides one illustration of this point. Prior to the 1964 Civil Rights Act, the Duke Power Company had an explicit policy of excluding blacks from all but the most undesirable jobs. After its passage, the company used various tests and devices to exclude blacks. In the *Griggs* case, the U.S. Supreme Court recognized that businesses have the right and the need to establish standards for recruiting the best qualified candidates. Sometime these standards produce racially discriminatory outcomes. When this happens, the Court requires businesses to demonstrate that the standards are fair—that is, nonarbitrary and job-related. If they are unrelated to the job, then they are arbitrary and discriminatory. The Court held as discriminatory the use of a personality test and a high school diploma to select candidates for a janitorial job because these standards were unrelated to the job and because they discriminated against blacks.

The Sheet Metal Workers case provides another illustration. After being ordered to stop excluding blacks, this union deliberately adopted a range of subtle practices designed to continue this policy. These practices included recruiting from all-white locals, recruiting on the basis of test scores but providing test preparation classes for white applicants only, and accepting only those applicants with recommendations from those already in the union—white males.

Lipsky (1980) discussed the manner in which racial stereotypes become bureaucratized by street-level bureaucrats. These bureaucrats—teachers, police officers, social workers, lower court judges—operate under conditions of enormous stress and little information. They have to make rapid and critical decisions affecting the lives of large numbers of people and often their own safety. Lacking adequate information and pressed by the need to make quick and critical decisions, they incorporate racial stereotypes in their daily decision-making activities. This incorporation of stereotypes routinizes the decision-making process, enhancing the speed and efficiency of making decisions and reducing the chance of errors. However, racially discriminatory impacts result from the incorporation of these stereotypes into bureaucratic routines. For example, teachers and school administrators often routinely exclude blacks from honors classes and disproportionately place them into slower-paced classes. School systems incorporate culturally biased tests that place a disproportionately high percentage of blacks into classes for the educable mentally retarded. Police working on the street, in dangerous situations, must make quick decisions; lacking any information on potentially dangerous suspects, police routinely react to black men with greater force. Juvenile court judges, lacking information on the hundreds of delinquents appearing before them, must make quick decisions on whether to incarcerate. The quick decisions rule is to give probation to those arrestees who are in school and from two-parent homes and to incarcerate those who have dropped out of school or are from one-parent homes. Lipsky claimed that collectively these bureaucratic routines have profound class and racially discriminatory impacts. They constitute the bureaucratization of racism.

Drug policies provide a good example of bureaucratic racism. Federal law mandates that those individuals convicted for the possession of 5 or more grams of crack cocaine get a minimum of 5 years in prison. At the same time, those convicted of possessing 300, 400, or 500 grams of cocaine often receive less than a year of imprisonment. The rationale behind this policy is that crack is associated with street violence and the destruction of communities, whereas cocaine is not. The stiffer penalty for crack is said to give the justice system the power to attack the source of the more serious forms of crime in this society—those associated with crack.

Crack—the cheaper derivative of cocaine made from cocaine and baking soda—has become the preferred drug among inner-city drug users. Cocaine is more popular among affluent suburban drug users. There are two negative effects of the drug policy that targets crack over cocaine. First, this policy focuses police resources on the lowest level drug dealer who sells the crack on the street corner and diverts police resources away from the higher level drug dealers, the major suppliers of the source of the inner-city drug problem—cocaine, the raw product. Second, this policy has profound racial and class biases. It contributes to dramatic increases in the number of incarcerated low income African Americans. According to a report by The Sentencing Project, blacks constituted about 12% of the population, 13% of monthly drug users, 33% of drug arrestees, but 55% of those convicted and 74% of those sentenced for drug posses- sion (Mauer and Huling 1995, p. 12). This policy has little effect on the drug problem. It has a profound racially discriminatory impact on blacks. Because it involves unjust and racially biased outcomes resulting from the practices of large, powerful, and presumptively rational organiza- tions—Congress, the courts, and law enforcement agencies—it con- stitutes bureaucratic or institutional racism.

Scapegoat Racism

Feagin and Vera (1995) provided an excellent example of scapegoat racism in their discussion of the rise of antiblack violence in Dubuque, Iowa, in the early 1990s. After race hate graffiti were on the garage of a black family, the city of Dubuque created a Constructive Integration Task Force in 1989. The Task Force developed a plan for attracting more black families to the city. Private sector employers were to create affirm- ative action initiatives, and the city planned to set aside money to help black families relocate. The city's economy had undergone post-Fordist changes, especially massive losses of industrial jobs, in the late 1970s and early 1980s, these being replaced by lower paying service-sector jobs in the 1980s and 1990s. The proposal called on private firms to recruit only where there were job vacancies (Feagin and Vera 1995, p. 21).

Reaction to this proposal was violent. Crosses were burned on the lawns of at least 12 black families, and bricks were thrown through some windows. Whites arrested for the racial violence claimed that the crosses expressed the white community's alarm over the job losses they expected from the integration plan.

A leader of the Neo-Nazi Nationalist Movement, Richard Barrett, came to Dubuque to exploit the conflict. He said that "Kingism (a reference to Martin Luther King) means loser take all" (Feagin and Vera 1995, p. 23). This statement is an obvious reference to affirmative action. Thousands of white residents signed petitions against the proposal. They referred to it as a form of forced integration. Violence broke out in other parts of the state.

The assault on the few black families in Dubuque and on the modest integration plan was not rational. Neither posed a threat to white jobs. One psychoanalytical explanation is this: Whites—fearful over job losses, insecure over the descending status of middle-class workers, and anxious over a bleak future—are using blacks and programs perceived to benefit blacks as scapegoats. This case illustrates the negrophobia behind the new race politics.

Thomas and Mary Edsall (1992), in *Chain Reaction,* presented another case that illustrates this scapegoating racism. It is based on focus group surveys of white Democrats conducted by a Democratic party polling firm, the Analysis Group. The summary explains why white Democrats are defecting from the party and the role race plays in the defection:

> These white Democratic defectors express a profound distaste for blacks, a sentiment that pervades almost everything they think about government and politics. . . . Blacks constitute the explanation for their (white defectors') vulnerability and for almost everything that has gone wrong in their lives; not being black is what constitutes being middle class; not living with blacks is what makes a neighborhood a decent place to live. These sentiments have important implications for Democrats, as virtually all progressive symbols and themes have been redefined in racial and pejorative terms. . . . The special status of blacks is perceived by almost all of these individuals as a serious obstacle to their personal advancement. Indeed, discrimination against whites has become a well-assimilated and ready explanation for their status, vulnerability and failures. (quoted in Edsall and Edsall, p. 182)

Many of these interviewees live in lily-white, upwardly mobile, suburban neighborhoods in Macomb County, adjacent to Wayne County and the city of Detroit. Interviewees blamed their insecure status on blacks and programs designed to benefit blacks. They saw affirmative action and welfare as black programs, responsible for white job losses. They opposed the Democratic party because they saw this party as supporting blacks, women, welfare recipients, and other people not like them (white males).

For the most part, interviewees operate within a cultural context that attaches specific meaning and emotions to blacks and whites. Within this context, whites symbolize higher status, pure, moral, and hard-working people; and blacks symbolize lower status, impure, amoral, lazy, and otherwise undesirable people. This paradigm focuses on blacks as a source of white vulnerability, financial stress, or lack of advancement and blames blacks for other things that may go wrong in the lives of whites. This paradigm makes blacks the lightning rod for white frustrations, failures, anxieties, and hostilities. At the same time, this cultural paradigm blots out the role of the corporate sector and of federal policies benefiting the upper stratum. This cultural paradigm is racist insofar as it explains social phenomena in terms of race, and it brews a kettle full of racial emotions. This case illustrates the intense antiblack hostility to and the passionate aversion for blacks undergirding contemporary racist culture.

Racist Imagery

Racist imagery is subtle and subconscious; that is, it entails the presence of dehumanizing images of blacks operating in the unconscious white mind but affecting conscious decisions. The old images included Black Sambo, Stepin Fetchit, and other childlike, inarticulate, black characters. The images also included crazed, bull-like, black characters, driven mad by freedom. Today's images include those of the black underclass: crazed, uncontrollable, powerful, violent, drug-addicted black men; promiscuous black women; and black welfare queens. These images move in the dark recesses of the collective unconscious mind. Although they are often invisible, they explain racially motivated behavior.

Several examples offer the best explanation for extreme racial behavior. One example is the videotaped beating of Rodney King, which appears irrational. The world was dumbfounded by both the beating and the initial acquittal of the officers involved. Defenders of the accused officers claimed that King appeared dangerous, that he lurched forward toward the police, that he refused to surrender. Nevertheless, the continued beating of a subdued and broken King makes sense only in the context of a particular image of King. It makes no sense if King appeared white, middle class, and innocuous. To say that King was beaten because he was black and the officers were racist explains little. However, a different picture comes into focus when we consider a number of factors. First, an officer referred to a black family as looking like gorillas in the mist. Second, officers claimed that they believed King was on drugs. Third, we occasionally see on television or on the movie screen images of crazed, uncontrollable, powerful, violent, drug-addicted black men attacking police officers. The fact that an officer referred to a black family as gorillas indicates that the policemen operated in a framework that viewed blacks as profoundly different from whites. The fact that they were concerned that King was on drugs points to the television or movie images of insane, violent, drug-addicted black men. The presence of these images in the minds of both the officers and the jurors who initially acquitted them provides a plausible explanation for the not guilty verdict. With these images, the beating appears as a rational response to a fear image.

Another example of racist imagery is found in the cases of white culprits falsely accusing imaginary black males. One case occurred in Boston in the fall of 1989. A white male, Charles Stuart, shot and killed his wife, wounded himself, and claimed that a black male had committed the crime. Whites were outraged. White police officers called for the reinstatement of the death penalty. They found and arrested a black male who fit the description provided by Mr. Stuart. Later, Stuart committed suicide. His brother, Matthew, confessed that he knew that Stuart had committed the crime and lied about the story of black male assailants (Feagin and Vera 1995, pp. 62-70). A similar case occurred in Milwaukee, Wisconsin, in the spring of 1992. A white male, Jesse Anderson, killed his wife and concocted a story about two black males who had attacked him and his wife in a parking lot. Anderson was later convicted. Another case happened in Union, South Carolina, in the fall of 1994. A white woman, Susan Smith, drowned her two children and then claimed a black male hijacked her car with the children in it. Still another, lesser known case occurred at the University of Toledo in the winter of 1992, when a white male police officer shot and killed a white female student. Apparently, the officer called the campus police, disguised his voice, and reported that a group of black males were accosting a cabdriver on campus. The call turned out to be a ruse to create the impression that the murder was a random act of violence committed by black men. The white officer was later arrested, tried, and convicted.

For an adult to commit a violent crime and fabricate a story that blames the crime on the random violent act of a black man, two conditions must be present. First, the adult must believe that random acts of black violence are widespread—that there are many dangerous and erratic black men out there in the streets of urban areas, waiting to commit acts of violence. The presence of this image of black men is key to understanding these cases. Second, the adult must feel that this belief or image is held by a great many rational people, including those in authority. The point is that these cases indicate the presence, in the collective unconscious mind, of images of dangerous, fearsome, and insane black men who commit arbitrary acts of violence that threaten white society.

Ideological Racism

Ideological racism functions more directly to legitimize a racially oppressive order. It is reflected in academic theories that explain black subordination in ways that (a) alienate the oppressed from the rest of society, (b) denigrate the oppressed, (c) desensitize society to the suffering of the oppressed, and (d) shift blame from the role of capital in contributing to declining opportunities and place that blame on the victims of oppression themselves.

There are several examples of ideological racism. One is the conservative *culture of poverty* thesis, which defines the lower class in terms of behavior and values. Banfield (1974), a proponent of this thesis, described the lower class as a group with behavioral and psychological deficits. His definition of the lower class included the permanently unemployed, long-term welfare recipients, drug addicts, dope dealers, street muggers, prostitutes, and pimps. He contrasted the values and behavior of the lower class with those of the middle class. He claimed that the middle class is future oriented whereas the lower class is present oriented. He blamed members of the lower class for their own poverty or unemployment. Banfield (p. 54) said that the lower-class male is improvident and irresponsible and therefore likely to be unskilled and to move from one dead-end job to another.

More contemporary theorists use the expression *the black underclass,* although the definition of this class is the same as Banfield's definition of the lower class. Auletta (1983) defined the underclass as that proportion of the poor that will not assimilate into the mainstream of American society: the long-term welfare recipients, the hostile street criminals, high school dropouts, drug addicts, hustlers, drifters, the homeless. Charles Murray (1984), in *Losing Ground,* argued that the ideology and policies of the 1960s shifted blame for poverty from the poor to society and altered social incentives in ways that now encourage dysfunctional behavior. He argued that generous welfare benefits provided incentives for women to have babies out of wedlock and liberal crime programs reduced the penalties for crime. Murray (p. 118) added, "blacks widely rejected the legitimacy of white norms and white laws."

Although these theories are not inherently racist, they blame the poor for their poverty. They shift attention away from the role of capital and systemic processes in generating unemployment and poverty. They alienate poor people from the rest of society. They characterize the oppressed as pathological and describe them in terms that make them appear as the antithesis of the middle class. This characterization of the poor practically demonizes them. Although these theories are not racist, they support racist images of lazy, amoral, crazy, and dangerous blacks crowded in the inner cities. They influence the construction of racist discourse and racist worldviews.

Eugenics and scientific racism are examples of inherently racist ideologies. Although these ideologies were buried a long time ago, they have recently been exhumed.

Herrnstein, Murray, and the New Eugenics

The old eugenics theory functioned to rationalize as natural, biologically determined, and inevitable the existing racial and ethnic hierarchy. It provided pseudoscientific support for some of the most dehumanizing racial stereotypes. It exonerated society, detracted attention from racially oppressive and exploitative arrangements, desensitized society to the suffering of the most subordinated groups, and blamed them for their own oppression.

Eugenics emerged out of craniology, a discipline that involved measuring skulls. The general belief of this discipline was that there were superior races with large brains and inferior races with small brains. The superior races, typically upper-class whites, exhibited higher levels of intelligence, morals, and ethical behavior; the inferior races, more likely lower-class blacks, have low levels of intelligence, base morals, and unethical behavior. Because of their low intelligence, the inferior races were subject to higher levels of poverty, violent crime, drug abuse, and promiscuity. Eugenics theory maintained that intelligence, moral behavior, and social class are associated with race and determined by genes. This theory suggests that blacks are poor and likely to commit crimes because they have inferior genes.

The demon of eugenics has long been exorcised from mainstream scholarship, refuted by careful scientific and social science research. A number of scholars, most notably Gould (1993), have documented a history of anomalies, errors, and falsifications in this pseudoscience. Most interesting is the Army IQ test that found northern blacks scored higher than southern whites. This discovery—ignored by proponents of eugenics who insisted that whites were superior to blacks and that IQ was hereditary—eventually convinced most social theorists to reject eugenics. Geneticists and biologists have long since rejected the notion that genetic traits are fixed and unchangeable. They have discovered that environmental factors alter not only traits, but genes themselves. Moreover, researchers have found that changing a teacher's expectations of a student can affect that student's performance on intelligence tests by as much as a 15 points (Rosenthal 1992).

Herrnstein and Murray (1994) exhumed the old eugenics demon with the publication of their *Bell Curve*. They insisted—although with much initial hedging and hesitation—that cognitive ability is substantially heritable (p. 23). They maintained that IQ varies with racial groups, with Asians scoring the highest, whites not far behind, and Africans and African Americans scoring well below whites. They concluded that IQ differences are fixed, that there is little that can be done about them, and that they account for much of the variation in social behavior: poverty, labor force nonparticipation, welfare, crime, and so on. Their policy implications are to eliminate all the old liberal programs based on notions of the equality of human potentials and the desirability of equal opportunity.

The Bell Curve had the veneer of a major academic work. Herrnstein and Murray covered a wide range of social science literature on the subject of race, class, and cognitive ability. They acknowledged works that disagreed with their conclusions. They used an extensive database, the National Longitudinal Survey with a sample of 12,000 subjects ages 14 to 22. However, when we move beyond the veneer, we find a number of problems: statistical weaknesses, logical fallacies, and blatant prejudices.

Herrnstein and Murray (1994) reached strong conclusions with data that are statistically weak. For example, for most of their regression formulas, their correlation of determination, R squared, is less than .20 or 20%. That is, their formulas explain less than 20% of the variation in the dependent variables. For the basic formulas for poverty, unemployment, and family status, R squared is less than 11% (pp. 596-602). This figure is too low to support any conclusions concerning a connection between cognitive ability and poverty, unemployment, or family status. Of course, this weakness is buried in the appendix, with a rationale on why we should ignore R squared.

There are many fallacies in Herrnstein and Murray's arguments. For example, they claimed that IQ is related to unemployment, poverty, crime, and female-headed households. They conceded that scores on achievement tests have improved, yet for the time period covered by their study, unemployment rates, poverty rates, crime rates, and female-headed household rates have all increased. This trend contradicts their conclusions.

The whole notion that an intelligence test produces a bell curve is a fallacy. Intelligence tests lack construct validity. They do not measure the various dimensions of mental ability that make up intelligence. Alfred Binet, the originator of the Stanford-Binet intelligence test, claimed that intelligence was too complex a phenomenon to be measured by a single score. Beyond the upper and lower ends of performance, there is not much variation in human mental potential.

Binet's test was designed to identify those at the lower end to select them for special educational programs. When his test was initially constructed, it did not produce a bell curve. Achievement tests, like Binet's, were rewritten and rewritten and rewritten until they produced the bell curve. The bell curve—like the notion of a hierarchy of intelligence and like most of Herrnstein and Murray's arguments—is an artificial construct.

Examples of blatant prejudice found in this book come primarily from the major sources cited to support the authors' infamous conclusions. For example, Herrnstein and Murray insisted that Africans have IQs well below other racial groups. They relied on the authority of Richard Lynn (1991) to support this contention. Lynn compiled the results of a number of studies measuring the intelligence of Africans. One study, conducted by Crawford-Nutts, was based on the Progressive Matrices examination scores of Zambian miners and black Soweto high school students. In an analysis of Lynn's report, Kamin (1995) pointed out a number of problems that raise serious questions about Lynn's, as well as Herrnstein and Murray's, objectivity. First, the Zambian mean score was well below the norm, whereas the black Soweto mean score was above the mean score of same-age U.S. whites. The Soweto results contradicted conclusions about black inferiority. Second, Lynn used the Zambian score but disregarded the Soweto scores. At best, Lynn's approach is racial propaganda or biased research driven by a strong prejudice against blacks and a need to believe in their genetic inferiority. At worst, Lynn's research arises out of a malicious and dishonest effort to demonstrate the genetic inferiority of blacks. Kamin found other methodological problems with Lynn's works. Lynn omitted other studies and subjectively assigned IQ scores to other groups. Kamin (1995, p. 86) concluded, "Lynn's distortions and misrepresentations of that data constitute a truly venomous racism, combined with scandalous disregard for scientific objectivity." Nevertheless,

Herrnstein and Murray used Lynn's study as proof of the low intelligence of Africans. Herrnstein and Murray's book attempts to legitimize pseudo-science and malicious racism.

Herrnstein and Murray (1994) presented a refined and repackaged form of the old eugenics. Indeed, most of the authors cited to support their theories were recipients of grants from the Pioneer Fund, an old eugenics organization (Lane 1994, pp. 14-19). Although Herrnstein and Murray defended their sources, their defense reveals a more obscene racism. For example, they said of J. Philippe Rushton of the University of Western Ontario, "Rushton starts with the well-established observation in biology that species vary in their reproductive strategies" (Herrnstein and Murray, p. 642). They maintained that Rushton is not a crackpot or a bigot (Herrnstein and Murray, p. 643). However, they provided a peculiar summary of his works:

> Rushton argues that the differences in the average intelligence test scores among East Asians, blacks, and whites are not only primarily genetic but part of a complex of racial differences that includes such variables as brain size, genital size, rate of sexual maturation, length of the menstrual cycle, frequency of sexual intercourse, gamete production, sexual hormones. . . . The ordering of the races, he further argues, has an evolutionary basis; hence these ordered racial differences must involve genes. (p. 652)

In other words, what Herrnstein and Murray (1994) said here, using Rushton, is that black men, compared with other races of men, have small brains and large penises. This is an old, malicious racist belief with absolutely no scientific basis, couched in new academic language. The fact that Herrnstein and Murray have been received with any credibility points to the persistence of racist beliefs in American culture and the strong need among European Americans to see African Americans as biologically and genetically inferior.

Dinesh D'Souza

Another example of a contemporary effort to exhume the rotting body of old racism is found in Dinesh D'Souza's book, *The End of Racism: Principles for a Multiracial Society* (1995). D'Souza breathed new life into every mummified racist theory from polygenisms to eugenics. He connected these theories with a thread of white or Aryan supremacy.

D'Souza (1995) intimated that the Aryans are genetically superior to other races, that they produced superior civilizations and conquered inferior ones. He added that this view of superior and inferior races has been well-grounded in legitimate science. He argued that the belief in black inferiority was not an irrational prejudice, grounded in emotions, but was validated by the academic community and legitimized by physicians, great scientists, and philosophers. He cited the surgeon Charles White, who, in the late 18th century, claimed that Africans have small brains and large penises (D'Souza, p. 125). He pointed out that Hegel, Hume, Kant, and other major thinkers believed that blacks were inferior and produced no civilizations.

D'Souza (1995) insisted that Europeans are superior to Africans and Native Americans; that this superiority is genetically based; and that it explains the technological superiority of Europeans over other races and the ability of Europeans to conquer other races. Citing Curtin and McNeil, D'Souza (p. 55) said that, at the time Columbus discovered America, "the most advanced communities of American Indians and African blacks were between one and four thousand years behind the West in technological development." He claimed these racist beliefs were held by most rational, progressive, and respectable people until World War II.

D'Souza (1995) argued that events surrounding World War II allowed liberal relativists to challenge and delegitimize scientific racism. His argument is as follows: Scientific racism is a legitimate theory well-grounded in object science. Unfortunately, overzealous political leaders like Hitler adopted this science for their own political ends. D'Souza claimed that scientists were embarrassed by Hitler's association with scientific racism. Nevertheless, by the end of the war, the world came to associate Nazism with mass destruction and genocide. Because of scientific racism's association with Hitler, racism became vulnerable to attack by liberal relativists. These liberal relativists included anthropologists such as Franz Boas, Ruth Benedict, and Margaret Mead who rejected the notion of superior and inferior races and attacked scientific racism. According to D'Souza, Boas and his students lobbied the American Anthropological Association to pass a resolution denouncing racism and declaring the equality of humankind. D'Souza claimed that Myrdal's ([1948] 1975) study operated in the new antiracist context, as Myrdal condemned prejudice and discrimination as irrational. D'Souza insisted that the liberal antiracism perspective became popular not because it was grounded in science or reason, but because it unfairly associated scientific racism, a perfectly valid theory, with fascism, an overly zealous and destructive political movement. According to him, liberals simply depicted racists as irrational barbarians.

D'Souza (1995) defended Herrnstein and Murray (1994). He stated,

> Yet *The Bell Curve* makes a strong case that cannot be ignored. Whatever the book's shortcomings, it remains an undisputed fact that the fifteen-point IQ difference between blacks and whites has remained roughly constant for more than three quarters of a century, even though the environmental conditions for African Americans have vastly improved during that period. (p. 475)

He even reiterated Rushton's discussion that black males have small brains and large penises. However, D'Souza claimed that he is not a rigid genetic determinist. For D'Souza, black intellectual inferiority is a function of both inferior genes and pathological culture. He attributed high rates of murder, drug abuse, female-headed households, and other social problems in the black community to a barbarous culture or a crisis of civilization. He differed with Herrnstein and Murray in that he placed more importance on the role of culture and civilization and less on genes.

D'Souza (1995, p. 464) conceded that theories of scientific racism inspired genocide but was not troubled by this racism-genocide connection. He argued that any theory can inspire mass murder and claimed that, in the name of egalitarianism, Mao in China and Stalin in Russia engaged in human extermination at a level that exceeded Hitler.

D'Souza's (1995) book is a passionate defense of scientific racism. He wrote, "Racism is what it always was: an opinion that recognizes real civilizational differences and attributes them to biology" (p. 537). He depicted craniology, polygenism, and eugenics as legitimate scientific theories (p. 127). Whereas he supported the notion that blacks are biologically inferior to other groups and he associated biological inferiority with cultural inferiority, he placed more emphasis on culture than biology. D'Souza (p. 556) concluded that "what blacks need to do is to 'act white,' which is to say, to abandon idiotic Back to Africa schemes and embrace mainstream cultural norms, so that they can effectively compete with other groups."

Scientific racism died a long time ago. It was weakened by the many scholars who have acknowledged that black and white differences on standardized achievement test scores have declined significantly over the past three decades—a point conceded even by Herrnstein and Murray but ignored by D'Souza. It was bludgeoned by the Army IQ tests showing that northern blacks scored higher than southern whites. It was assaulted by objective scientists who demonstrated that craniology was a fraud perpetrated by scientists insistent on proving that blacks had smaller brains than whites; there were no differences in the skull capacity of blacks and whites.

Scientific racism is not only a pseudoscience, it dehumanizes oppressed people, desensitizes society to their suffering, and fuels the impulse toward human destructiveness. The association between scientific racism and fascism or genocide was no accident. Genocide was the natural consequence of a view that explained social problems in terms of the presence of a genetically defective subhuman species whose members function like parasites on society. The simple solution arising from this perspective was to remove the species.

It is amazing that D'Souza attempted to resuscitate and legitimize scientific racism—views that are most demeaning and humiliating to African Americans. These views speak to an irrepressible contempt for blacks and a persistent social need to justify the existence of racial hierarchy as natural and inevitable.

The astonishing thing about D'Souza's (1995) and Herrnstein and Murray's (1994) books is how well they have been received by the media. Of course, this is not the first time in U.S. history that racist perspectives have been promoted by the media. It indicates a strong need in this country to justify a racial hierarchy. It also points to strong political opposition to racial equality.

Capital and Racist Ideology

Historically, members of the upper class have played a role in the construction and dissemination of racist ideology. In the past, members of this class have been more directly involved in the construction of ideas legitimizing the established order. Today the corporate sector tends to be more indirectly involved in this construction by supporting conservative think tanks. These think tanks include organizations such as the Adolph Coors Foundation, the American Enterprise Institute, the Heritage Foundation, the Hoover Institute, the J. Howard Pew Foundation, and many others.

Over the past 10 to 15 years, corporate contributions to these think tanks have increased dramatically. Consider the American Enterprise Institute (AEI) for example. The budget for this Institute increased by more than 10 fold since 1970 (Vogel 1989, p. 224; Greider 1993, p. 48).

AEI sponsors include "the largest banks and corporations in America: AT&T contributed $125,000, Chase Manhattan Bank gave $171,000, Chevron donated $95,000, CitiCorp, $100,000, Exxon, $130,000, General Electric, $65,000, General Motors, $100,000, and Procter & Gamble, $165,000" (Greider, p. 48).

Many of these corporation-sponsored think tanks have contributed either indirectly or directly, to the formation of racist ideology. Most of the studies coming from these think tanks oppose government regulations including civil rights policies. For example, Thomas Sowell, a Hoover Institute fellow, has published several pieces arguing that market forces are more effective and constructive in eliminating discrimination than government civil rights regulations. For another example, the Smith Richardson Foundation provided the funds that enabled George Gilder to write *Wealth and Poverty* (1981), a study that denied the existence of discrimination and deplored the harmful effects of civil rights policies.

The Pioneer Foundation founded by a $5 million endowment left by a textile owner, Wickliffe Draper, is a more extreme example of the connection between the corporate sector and racist ideology. The mission of this foundation is to support eugenics studies or research demonstrating the genetic superiority or inferiority of racial groups. Directors of this foundation have maintained that African Americans "are at the bottom of most socioeconomic measures not because of traumas they have faced as a race but largely because they are genetically deficient" (Sedgwick 1995, p. 48). This foundation has given more than $1 million to Arthur Jensen, who argues that the low academic performance of African Americans is attributable to genetic deficiencies (Miller 1995, p. 173). The fund has also given grants to William Shockley, a Nobel Prize-winning physicist who advocated the sterilization of intellectually inferior people (Sedgwick, p. 146). The fund also has had ties with the White Citizens Council and the American Nazi Party (Miller, p. 173).

Although the Pioneer fund may be an extreme example of the link between the corporate sector and racist ideology, other conservative but more reputable think tanks have exhibited similar connections. The AEI is a prime example. AEI funding enabled D'Souza (1995) to write and publish his racist treatise, *The End of Racism*. Charles Murray is an AEI fellow. The AEI has also supported the marketing of *The Bell Curve* (Kamin 1995, pp. 99-100). The role of the AEI in supporting these books and authors functioned to legitimize their racist ideology. It also connects the corporate sector with the formation of this ideology.

Symbolic Racism and the O. J. Simpson Trial

Sometimes social or political events become symbols representing particular beliefs or meaning. Symbols do not automatically represent beliefs. Rather people project meaning or beliefs onto events and then use the events to symbolize the beliefs (Edelman 1980). These beliefs do not appear out of a vacuum. They emerge out of a particular cultural context with particular assumptions about the world, particular experiences, and particular feelings shared by a mass of people.

Symbolic racism arises out of a racist cultural context undergirded by racist assumptions, feelings, and images. This form of racism involves the construction and use of symbols embodying beliefs that degrade oppressed racial groups and blame them for their own oppression. The O. J. Simpson trial illustrates some aspects of symbolic racism. Simpson was arrested and tried for murdering his ex-wife, Nicole Brown Simpson, and her friend, Ronald Goldman.

This trial had different symbolic meaning for blacks than it did for whites. For many African Americans, the trial symbolized a black man's struggle against an unjust and racist criminal justice system—a system with police who use excessive force against blacks and who lie and plant evidence to guarantee convictions. For many whites, the Simpson trial symbolized white victimization. That is, it symbolized whites victimized by a black man who killed a white woman and a white man; by a black attorney who played the race card or cried racism to get an acquittal; and by a predominantly black jury lacking the technical knowledge and the objectivity to find the man guilty.

For the most part, this trial was a tremendous contest between the prosecution and the defense team. The prosecution presented a convincing case that Simpson had exhibited a pattern of severe spousal abuse leading to the murder. They found physical evidence linking him to the crime. They found blood in his Ford Bronco, a bloody sock in his bedroom, and a bloody glove on the ground outside his home. At the crime scene, they found blood matching Simpson's blood, bloody footprints matching O. J. Simpson's shoes, and a knit cap with strands of Simpson's hair. They had enough physical evidence to convict him. Moreover, they demonstrated that Simpson had the opportunity and the motive for committing the murders.

The defense team presented material and witnesses suggesting that the police tampered with the evidence to ensure Simpson's arrest and conviction:

1. A police investigation videotape of Simpson's bedroom makes it seem that the blood-stained sock was not on the rug in front of the bed where it was discovered by the police at a later time.
2. In his testimony, Detective Philip Vannatter admitted carrying Simpson's blood in a vial for several hours and transporting it from the downtown Los Angeles police headquarters to Simpson's home, more than 15 miles away.
3. A lab technician's testimony suggested that about one and one half milliliters of Simpson's blood was missing from the police laboratory vial.
4. In tape recordings, Los Angeles Police Detective Mark Fuhrman indicated that he and other police officers had on a number of occasions lied and planted evidence in order to secure arrests and convictions, that they held blacks in contempt, that they often referred to blacks as niggers, and that they sometimes beat black suspects unmercifully.

Defense attorneys demonstrated that the practice of detectives lying and planting incriminating material was not uncommon and that it appeared that the police had tampered with the evidence in this case. At one point in the trial, Judge Lance Ito suggested that police detectives had acted with a reckless disregard for the truth. The defense team offered a credible motive for why the detectives planted evidence—the police believed Simpson was guilty and they wanted to secure an arrest and conviction.

Despite the vigorous defense, one can reasonably conclude that O. J. Simpson committed the murders; the evidence still points to him. However, Judge Ito instructed jury members that their task was not to say who *probably* committed the murders, but to determine whether Simpson was guilty beyond any reasonable doubt. To obtain an acquittal, all that was required was for the defense team to present a case that raised a reasonable doubt. This requirement is consistent with state law. It arose out of long-standing principles that it is better for a guilty man to go free than it is for an innocent man to hang and that the tyranny of a police state is worse than the acquittal of the guilty.

Aside from these principles, there are many ways in which discussions surrounding this trial could have been framed. They could have focused on the results of sloppy, unprofessional, and unethical police behavior; the impact of having the best attorneys money could buy; the importance of dramatic presentations in affecting the trial's outcome; or the consequences of having blatantly racist officers in a police department. Instead, the media focused on white rage or a white backlash arising from white victimization.

Illustrating the extent of this backlash or rage in an article published by *The Nation,* Alexander Cockburn (1995) cited a number of comments made by whites on television talk shows and in newspaper columns. He quoted one Pasadena, California, talk show caller who said that blacks should be barred from serving on juries "because they don't have the brains of a dog" (p. 492)." Cockburn cited a caller on the Bob Grant show who said the jurors had an average IQ of 75. Bob Grant agreed. Cockburn (p. 492) quoted Rush Limbaugh saying that the verdict was "not so much about race as it is about stupidity . . . about low IQs on the jury." Cockburn suggested that this was harvest time for *The Bell Curve.* He summarized the views of a number of columnists who blamed the verdict on black biases against whites. He cited an article written by Michael Lind and published in *The New Republic,* which called the present system of jury selection barbaric. According to Cockburn, (p. 492), the editors of *The New Republic* described Johnnie Cochran as a "repulsive" symbol who "exploits the basest elements of the human psyche for money."

Assuming that Simpson is guilty, why would whites become angry at blacks over his acquittal? Why not become angry at racist cops, the power of money, incompetent police investigators, or zealous lawyers? The answer lies in the cultural context out of which the trial came to symbolize white victimization. This context is filled with images of dangerous black males and anxiety over blacks acquiring too much power. It is related to an old racist white/black dichotomous discourse in which whites are objective, blacks emotional; whites are intelligent, blacks dull-minded; whites are controlled and sophisticated, blacks impulsive and uneducated; whites are superior, blacks, inferior. This white victimization symbol rests on the assumptions that charging racism is a sinister way in which blacks advance themselves and their interest at the expense of whites; that racism is largely a thing of the past; that conspiracy theories are absurd; that blacks generally lack the education required to understand DNA testing; and that a predominantly black jury is unlikely to convict an accused black man. It rests on the pervasive fear and myth that blacks are acquiring too much power and advancing themselves at the expense of whites. It appears that these images, anxieties, fears, and assumptions—undergirding the dominant culture and projected onto the trial—contributed to the construction of the white victimization symbol.

The use of this trial to symbolize white rage and white victimization serves the same function as ideological racism. It shifts attention away from systemic sources of racial oppression and places the blame for this oppression on the oppressed themselves. It intimates that black jurors are responsible for injustices in the system. It suggests that blacks have far more power than they actually have. If Simpson had any power at all, it arose from his wealth, not his blackness. The experience of O. J. Simpson, whose defense cost millions of dollars, contrasts sharply with the reality of poor blacks processed in the criminal justice system in cities across the country.

The white victimization symbol diverts attention away from rather disturbing figures on race and the criminal justice system. These figures indicate that more than 30% of black males between the ages of 20 and 29 are in prison and jail or on probation and parole; more blacks from this age group are in state and federal prisons than their whites age peers (Mauer and Huling 1995). Figures also reveal that the incarceration rate for black men in the United States is higher than the incarceration rates for almost every other group in the world (Currie 1985).

The federal prosecution of drug offenders provides an illustration of systemic racial biases in the criminal justice arena. For example, Mauer and Huling (1995, p. 10) reported that despite the fact that the majority of crack users in the area are white, "not a single white offender had been convicted of a crack cocaine offense in the federal courts serving the Los Angeles metropolitan area since 1986." This pattern is not unique to Los Angeles. It is found in about 17 states and in almost half the federal district courts (Mauer and Huling; "Report Finds Whites" 1995).

The use of the O. J. Simpson trial to symbolize a system that is biased against whites and in favor of blacks perverts the reality of black oppression. It exemplifies symbolic racism. It emerged from an inherently racist cultural context.

The Farra-colonization of the Million Man March

The Million Man March on October 16, 1995, also illustrated aspects of symbolic racism. For many black men, the march symbolized black unity and efficacy, a willingness of black men to stand together against destructive forces in their community—violence, drug abuse, and the disintegration of the two-parent family. For many whites, the march symbolized black separatism and black racism.

Media attention surrounding this march focused on Minister Louis Farrakhan. One black journalist called this treatment the Farra-colonization of the March. This targeting of Farrakhan shifted attention away from the racism deeply rooted in American culture and focused almost exclusively on issues surrounding this single leader. Several problems arose from this treatment.

First, this treatment ignored the extent to which Farrakhan and other leaders of the march were products of American culture. Their ideas were not much different from those of the Christian Coalition supporting the Republican party. They emphasized self-help, family values, and independence from government. The bigotry evident in the speeches of Farrakhan was rooted in the racist dimension of American culture. This dimension of American culture explains differences in human behavior in terms of racial differences. In this cultural perceptual framework, human oppression is not explained in terms of systemic arrangements. It is explained in terms of other people—blacks, Jews, whites, and so on. The views that blacks are intellectually inferior, that Jews are responsible for the slave trade, or that whites are devils arise out of race modes of thinking, common in racist cultures.

Second, the targeting of Farrakhan reveals biases in the media. The media have been quite critical of Farrakhan, especially his anti-Semitic and misogynous remarks. Of course, this criticism is important because anti-Semitism and misogyny are like racism—they are forms of oppression in and of themselves, and they divert attention away from systemic aspects of oppression. Nonetheless, representatives of the media have posed a number of questions to Farrakhan that they have been reluctant to pose to white leaders with comparable perspectives. For example, they frequently asked if Farrakhan was a bigot or if he was dividing America. However, when David Duke ran for governor of Louisiana on an antiaffirmative action and antiwelfare platform, rarely did the media ask these questions. When Pat Buchanan ran on an anti-immigrant, antilesbian, antigay, and anti-people unlike Pat Buchanan campaign, rarely did the media ask if he was a bigot or if he was dividing America. *Time* magazine called Buchanan a "hell raiser" but not a bigot. When Jesse Helms aired his black hands replacing white hands campaign ads, rarely did the media ask if he was a bigot attempting to divide America. When Bush revealed his Willie Horton campaign ads, rarely did the media ask if he was a bigot dividing America.

Third, the focus on Farrakhan shifted attention away from the problems that impelled people to march and redefined the problem as Farrakhan.

These conditions include high rates of poverty, violence, and incarceration among black males; the negative images of blacks portrayed in the media; and other forms of racism. The march was a reaction to an America that is divided along racial lines and to racism deeply imbedded in American culture. The focus on Farrakhan transforms the problem of racial oppression into a problem of a racist, anti-Semitic, and misogynous black leader. This Farra-colonization of the march is a form of symbolic racism.

To some extent, the march was an awkward struggle against racial oppression led by conservative religious leaders who were products of the same racist culture they were struggling against. Nevertheless, the Farra-colonization of the Million Man March diverted attention away from the oppression the marchers were reacting against.

RACISM AND ADVANCED CAPITALISM

In every era, from slavery to advanced capitalism, racism arose out of oppressive and exploitative economic arrangements in which wealth was concentrated in a dominant class. This class played a leading role in generating discourse and ideology to legitimize these oppressive arrangements and to convince other classes to support the established order. This class also used the state to protect these arrangements. This discourse, ideology, and state action sustained oppressive arrangements and contributed to the formation of racist culture.

Changes in modes of production generated changes in forms of oppression and types of racism. Also, shifts in political power precipitated changes in the role of the state and in the formation of racist culture. The old racism died with the disintegration of the sharecropping system and the relative success of the civil rights movement. Nevertheless, a new form of racism emerged out of new exploitative and oppressive arrangements—meta-racism.

The old exploitative mechanism of industrial capitalism and the Fordist period gave way to new post-Fordist, exploitative processes. The corporate sector found new ways to extract more surplus value from labor, new ways to reduce the costs of labor, and new ways to diminish the power of labor unions. In their drive to accumulate wealth, corporations engaged in more flexible capital investment strategies. They closed down many production facilities where labor costs were high and unions strong. They relocated in areas of cheap labor and nonexistent unions. They sub-contracted with peripheral firms and eliminated core sector jobs. They used mergers and bankruptcy to undermine unions and reduce labor costs. They attacked unions directly at the negotiating table.

These economic changes contributed to the rise of the new racism in several ways. First, economic changes influenced shifts in political power. These changes contributed to greater concentrations of wealth in the upper stratum and the decline of organized labor. These changes meant a weakening of civil rights forces and a strengthening of conservative forces. The corporate sector is now more politically active than ever before. It contributes more resources to conservative think tanks committed to generating studies and ideas supporting the established order. Some of the works from these research institutes contributed to the formation and dissemination of racist ideology. The corporate sector also supports political leaders who have used racist imagery and discourse in ways that encouraged the rise of racism.

Second, these economic changes, combined with institutional practices, produced new racially oppressive arrangements characterized by black poverty substantially concentrated in inner cities. This concentrated black poverty is not simply a function of impersonal market forces nor the unintended effects of a global economy. This poverty is associated with the uneven economic development of advanced capitalism. It is the result of the impact of the shift from the Fordist to the post-Fordist period. It is related to deliberate decisions of corporate leaders—decisions calculated to depress wages and weaken labor power. These decisions affected black workers most severely. Also, Squires (1990, p. 202) contended that the corporate sector deliberately avoided locating new industrial development in areas with large black populations:

> Industrial development specialists in several state governments have reported that managers of corporations seeking locations for new sites often request that areas with substantial minority populations be eliminated from consideration. The stated concerns are that blacks are more susceptible to union organizing drives and that if there are fewer minorities there will be fewer equal opportunity obligations with which to contend.

Post-Fordist changes, uneven development, and an aversion to locating industrial development in central cities have contributed to the marginalization of black workers. These factors, in conjunction with housing segregation and labor market discrimination, produced black poverty, substantially concentrated in inner cities. This visible aspect of racial oppression contributed directly to the formation of the new racism, especially when political leaders justified this poverty in ways that further denigrated African Americans.

Third, conservative forces contributed to racist discourse in the process of justifying the growth of concentrated black poverty. This discourse alienated poor blacks from the larger community and desensitized its members to the plight of the poor. This discourse involved images of black welfare queens, dangerous black males addicted to drugs and driven by uncontrollable rage, incompetent blacks given undeserved jobs through affirmative action, lazy black males who prefer to hang out on street corners, and other denigrating figures. This discourse contributed to the formation of the new racist culture, as it was popularized in the media. It influenced most sectors of society—classes, groups, and institutions— which in turn operate to maintain existing racially oppressive arrangements. The culture encourages the maintenance of racial segregation in metropolitan areas and of racial discrimination in urban labor markets.

Fourth, post-Fordist changes generated a pervasive sense of anxiety and insecurity, especially among middle-class workers. This anxiety and insecurity made people more susceptible to new forms of racism. It contributed to scapegoating—pure hostility against blacks. It has fueled the assault on affirmative action.

In the final analysis, exploitative and oppressive economic arrangements contributed to the formation of racial politics and racist culture. This racism will continue into the 21st century unless there is another major social movement or unless shifts in political power occur that counterbalance the dominant position of the corporate sector—the sector today most resistant to fairer ways of distributing societal resources.

References

Adorno, Theodor, Else Frenkel-Brunswik, Daniel Levinson, and R. Nevitt Sanford. 1950. *The Authoritarian Personality.* New York: Harper.

Allen, Theodore W. 1994. *The Invention of the White Race.* Vol. 1, *Racial Oppression and Social Control.* New York: Verso.

Allport, Gordon. 1979. *The Nature of Prejudice.* Reading, MA: Addison-Wesley.

Amaker, Norman. 1988. *Civil Rights and the Reagan Administration.* Washington, DC: Urban Institute Press.

Aristotle. 1969. *Politics and Poetics,* translated by Benjamin Jowett and Thomas Twining. New York: Viking.

Ashton, Patrick J. 1978. "The Political Economy of Suburban Development." In *Marxism and the Metropolis: New Perspectives in Urban Political Economy,* edited by William Tabb and Larry Sawers. New York: Oxford University Press.

Auletta, Ken. 1983. *The Underclass.* New York: Vintage.

Banfield, Edward. 1974. *The Unheavenly City Revisited.* Boston: Little, Brown.

Baron, Paul and Paul Sweezy. 1968. *Monopoly Capital: An Essay on the American Economic and Social Order.* New York: Monthly Review Press.

Beard, Charles. 1941. *An Economic Interpretation of the Constitution.* New York: Macmillan.

Becker, Gary. 1957. *The Economics of Discrimination.* Chicago: University of Chicago Press.

Bell, Derrick. 1973. *Race, Racism, and American Law.* Boston: Little, Brown.

———. 1987. *And We Are Not Saved: The Elusive Quest for Racial Justice.* New York: Basic Books.

Bellah, Robert, Richard Madsen, William Sullivan, Ann Swidler, and Steven Tipton. 1986. *Habits of the Heart: Individualism and Community in American Life.* New York: Harper & Row.

Bennett, Lerone. 1970. *Before the Mayflower: A History of the Negro in America 1619-1964.* Baltimore, MD: Penguin.

Bettelheim, Bruno. 1967. *The Informed Heart.* New York: Avon.

Billings, Dwight B. 1979. *Planters and the Making of a "New South": Class, Politics, and Development in North Carolina, 1865-1900.* Chapel Hill: University of North Carolina Press.

Blauner, Robert. 1972. *Racial Oppression in America.* New York: Harper & Row.

Bloom, Jack M. 1987. *Class, Race, and the Civil Rights Movement.* Indianapolis: Indiana University Press.

Bluestone, Barry and Bennett Harrison. 1982. *The Deindustrialization of America: Plant Closings, Community Abandonment, and the Dismantling of Basic Industry.* New York: Basic Books.

Blumberg, Paul. 1981. *Inequality in an Age of Decline.* Oxford, UK: Oxford University Press.

Boggs, James and Grace Boggs. 1970. *Racism and the Class Struggle: Further Pages From a Black Worker's Notebook.* New York: Monthly Review Press.

Bonacich, Edna. 1976. "Advanced Capitalism and Black/White Race Relations in the United States: A Split Labor Market Interpretation." *American Sociological Review* 41(February):34-51.

Bosmajian, Haig. 1983. *The Language of Oppression.* New York: University Press of America.

Bottomore, Tom. 1985. *Theories of Modern Capitalism.* London: Allen and Unwin.

Bradley, Michael. 1991. *The Iceman Inheritance: Prehistoric Sources of Western Man's Racism, Sexism, and Aggression.* New York: Kayode.

Brooks, Thomas. 1971. *Toil and Trouble: A History of American Labor.* New York: Dell.

Brown v. Board of Education (Brown I), 347 U.S. 483, 1954.

Brown v. Board of Education (Brown II), 349 U.S. 294, 1955.

Buchanan v. Warley, 245 U.S. 60, 1917.

Buck, Solon. 1913. *The Grange Movement: A Study of Agricultural Organization and Its Political, Economic, and Social Manifestations, 1870-1880.* Lincoln: University of Nebraska.

Bullock, Charles III and Charles Lamb. 1984. *Implementation of Civil Rights Policy.* Monterey, CA: Brooks/Cole.

Bush, George. 1991. "Message to the Senate Returning Without Approval the Civil Rights Act of 1990" (October 22, 1990). Pp. 1437-39 in *Public Papers of the Presidents of the United States: George Bush, Book II.* Washington, DC: Government Printing Office.

Butchers' Benevolent Association v. Crescent City Livestock Landing and Slaughterhouse Co., 83 U.S. 36, 1873.

Camejo, Peter. 1976. *Racism, Revolution, Reaction, 1861-1877: The Rise and Fall of Radical Reconstruction.* New York: Monad.

Carmichael, Stokely and Charles Hamilton. 1967. *Black Power.* New York: Random House.

Carnoy, Martin. 1984. *The State and Political Theory.* Princeton, NJ: Princeton University Press.

Cash, W. J. 1941. *The Mind of the South.* New York: Vintage.

Castells, Manuel. 1980. *The Economic Crisis and American Society.* Princeton, NJ: Princeton University Press.

Cell, John W. 1982. *The Highest Stage of White Supremacy: The Origins of Segregation in South Africa and the American South.* Cambridge, UK: Cambridge University Press.

Center for Popular Economics. 1986. *Economic Report of the People.* Boston: South End Press.

Cherry, Robert. 1989. *Discrimination: Its Economic Impact on Blacks, Women, and Jews.* Lexington, MA: Lexington Books.

Chomsky, Noam. 1985. *Turning the Tide: U.S. Intervention in Central America and the Struggle for Peace.* Boston: South End Press.

City of Richmond v. J. A. Croson Co., 488 U.S. 469, 1989.

Civil Rights Cases, 109 U.S. 3, 1883.

Clark, Kenneth. 1965. *Dark Ghetto: Dilemmas of Social Power.* New York: Harper and Row.

Clyatt v. United States, 197 U.S. 209, 1905.

Cockburn, Alexander. "White Rage: The Press and the Verdict." *The Nation* 261(14):491-92.

Cooper, William, Jr. 1983. *Liberty and Slavery.* New York: Knopf.

Cox, Oliver. 1970. *Caste, Class, and Race: A Study in Social Dynamics.* New York: Monthly Review Press.

Currie, Elliott. 1985. *Confronting Crime: An American Challenge.* New York: Pantheon.

Daniel, Pete. 1972. *The Shadow of Slavery: Peonage in the South 1901-1969.* Chicago: University of Illinois Press.

Danielson, Michael. 1976. *The Politics of Exclusion.* New York: Columbia University Press.

Darden, Joe. 1987. "Choosing Neighbors and Neighborhoods: The Role of Race in Housing Preference." Pp. 15-42 in *Divided Neighborhoods: Changing Patterns of Racial Segregation,* edited by G. Tobin. Beverly Hills, CA: Sage.

Darden, Joe, Richard Child Hill, June Thomas, and Richard Thomas. 1987. *Detroit: Race and Uneven Development.* Philadelphia: Temple University Press.

Derrida, Jacques. 1981. *Positions.* Chicago: University of Chicago Press.

D'Souza, Dinesh. 1995. *The End of Racism: Principles for a Multiracial Society.* New York: Free Press.

Dollard, John. 1949. *Caste and Class in a Southern Town.* New York: Doubleday.

Dred Scott v. Sandford, 60 U.S. (19 How.) 393, 1857.

Du Bois, W. E. B. 1969a. *Black Reconstruction in America 1860-1880.* New York: Atheneum.

———. 1969b. *The World and Africa.* New York: International Publishers.

Duncan, David (Ed.). 1908. *Life and Letters of Herbert Spencer.* New York: Appleton.

Dye, Thomas and Harmon Ziegler. 1996. *The Irony of Democracy: An Uncommon Introduction to American Politics.* Belmont, CA: Wadsworth.

Dyer, Thomas. 1980. *Theodore Roosevelt and the Idea of Race.* Baton Rouge: Louisiana State University Press.

Edelman, Murray. 1980. *The Symbolic Uses of Politics.* Urbana: University of Illinois Press.

Edsall, Thomas with Mary Edsall. 1992. *Chain Reaction: The Impact of Race, Rights, and Taxes on American Politics.* New York: Norton.

Edwards, Richard, Michael Reich, and Thomas Weisskopf. 1978. *The Capitalist System: A Radical Analysis of American Society.* Englewood Cliffs, NJ: Prentice Hall.

Engels, Friedrich. 1877/1973. *The Conditions of the Working Class in England: From Personal Observation and Authentic Sources.* Moscow: Progress Publishers.

———. 1877/1975. *AntiDuhring.* Moscow: Progress Publishers.

Erikson, Erik. 1963. *Childhood and Society.* New York: Norton.

Fainstein, Norman. 1986-1987. "The Underclass/Mismatch Hypothesis as an Explanation for Black Economic Deprivation." *Politics and Society* 15:403-51.

Fanon, Frantz. 1967. *Black Skin, White Masks.* New York: Grove Weidenfeld.

Farley, John. 1987. "Segregation in 1980: How Segregated Are America's Metropolitan Areas?" Pp. 95-114 in *Divided Neighborhoods: Changing Patterns of Racial Segregation,* edited by G. Tobin. Beverly Hills, CA: Sage.

Farley, Reynolds. 1976. "Detroit Area Study." Department of Sociology (monograph), University of Michigan, Ann Arbor.

———. 1984. *Blacks and Whites: Narrowing the Gap?* Cambridge, MA: Harvard University Press.

Farley, Reynolds, S. Bianchi, and D. Colasanti. 1979. "Barriers to the Racial Integration of Neighborhoods: The Detroit Case." *Annals of the AAPSS* 441:97-113.

Feagin, Joe R. and Clairece B. Feagin. 1986. *Discrimination American Style: Institutional Racism and Sexism.* Malabaar, FL: Robert E. Krieger.

Feagin, Joe R. and Hernan Vera. 1995. *White Racism: The Basics.* New York: Routledge.

Feins, J. D., R. G. Bratt, and R. Hollister. 1981. *Final Report of a Study of Racial Discrimination in the Boston Housing Market.* Cambridge, MA: Abt.

Fields, Barbara. 1982. "Ideology and Race in American History." Pp. 143-77 in *Region, Race, and Reconstruction: Essays in Honor of C. Vann Woodward,* edited by J. M. Kousser and J. M. McPherson. New York: Oxford University Press.

Firefighters Local Union No. 1784 v. Stotts, 467 U.S. 561, 1984.

Flug, Michael. 1987. "Organized Labor and the Civil Rights Movement of the 1960s: The Case of the Maryland Freedom Union." Unpublished manuscript.

Fogel, Robert W. and Stanley L. Engerman. 1974. *Time on the Cross: The Economics of American Negro Slavery.* Boston: Little, Brown.

Foner, Philip S. 1981. *Organized Labor and the Black Worker 1619-1981.* New York: International Publishers.

———. 1982. *Organized Labor and the Black Worker 1619-1981.* New York: International Publishers.

Foucault, Michael. 1972. *The Archaeology of Knowledge.* New York: Pantheon.

———. 1980. *Power/Knowledge: Selected Interviews and Other Writings. 1972-1977.* New York: Pantheon.

Franklin, John Hope. 1969. *From Slavery to Freedom: A History of Negro Americans.* New York: Vintage.

Fredrickson, George. 1971. *Black Image in the White Mind: The Debate on Afro-American Character and Destiny, 1817-1914.* New York: Harper & Row.

Fredrickson, George M. 1982. *White Supremacy: A Comparative Study in American and South African History.* New York: Oxford University Press.

Freeman, Alan David. 1978. "Legitimizing Racial Discrimination Through Antidiscrimination Law: A Critical Review of Supreme Court Doctrine." *Minnesota Law Review* 62:1049-1119.

Fromm, Erich. 1965. *Escape From Freedom.* New York: Avon.

———. 1971. *Beyond the Chains of Illusions: My Encounter With Marx and Freud.* New York: Simon and Schuster.

———. 1980. *Greatness and Limitations of Freud's Thought.* New York: Mentor.

Fullilove v. Klutznick, 448 U.S. 448, 1980.

Fusfeld, Daniel R. and Timothy Bates. 1984. *The Political Economy of the Urban Ghetto.* Carbondale: Southern Illinois University Press.

Genovese, Eugene D. 1989. *The Political Economy of Slavery: Studies in the Economy and Society of the Slave South.* Middletown, CT: Wesleyan University Press.

Geschwender, James A. 1979. *Class, Race, and Worker Insurgency: The League of Revolutionary Black Workers.* Cambridge, UK: Cambridge University Press.

Gilder, George. 1981. *Wealth and Poverty.* New York: Basic Books.

Glazer, Nathan. 1978. *Affirmative Discrimination: Ethnic Inequality and Public Policy.* New York: Basic Books.

Glazer, Nathan and Daniel Patrick Moynihan. 1970. *Beyond the Melting Pot: The Negroes, Puerto Ricans, Jews, Italians, and Irish of New York City.* Cambridge: MIT Press.

Goldberg, David Theo. 1990. "Social Formation of Racist Discourse." Pp. 225-318 in *Anatomy of Racism,* edited by David Theo Goldberg. Minneapolis: University of Minnesota.

Gordon, David. 1978. "Capitalist Development and the History of American Cities." Pp. 25-63 in *Marxism and the Metropolis: New Perspectives in Urban Political Economy,* edited by W. K. Tabb and L. Sawers. New York: Oxford University Press.

Gordon, David, Richard Edwards, and Michael Reich. 1982. *Segmented Work, Divided Workers: The Historical Transformations of Labor in the United States.* New York: Cambridge University Press.

Gordon, Milton. 1964. *Assimilation in American Life: The Role of Race, Religion, and National Origins.* New York: Oxford University Press.

Gossett, Thomas F. 1971. *Race: The History of an Idea in America.* New York: Schocken.

Gough, Ian. 1985. *The Political Economy of the Welfare State.* London: Macmillan.

Gould, Steven. 1993. *The Mismeasurement of Man.* New York: Norton.

Gouldner, Alvin. 1982. *Two Marxisms: Contradictions and Anomalies in the Development of Theory.* New York: Oxford University Press.

Gramsci, Antonio. 1980. *Selections from the Prison Notebooks of Antonio Gramsci.* New York: International Publishers.

Greer, Edward. 1979. *Big Steel: Black Politics and Corporate Power in Gary, Indiana.* New York: Monthly Review Press.

Greider, William. 1993. *Who Will Tell the People: The Betrayal of American Democracy.* New York: Simon and Schuster.

Griggs v. Duke Power Company, 401 U.S. 424, 1971.

Habermas, Jurgen. 1975. *Legitimation Crisis.* Boston: Beacon.

Hall, Edward. 1981. *Beyond Culture.* New York: Doubleday.

Hall v. DeCuir, 95 U.S. 485, 1878.

Harrison, Bennett and Barry Bluestone. 1990. *The Great U-Turn: Corporate Restructuring and the Polarizing of America.* New York: Basic Books.

Harvey, David. 1993. *The Condition of Postmodernity: An Enquiry into the Origins of Cultural Change.* Cambridge, UK: Blackwell.

Helper, Rose. 1969. *Racial Policies and Practices of Real Estate Brokers.* Minneapolis: University of Minnesota Press.

Herrnstein, Richard and Charles Murray. 1994. *The Bell Curve: Intelligence and Class Structure in American Life.* New York: Free Press.

Hill, Herbert. 1985. *Black Labor and the American Legal System: Race, Work, and the Law.* Madison: University of Wisconsin Press.

Hills v. Gautreaux, 425 U.S. 284, 1976.

Hofstadter, Richard. 1948. *The American Political Tradition.* New York: Vintage.

Hudson, William. 1995. *American Democracy in Peril: Seven Challenges to America's Future.* Chatham, NJ: Chatham House.

Independent Federation of Flight Attendants v. Zipes, 491 U.S. 105, 1989.

James v. Valtierra, 404 U.S. 137, 1971.

Janda, Kenneth, Jeffrey M. Berry, and Jerry Goldman. 1995. *The Challenge of Democracy: Government in America.* Boston: Houghton Mifflin.

Jargowsky, Paul A. and Mary Jo Bane. 1991. "Ghetto Poverty in the United States, 1970-1980." Pp. 235-73 in *The Urban Underclass,* edited by C. Jencks and P. Peterson. Washington, DC: Brookings Institution.

Jaynes, Gerald K. and Robin M. Williams. 1989. *A Common Destiny: Blacks and American Society.* Washington, DC: National Academy Press.

Jefferson, Thomas. 1955. *Notes on the State of Virginia.* Chapel Hill: University of North Carolina Press.

Jencks, Christopher. 1991. "Is the American Underclass Growing?" Pp. 235-73 in *The Urban Underclass,* edited by Christopher Jencks and Paul E. Peterson. Washington, DC: Brookings Institution.

Jencks, Christopher and Paul E. Peterson, eds. 1991. *The Urban Underclass.* Washington DC: Brookings Institution.

Johnson v. Transportation Agency, 480 U.S. 616, 1987.

Jones, Bryan D. 1983. *Governing America: A Policy Focus.* Boston: Little, Brown.

Jordan, Winthrop. 1968. *White Over Black: American Attitudes Toward the Negro 1550-1812.* Chapel Hill: University of North Carolina Press.

Judd, Dennis. 1979. *The Politics of American Cities: Private Power and Public Policy.* Boston: Little, Brown.

Kamin, Leon. 1995. "Lies, Damned Lies, and Statistics." Pp. 81-105 in *The Bell Curve Debate: History, Documents, Opinions,* edited by R. Jacoby and N. Glauberman. New York: Times Books.

Kasarda, John. 1985. "Urban Change and Minority Opportunities." Pp. 33-68 in *The New Urban Reality,* edited by P. Peterson. Washington, DC: Brookings Institution.

Katz, Phyllis A. and Dalmas A. Taylor, eds. 1988. *Eliminating Racism: Profiles in Controversy.* New York: Plenum.

Katzman, David M. 1975. *Before the Ghetto: Black Detroit in the Nineteenth Century.* Urbana: University of Illinois Press.

Katznelson, Ira. 1981. *City Trenches: Urban Politics and the Patterning of Class in the United States.* Chicago: University of Chicago Press.

Key, V. O. 1984. *Southern Politics in State and Nation.* Knoxville: University of Tennesse Press.

Kirschenman, Joleen and Kathryn M. Neckerman. 1991. "We'd Love to Hire Them, But . . . ": The Meaning of Race for Employers." Pp. 203-34 in *The Urban Underclass,* edited by C. Jencks and P. Peterson. Washington, DC: Brookings Institution.

Knowles, Louis and Kenneth Prewitt, eds. 1970. *Institutional Racism.* Englewood, NJ: Prentice Hall.

Kolko, Gabriel. 1963. *The Triumph of Conservatism: A Reinterpretation of American History, 1900-1916.* London: Free Press of Glencoe.

Kousser, J. Morgan. 1974. *The Shaping of Southern Politics Suffrage Restriction and the Establishment of the One-Party South, 1880-1910.* New Haven, CT: Yale University Press.

Kovel, Joel. 1984. *White Racism: A Psychohistory.* New York: Columbia University Press.

Kozol, Jonathan. 1991. *Savage Inequalities: Children in America's Schools.* New York: Harper Perennial.

Kuhn, Thomas. 1975. *The Structure of Scientific Revolutions.* Chicago: University of Chicago Press.

Kusmer, Kenneth. 1976. *A Ghetto Takes Shape: Black Cleveland, 1870-1930.* Urbana: University of Illinois Press.

Lane, Charles. 1994. "The Tainted Sources." Pp. 125-39 in *The Bell Curve Debate: History, Documents, Opinions,* edited by R. Jacoby and N. Glauberman. New York: Times Books.

Lasch, Christopher. 1979. *The Culture of Narcissism: American Life in an Age of Diminishing Expectations.* New York: Norton.

Latham, Frank B. 1969. *The Rise and Fall of Jim Crow, 1865-1964: The Negro's Long Struggle to Win the "Equal Protection of the Laws."* New York: Franklin Watts.

Levy, Frank. 1988. *Dollars and Dreams: The Changing American Income Distribution.* New York: Norton.

Liggio, Leonard, 1976. "English Origins of Early American Racism." *Radical History Review* 3(1):1-36.

Lindblom, Charles. 1977. *Politics and Markets: The World's Political-Economic Systems.* New York: Basic Books.

Lineberry, Robert. 1986. *Government in America: People, Politics, and Policy.* Boston: Little, Brown.

Lipset, Seymour Martin. 1963. *Political Man: The Social Bases of Politics.* New York: Anchor.

Lipsky, Michael. 1980. *Street-Level Bureaucracy: Dilemmas of the Individual in Public Services.* New York: Russell Sage.

Local 28 of the Sheet Metal Workers v. Equal Employment Opportunity Commission, 478 U.S. 421, 1986.

Locke, John. 1980. *Second Treatise of Government.* Indianapolis, IN: Hackett.

Logan, Rayford. 1965. *The Betrayal of the Negro.* New York: Collier-Macmillan.

Long, Edward. 1972. *The History of Jamaica.* New York: Arno.

Lorance v. AT&T Technologies, 400 U.S. 900, 1989.

Loving v. Virginia, 388 U.S. 1, 1967.

Lowi, Theodore J. and Benjamin Ginsberg. 1994. *American Government: Freedom and Power.* New York: Norton.

Lukacs, Georg. 1975. *History and Class Consciousness: Studies in Marxist Dialectics,* 4th ed. Cambridge: MIT Press.

Lynn, Richard. 1991. "Race Differences in Intelligence: A Global Perspective." *Mankind: A Quarterly* 31: 254-296.

McDonald, Forrest, Leslie Decker, and Thomas Govan. 1972. *The Last Best Hope: A History of the United States: 1815-1970.* Reading, MA: Addison-Wesley.

McKitrick, Eric L., ed. 1963. *Slavery Defended: The Views of the Old South.* Englewood Cliffs, NJ: Prentice Hall.

McLaurin, Melton. 1971. *Paternalism and Protest.* Westport, CT: Greenwood.

Main, Jackson T. 1965. *The Social Structure of Revolutionary America.* Princeton, NJ: Princeton University Press.

Mandel, Ernest. 1973. *An Introduction to Marxist Economic Theory*. New York: Pathfinder.

Mandle, Jay. 1992. *Not Slave, Not Free: The African American Economic Experience*. Durham, NC: Duke University Press.

Marable, Manning. 1986. *Race, Reform, and Rebellion: The Second Reconstruction in Black America, 1945-1982*. Jackson: University Press of Mississippi.

Martin v. Wilks, 490 U.S. 755, 1989.

Marx, Karl. 1852/1959a. "The Eighteenth Brumaire of Louis Bonaparte." Pp. 320-48 in *Marx and Engels: Basic Writings on Politics and Philosophy*, edited by L. Feuer. New York: Anchor.

———. 1859/1959b. "Excerpt from *A Contribution to the Critique of Political Economy*." Pp. 42-46 in *Marx and Engels: Basic Writings on Politics and Philosophy*, edited by L. Feuer. New York: Anchor.

———. 1888/1974. "Thesis on Feuerbach." Pp. 121-23 in *The German Ideology: Part One*, edited by C. J. Arthur. New York: International Publishers.

———. 1867/1975. *Capital: A Critical Analysis of Capitalist Production*. Vol. 1. New York: International Publishers.

Massey, Douglas and Nancy Denton. 1993. *American Apartheid: Segregation and the Making of the Underclass*. Cambridge, MA: Harvard University Press.

Mauer, Marc and Tracy Huling. 1995. *Young Black Americans and the Criminal Justice System: Five Years Later*. Washington, DC: The Sentencing Project.

Meier, August and Elliott Rudwick. 1973. *CORE: A Study in the Civil Rights Movement, 1942-1968*. New York: Oxford University Press.

———. 1981. *Black Detroit and the Rise of the UAW*. Oxford, UK: Oxford University Press.

Miller, Adam. 1995. "Professors of Hate." Pp. 162-78 in *The Bell Curve Debate: History, Documents, Opinions*, edited by R. Jacoby and N. Glauberman. New York: Times Books.

Missouri ex rel. Gaines v. Canada, 305 U.S. 337, 1938.

Mitchell, Broadus and George Mitchell. 1930. *The Industrial Revolution in the South*. Baltimore, MD: The Johns Hopkins University Press.

Moore, Barrington. 1966. *Social Origins of Dictatorship and Democracy*. Boston: Beacon.

Morgan, Edmund. 1975. *American Slavery, American Freedom: The Ordeal of Colonial Virginia*. New York: Norton.

Murray, Charles. 1984. *Losing Ground: American Social Policy, 1950-1980*. New York: Basic Books.

Myrdal, Gunnar. [1948] 1975. *An American Dilemma: The Negro Problem & Modern Democracy*. Vol. 1. New York: Pantheon.

Naim v. Naim, 27 SE.2d. 749, 756, 1955.

Nash, Gary. 1990. *Race and Revolution*. Madison, WI: Madison House.

Nathan, Richard. 1987. "Will the Underclass Always Be With Us?" *Society* 24(3):57-62.

Northrup, Herbert R. 1944. *Organized Labor and the Negro*. New York: Harper & Brothers.

Oakes, James. 1982. *The Ruling Race: A History of American Slaveholders*. New York: Knopf.

O'Connor, James. 1973. *The Fiscal Crisis of the State*. New York: St. Martin's.

Omi, Michael and Howard Winant. 1990. *Racial Formation in the United States: From the 1960s to the 1980s.* New York: Routledge.

Pace v. Alabama, 106 U.S. 583, 1883.

Parenti, Michael. 1988. *Democracy for the Few.* New York: St. Martin's.

Park, Robert. 1974. *The Collected Papers of Robert Ezra Park.* New York: Arno.

Patterson v. McLean Credit Union, 491 U.S. 164, 1989.

Pettigrew, Thomas. 1979. "The Changing—Not Declining—Significance of Race." In *The Caste and Class Controversy,* edited by C. Willie. Bayside, NY: General Hall.

Phillips, William D. and Carla R. Phillips. 1992. *The Worlds of Christopher Columbus.* Cambridge, UK: Cambridge University Press.

Pinderhughes, Dianne M. 1987. *Race and Ethnicity in Chicago Politics: A Reexamination of Pluralist Theory.* Urbana: University of Illinois Press.

Piore, Michael J. 1977. "The Dual Labor Market: Theory and Implications." Pp. 93-97 in *Problems in Political Economy: An Urban Perspective,* edited by D. Gordon. Lexington, MA: D. C. Heath.

Piven, Frances Fox and Richard A. Cloward. 1972. *Regulating the Poor: The Functions of Public Welfare.* New York: Vintage.

Plessy v. Ferguson, 163 U.S. 537, 1896.

Prewitt, Kenneth and Alan Stone. 1973. *The Ruling Elites: Elite Theory, Power, and American Democracy.* New York: Harper & Row.

Quinn, D. B. 1965. *Elizabethans and the Irish.* Ithaca, NY: Cornell University Press.

Rabinowitz, Howard N. 1992. *The First New South 1865-1920.* Arlington Heights, IL: Harlan Davidson.

Reed, Merl E. 1991. *Seedtime for the Modern Civil Rights Movement: The President's Committee on Fair Employment Practices, 1941-1946.* Baton Rouge: Louisiana State University Press.

Regents of the University of California v. Bakke, 438 U.S. 265, 1978.

Reich, Michael. 1977. "The Economics of Racism." Pp. 183-88 in *Problems in Political Economy: An Urban Perspective,* edited by D. Gordon. Lexington, MA: D. C. Heath.

———. 1981. *Racial Inequality: A Political Economic Analysis.* Princeton, NJ: Princeton University Press.

Reich, Robert. 1988. *Tales of a New America: The Anxious Liberal's Guide to the Future.* New York: Vintage.

———. 1992. *The Work of Nations.* New York: Vintage.

Reich, Wilhelm. 1970. *The Mass Psychology of Fascism.* New York: Farrar, Straus & Giroux.

"Report Finds Whites Seldom Get Severe Penalties Blacks Get for Selling, Using Crack Cocaine." 1995, June 12. *Jet* 88:33.

Rich, Wilbur. 1982. *The Politics of Urban Personnel Policy: Reformers, Politicians, and Bureaucrats.* Port Washington, NY: National University Publications.

———. 1989. *Coleman Young and Detroit Politics: From Social Activist to Power Broker.* Detroit: Wayne State University Press.

Roediger, David. 1991. *The Wages of Whiteness: Race and the Making of the American Working Class.* New York: Verso.

Rosenthal, Robert. 1992. *Pygmalion in the Classroom: Teacher Expectation and Pupils' Intellectual Development.* New York: Irvington.

Roth, Cecil. 1972. *A History of the Jews: From Earliest Times Through the Six-Day War.* New York: Schocken.

Ryan, William. 1982. *Equality.* New York: Vintage.

San Antonio Independent School District v. Rodriguez, 411 U.S. 1, 1973.

Sassen-Koob, Saskia. 1984. "The New Labor Demand in Global Cities." In *Cities in Transformation: Class, Capital, and the State,* edited by Michael Smith. Beverly Hills, CA: Sage.

Saxon, Alexander. 1990. *The Rise and Fall of the White Republic.* London: Verso.

Schattschneider, E. E. 1975. *The Semisovereign People: A Realist's View of Democracy in America.* Hinsdale, IL: Dryden.

Sedgwick, John. 1995. "Inside the Pioneer Fund." In *The Bell Curve Debate: History, Documents, Opinions,* edited by R. Jacoby and N. Glauberman. New York: Times Books.

Shelley v. Kraemer, 334 U.S. 1, 1948.

Shugg, Roger W. [1939] 1968. *Origins of Class Struggle in Louisiana: A Social History of White Farmers and Laborers During Slavery and After 1840-1875.* Baton Rouge: Louisiana State University Press.

Shulman, Steven. 1989. "Controversies in the Marxian Analysis of Racial Discrimination." *Review of Radical Political Economics* 21(4):73-82.

Sitkoff, Harvard. 1978. *A New Deal for Blacks: The Emergence of Civil Rights as a National Issue.* Vol. 1, *The Depression Decade.* New York: Oxford University Press.

Smedley, Audrey. 1993. *Race in North America: Origin and Evolution of a World View.* Boulder, CO: Westview.

Smith v. Allwright, 321 U.S. 649, 144, 1944.

Snowden, Frank. 1983. *Before Color Prejudice: The Ancient View of Blacks.* Cambridge, MA: Harvard University Press.

Sowell, Thomas. 1975. *Race and Economics.* New York: McKay.

———. 1981. *Markets and Minorities.* New York: Basic Books.

———. 1984. *Civil Rights: Rhetoric or Reality.* New York: Morrow.

Spencer, Herbert. 1891. *Essays: Political and Speculative.* London: Williams and Norgate.

Spero, Sterling D. and Abram L. Harris. 1931. *The Black Worker: The Negro and the Labor Movement.* New York: Columbia University Press.

———. 1968. *The Black Worker: The Negro and the Labor Movement.* New York: Atheneum.

Squires, Gregory D. 1990. "Economic Restructuring, Urban Development, and Race: The Political Economy of Civil Rights in 'Post Industrial' America: A Review Essay." *Western Political Quarterly* 43:201-17.

Stampp, Kenneth M. 1956. *The Peculiar Institution: Slavery in the Ante-Bellum South.* New York: Vintage.

———. 1965. *The Era of Reconstruction 1865-1877.* New York: Vintage.

Staples, Robert. 1987. *The Urban Plantation: Racism and Colonialism in the Post Civil Rights Era.* Oakland, CA: The Black Scholar Press.

Steinberg, Stephen. 1989. *The Ethnic Myth: Race, Ethnicity, and Class in America.* Boston: Beacon.

Stone, Clarence N. 1980. "Systemic Power in Community Decision Making: A Restatement of Stratification Theory." *American Political Science Review* 80:978-90.

Sweatt v. Painter, 339 U.S. 629, 1950.

Sweezy, Paul M. 1970. *The Theory of Capitalist Development: Principles of Marxian Political Economy.* New York: Monthly Review Press.

Swinton, David H. 1993. "The Economic Status of African Americans During the Reagan-Bush Era: Withered Opportunities, Limited Outcomes, and Uncertain Outlooks." In *The State of Black America 1993.* New York: National Urban League.

Tobin, Gary, ed. 1987. *Divided Neighborhoods: Changing Patterns of Racial Segregation.* Beverly Hills, CA: Sage.

Trelease, Allen W. 1971. *White Terror: The Ku Klux Klan Conspiracy and Southern Reconstruction.* New York: Harper and Row.

Turner, Margery, Michael Fix, and Raymond Struyk. 1991. *Opportunities Denied, Opportunities Diminished: Racial Discrimination in Hiring.* Washington DC: The Urban Institute.

Tuttle, William. 1982. *Race Riot: Chicago in the Red Summer of 1919.* New York: Atheneum.

U.S. Department of Commerce, Bureau of the Census. 1990a. *Census of Population and Housing: The Chicago SMSA.* Washington, DC: Government Printing Office.

U.S. Department of Commerce, Bureau of the Census. 1990b. *Census of Population and Housing: The Detroit SMSA.* Washington, DC: Government Printing Office.

U.S. Department of Commerce, Bureau of the Census. 1990c. *Census of Population and Housing: New York City SMSA.* Washington, DC: Government Printing Office.

U.S. Department of Commerce, Bureau of the Census. 1990d. *Census of Population and Housing: The Philadelphia SMSA.* Washington, DC: Government Printing Office.

United States v. Cruikshank, 92 U.S. (2 Otto) 542, 1876.

United States v. Mitchell, 335 F. Supp. 1004, 1971.

United States v. Paradise, 480 U.S. 149, 1987.

United States v. Reese, 92 U.S. (2 Otto) 214, 1876.

United Steelworkers of America v. Weber, 443 U.S. 193, 1979.

Village of Arlington Heights v. Metropolitan Housing Development Corporation, 492 U.S. 252, 1977.

Vogel, David. 1989. *Fluctuating Fortunes: The Political Power of Business in America.* New York: Basic Books.

Wallerstein, Immanuel. 1991. *Unthinking Social Science: The Limits of Nineteenth Century Paradigms.* Cambridge, MA: Polity Press.

Wards Cove Packing Co., Inc., v. Atonio, 490 U.S. 642, 1989.

Wayne, Michael. 1983. *The Reshaping of Plantation Society: The Natchez District, 1860-1880.* Baton Rouge: Louisiana State University Press.

Webster's New World Dictionary of the American Language. 1976. Englewood Cliffs, NJ: William Collins.

Welsing, Frances Cress. 1970. "The Cress Theory of Color-Confrontation and Racism." Monograph, Washington, DC.

West, Cornel. 1982. *Prophesy Deliverance: An Afro-American Revolutionary Christianity.* Philadelphia: Westminister.

Widick, B. J. 1989. *Detroit: City of Race and Class Violence.* Detroit: Wayne State University Press.

Wiener, Jonathan. 1978. *Social Origins of the New South: Alabama 1860-1985.* Baton Rouge: Louisiana State University Press.

Willhelm, Sidney. 1970. *Who Needs the Negro.* Garden City, NY: Anchor.

Williams, Eric. 1966. *Capitalism and Slavery.* New York: Capricorn Books.

Williams, Rhonda M. 1987. "Capital, Competition, and Discrimination: A Reconsideration of Racial Earnings Inequality." *Review of Radical Political Economics* 19(2):1-15.

Williamson, Joel. 1965. *After Slavery: The Negro in South Carolina During Reconstruction, 1861-1877.* Chapel Hill: University of North Carolina Press.

———. 1986. *Rage for Order.* Oxford, UK: Oxford University Press.

Willie, Charles, ed. 1979. *The Caste and Class Controversy.* Bayside, NY: General Hall.

Wilson, Carter A. 1992. "Restructuring and the Growth of Concentrated Poverty in Detroit." *Urban Affairs Quarterly* 28(2):187-205.

Wilson, James Q. 1992. *American Government: Institutions and Policies.* Lexington, MA: D. C. Heath.

Wilson, William Julius. 1980. *The Declining Significance of Race: Blacks and Changing Americans Institutions,* 2nd ed. Chicago: University of Chicago Press.

———. 1987. *The Truly Disadvantaged: The Inner City, the Underclass, and Public Policy.* Chicago: University of Chicago Press.

Wolkinson, Benjamin W. 1973. *Blacks, Unions, and the EEOC: A Study of Administrative Futility.* Lexington, MA: Lexington Books.

Woodward, C. Vann. 1951. *Origins of the New South 1877-1913.* Baton Rouge: Louisiana State University Press.

———. 1974. *The Strange Career of Jim Crow.* New York: Oxford University Press.

Wygant v. Jackson Board of Education, 476 U.S. 267, 1986.

Yinger, John. (1987) "Housing Market Discrimination and Black Suburbanization in the 1980s." Pp. 43-67 in *Divided Neighborhoods: Changing Patterns of Racial Segregation,* edited by G. Tobin. Beverly Hills, CA: Sage.

Zinn, Howard. 1990. *The People's History of the United States.* New York: Harper Perennial.

Zuch v. Hussey, 394 F. Supp. 1028, 1975.

Index

About the Author

Carter A. Wilson is Associate Professor in the Department of Political Science and Public Administration at the University of Toledo. He specializes in the areas of urban political economy, public policy and administration, and race and public policy. He has published articles in *Urban Affairs Quarterly, Administration & Society,* and *The Black Scholar.* He did much of the research for this volume at Denison University, where he lectured as a visiting scholar.